The Urban Threshold

The Urban Threshold

Growth and Change
in a Nineteenth-
Century American
Community

Stuart M.
Blumin

The University of Chicago Press
Chicago and London

HN
80
.K5
B55
1976

STUART M. BLUMIN is assistant professor of
history at Cornell University. He has taught
at Skidmore College and M.I.T. and is the
author of a number of scholarly articles.

The University of Chicago Press, Chicago 60637
The University of Chicago Press, Ltd., London

Library of Congress Cataloging in Publication Data

Blumin, Stuart M.
  The urban threshold.

  Bibliography: p.
  Includes index.
  1. Kingston, N.Y.—Social conditions. 2. Kingston,
N.Y.—Economic conditions. 3. Cities and towns—
United States—Case studies. 4. Urbanization—United
States—Case studies. I. Title.
HN80.K5 B55 1976   309.1'747'34   75-27891
ISBN 0-226-06169-8

To my mother and father

Contents

Tables

Figures

Preface

The case study of a single representative community has by now established itself as a scholarly genre, not only among the sociologists and anthropologists who first employed it, but among historians as well. Unlike the city or town "biography," which assumes that its subject is sufficiently interesting to warrant a mere chronicle of local events, the case study has at its core the urge to generalize, to other communities or to whole societies, on the basis of what is found in the particular place at a particular time. Recent books by such American historians as Charles S. Grant, Philip Greven, Kenneth A. Lockridge, John Demos, Merle Curti, Stephan Thernstrom, and Michael H. Frisch share this quality. What is important is not the specific history of Andover or Trempeleau County or Springfield, but the ways in which this history informs such general issues as colonial family relationships, frontier democracy, or the meaning of community in an urbanizing milieu. They share as well the idea, expressed or implied, that the study of the individual community reveals information that cannot be obtained at any other level of inquiry. The records of the General Court of Massachusetts Bay indicate how land was allocated to the proprietors of the town of Dedham, but only research in Dedham's own records can tell how that land was divided among the inhabitants, how it was farmed, and how it intersected with other aspects of the life of the community. National census tabulations quickly yield the quantitative dimensions of urban growth in nineteenth-century America, but only a careful reading of a variety of local documents can suggest ways of interpreting the consequences of growth to the daily lives of the new American urbanites. And finally, the historians who have written these case studies share the growing impulse to write history "from the bottom up"—to discuss the lives of ordinary, "anonymous Americans," and to stretch our historical vision across the whole spectrum of social classes.

The present study of the nineteenth-century Hudson Valley town of Kingston, New York, shares all three of these motifs. Like the case studies that have preceded it, *The Urban Threshold* is aimed at the discovery of general statements about American society, at the sorts of phenomena that reveal themselves only in the arena of the local community, and at the development of further insights into the lives of anonymous Americans. On the other hand, it differs in some of the specific questions it asks and is probably unique in the type of community it examines. In 1820, Kingston was a long-settled rural community, seven generations removed from its frontier experience, displaying all the characteristics of a rural town located at the center rather than the edge of society. In the decades that immediately followed, Kingston, like many other American communities touched by the transportation revolution, grew into a small but robust commercial city. What this book investigates is the consequences, to the individual members of the community and to the community itself, of the crossing of this urban threshold. In short, it is a case study, not of a frontier settlement, or a New England Town, or an emerging great city, but of the processes by which the typical American rural community became the typical American town.

A great many individuals and institutions have assisted me in my work, and I have long looked forward to this chance to acknowledge as many as possible. My greatest debt, by far, is to my wife, Deborah Adelman Blumin, who was the only person besides myself to participate in every stage of this study, from initial speculation, to archival research, to the editing of each of many drafts. I choose to thank her first, rather than at the traditional close of these acknowledgments, because her help went so far beyond (but certainly included) the usual moral support that authors invariably seek from their husbands or wives.

I am indebted to several organizations for their financial assistance. Research and data-processing costs were defrayed by a grant-in-aid from the American Council of Learned Societies, two grants from the Ford Program in Comparative Modernization at the Massachusetts Institute of Technology, and by a special grant of computer time from M.I.T.'s Information Processing Center. Time to write the first draft of this book was provided by an Old Dominion Fund fellowship, while both time and facilities were provided by a research fellowship at the Charles Warren Center for

Studies in American History at Harvard University. To the director, staff, and especially my colleagues at the Charles Warren Center, I owe a particularly warm expression of gratitude. Final costs of manuscript preparation were borne in part by the Meigs Fund of the Department of History, Cornell University.

Other individuals and institutions were helpful in a variety of ways. I would like to thank the staffs of the Widener, Lamont, and Baker Libraries of Harvard University, the New York State Library at Albany, the New York State National Guard at Albany, the New-York Historical Society, the Kingston Area Library, the Senate House Museum at Kingston, the Ulster County Historical Society, various departments of the Ulster County and City of Kingston governments, and sundry of Kingston's churches. Individuals at these institutions who deserve a personal note of thanks include the late Howard Crocker (who led me to local data archives and to trout streams with equal enthusiasm), Albert Spada, Caroline Matzen, Mildred Buddington, Herbert Cutler, Norwood Locke, Jay Hogan, Henry Peyer, and two very charming sisters, Cora and Pearl Rightmyer.

This study benefited greatly from the participation of two students. Sheila Bryson, then an undergraduate at Duke University, served as my research assistant during a highly significant phase of the study, the collection of data from the manuscript schedules of the Federal and New York State censuses. Somehow, Sheila managed to wade through thousands of census entries without losing either her accuracy or her keen eye for the special problems that these schedules so often present. Her superb job allowed me to write several chapters with more confidence than I would otherwise have been able to muster. Robert S. Litt, then an undergraduate at Harvard University, participated in a less conventional way. By utilizing my research for his senior honors essay (cited in the text), Bob became a particularly useful and engaging discussant of both the details and the ideas on which this study is based.

I would like also to single out a remarkable collection of men and women, the staff of the Information Processing Center at M.I.T. Carla Van Hoesen, Sally Kelly, Tom Van Vleck, Dick Steinberg, and Bob Burke, among others, combined an unfailing friendliness and eagerness to help with a staggering degree of professional expertise. Those who fear that massive computer systems will dehumanize the people who come into contact with them, or that the computer will replace the human brain, owe themselves a visit to the I.P.C.

Several scholars willingly gave me significant advice and criticism. Conversations with Stuart K. Witt were extremely useful at the very outset of the study, while Paul Holland provided invaluable assistance with the selection of statistical procedures. Clyde Griffen, Sam Bass Warner, Jr., Ronald P. Formisano, Henry Y. K. Tom, Simeon Crowther, and Henry Shapiro each read and criticized, to my great profit, all or part of various drafts. And finally, though Murray G. Murphey has not read a page of what follows, his influence may be found wherever my pen has touched paper. But this is something only his other former students can fully appreciate.

Ithaca, New York   S. M. B.

1   Introduction

Just before the outbreak of the Civil War, the total
urban population in the United States was a little more than six
million—about half of the average *increase* recorded every ten
years during the first half of the present century. Yet the forty years
or so preceding the Civil War were, in relative terms, the period of
the most rapid urbanization in the entire history of the United
States; this was the age when the foundations of an urban society
were firmly laid.[1] The most dramatic contributors to antebellum
urban growth were surely the largest cities, which grew during
these years from "walking cities" with 25,000, 50,000, or 100,000
inhabitants, to large, industrializing, and even suburbanizing cities
with as many as New York's 800,000.[2] In 1860 eight American cities
were larger than any had been forty years earlier, and the total
number of people living in cities of 100,000 or more had increased
from 123,000 to more than two and a half million.[3] Yet American
urbanization in the pre–Civil War period is by no means accounted
for by the growth of the largest cities. Equally significant was the
multiplication of smaller centers with 5,000, 10,000, or 20,000
inhabitants. In 1820 there had been only fifty-six incorporated
villages and towns numbering between 2,500 and 25,000 inhabitants. By 1860 there were some three hundred "urban places" of
between 2,500 and 10,000 population, and another sixty-eight of
between 10,000 and 25,000.[4] Viewed in conjunction with the larger
urban centers, these smaller cities and towns represent a filling out
of the urban landscape, a more complete articulation of the urban
regionalization that is the surest sign of a maturing urban society.
Viewed by themselves, they exemplify a significant, highly interesting, and much ignored transformation of the structure and meaning
of the smaller American community—for most of these little cities
(all but some of the older New England ports and the more recently
settled and rapidly growing frontier towns) grew during these years

1

out of local societies that had been rural and agricultural for years and even generations. Thus, while the nation as a whole was crossing the threshold of an urban age, its smaller cities were experiencing in their own tangible, day-to-day affairs the transition from rural to urban social organization.

Kingston, New York, was one of these small cities, and its history during the four decades preceding the Civil War is the history of a town that crossed the urban threshold after seven generations of rural life. Lying on the west bank of the Hudson River some ninety miles north of New York City, Kingston was settled just past the midpoint of the seventeenth century by a small band of farmers who ventured down the Hudson from the Manor of Rensselaerswyck to clear farms for themselves in the fertile valley of Esopus Creek. During its earliest years this frontier community, the only European settlement in the Mid–Hudson Valley, was known simply as Esopus and consisted of nothing more than farms. A village was not constructed in Esopus until 1658, five or six years after the original settlement, and this was a defensive affair, a stockade ordered built by Peter Stuyvesant, director general of New Netherlands, after relations between the white settlers and the Esopus Indians had deteriorated into armed conflict. This village, to which Stuyvesant gave the name Wiltwyck, remained after the "Esopus Wars" had ended and in a few years had transformed itself into an ordinary rural frontier community. Eventually, the stockade disappeared, Wiltwyck was renamed Kingston by the new British rulers of the province, and Kingston grew into a small city, one of a chain of secondary urban centers that now line both shores of the Hudson River between New York and Albany.[5]

As late as the 1820s, however, Kingston was still a distinctly rural town, with some 2,000 farm dwellers surrounding a village whose population had only recently passed 1,000. The catalyst of most of its growth was the Delaware and Hudson Canal, built during the 1820s from the anthracite fields of Pennsylvania to the Hudson Valley at the southern boundary of the town of Kingston. By 1840, after a decade of canal operations, the town's population had doubled to 6,000, with nearly all the increase concentrated in the old village and in a new village that was rapidly growing up next to it on the canal itself. By 1850 Kingston had passed 10,000, and in 1860 it reached 16,640. Whether it should be called a "city" in 1860 may be debated; but certainly it was a community that had been transformed, perhaps fundamentally, by what George Rogers Taylor has aptly called the transportation revolution.[6] And when the D & H Canal turned Kingston into a node within the emerging network of modern transportation, 175 years of rural social organization, of Dutch-American culture, of specific family names and institutions and village streets, lay in Kingston's past.

This book, then, is the study of a single, but not singular, American town. My purpose is to examine at close range—in the real environment of daily social life—the broad social and economic changes that swept across the American landscape during the decades preceding the Civil War. Rapid urbanization, the revolution in transportation, and the proto-industrial economy that was developing in and around the major cities because of the new inland transportation system, are only the most pertinent of these changes. Other developments, no less dramatic but perhaps less easily associated on the broader national level with urban growth, may also be examined and placed within the context of the growth of the particular community. For example, the early years of Kingston's rapid growth were also the Age of Jackson, and whether one prefers to attribute the political changes of this era to Jacksonian Democrats, Whigs, Anti-Masons, or Working Men, it is clear that by the 1840s the stage, style, and content of American political dialogue had changed dramatically. As both cause and effect of expanded (white) suffrage, a system of "mass politics" had emerged for the mobilization of public support for each of the nation's parties. Party-controlled newspapers were joined in this system to an increasingly well-articulated hierarchy of town, county, district, and state party committees, nominating conventions at all levels from municipal to national, torchlight parades, campaign clubs, and an appreciation of mass-appeal political symbols and slogans, from hickory poles and log cabins to "Tippecanoe and Tyler Too."[7] And as further indication, if any were needed, that political institutional development was but one phase of a more general phenomenon, we may point to similar changes in the organization of evangelical religion and social reform. William McLoughlin has called Charles Grandison Finney the first of the modern revivalists, by which he means that Finney brought American sinners to the anxious bench with the same spirit and many of the same techniques that brought American voters to the polls.[8] And so did less visible organizers, who built national societies for the organization of home missions, the distribution of Bibles and religious tracts, the abolition of slavery, the elimination of alcoholic drink, the reform of penal institutions, the better observance of the Sabbath—the eradication of all obstacles, large and small, that inhibited the realization of the millennium.[9] The essence of all these developments was their extralocal scope. Each of them, including the revivals, transcended the particular locality and in the process increased and intensified social activity oriented toward state, regional, and even national institutions. What was their influence upon the American community? The question is relevant to all types of communities, from the largest cities to the most static rural towns, but it should prove particularly interesting to raise in the context of a growing town, such as Kingston, that experienced its most critical internal institutional developments during this era of emerging mass parties and national reform societies.

Local growth and extralocal institutional development were not merely coincidental events, for both depended in large measure on the emerging network of canals, railroads, plank roads, and steamboat routes that brought ever closer economic and social communication to an expanding nation. Communication depended also on the closely related, no less dramatic revolution in the transportation of messages—the telegraph, the penny press, the more respectable city dailies, the village weeklies, and such nationally circulating magazines as Harper's, Godey's Lady's Book, Country Gentleman, and Frank Leslie's Illustrated. At the turn of the century there were perhaps 150 or 200 newspapers printed in the United States, nearly all of which were four-page weeklies.[10] But the tradition of local newspaper publishing was already gaining its foothold, even in the smaller towns, and as the nation grew and towns proliferated, the numbers of local presses more than kept pace. By the 1830s there were some 1,200 local papers; by 1860 there were more than 3,000, nearly 400 of which were city dailies.[11] Even more dramatic was the increase in the numbers and circulation of magazines—from a dozen small-circulation periodicals in 1800 to 600 or 700 by the 1850s, some of which maintained subscription lists reaching into the hundreds of thousands.[12] The transmission of words and pictures (to say nothing of telegraphic code) had changed no less remarkably than had the transportation of goods and people, and it was this revolution in both transportation and communications that provided the vehicles for the development of regional and national social and economic institutions.

Coincident with these institutional developments were changes in the class and ethnic structures, and these too may be examined in the context of the urbanizing community. At the bottom of the social and economic ladder two changes were becoming apparent. First, the development and consolidation of industrial production in larger and larger "manufactories" in and around the cities were beginning to produce a seemingly permanent class of wage earners, a trend which ran counter to the endlessly repeated proclamation that opportunities for advancement in America were open to all.[13] And second, there appeared for the first time in American history a major influx of foreign immigrants perceived by those who had preceded them as a significant threat to the Anglo-Saxon (or anglicized) white Protestant hegemony. Nearly two million Irish Catholics and one and a half million Catholic and Protestant Germans entered the United States between 1830 and 1860, most of them in the desperate condition of refugees from enclosure, eviction, revolution, and famine.[14] Meanwhile, at the opposite end of the ladder, successful merchants and manufacturers were amassing fortunes that had never before been seen in the New World. Though $100,000 was then a level of considerable wealth, there were a number of individual fortunes that reached much higher, even in a few instances into the millions. The appearance of these fortunes was no challenge to the idea of the United States as a land of opportunity (although most of the wealthy seem to have been born to at least moderately wealthy parents), but it did contradict those who saw this nation as one large, undifferentiated middle class.[15] And within the middle class itself there were also significant changes, as large numbers of families experienced a much improved style of living (including finer clothes, indoor plumbing, and vacation journeys to Niagara Falls, Saratoga Springs, and Atlantic City), while others, principally the once independent master craftsmen of the cities, sank into the wage-earning class.[16]

The fact that Kingston experienced all these changes in some degree makes it an excellent laboratory for the study of social change in antebellum America. And the further fact that its growth carried it across the urban threshold allows us to pursue the more particular question of how urban growth, improvements in transportation and communications, institutional development, and changes in local ethnic and class structures affected the life of the previously rural American community. Curiously, this is a subject that has thus far been almost entirely ignored, both by historians of the "town in American history," who have focused resolutely, almost militantly, on small towns that never grew,[17] and by more urban-minded historians, who have fixed most of their energies on cities, eastern and western, with little or no rural background. The old coastal cities, to be sure, remained relatively small throughout much of the seventeenth and eighteenth centuries, devoting fairly large amounts of their land to pastures, gardens, orchards, and even tillage, but each was dominated from the start by international commerce and provincial and imperial government rather than by farming, and none could realistically be considered rural in character.[18] Those inland cities that have attracted the attention of historians either grew up virtually overnight out of partly cleared forests or open prairies, or else they developed more gradually out of old trading centers that had been only partly committed to agriculture.[19] Few historians, if any, have asked how local growth, and the emerging national network of canals and railroads, might have affected the structure and life of old, rural communities whose economies were rooted in the soil and whose external contacts had been maintained over changeless rivers and nearly changeless roads by means of sloops and wagons that traveled no faster than those used a century or more earlier.[20]

Of course, there remains the matter of generalization. How typical was Kingston of other American towns? To what degree can we realistically generalize from the experiences of this one community to the larger history of antebellum American society? There has obviously been no such place as a "typical American town," even if we restrict this notion to the earliest years of the nineteenth century, when all but a handful of towns were little more than rural villages. All communities existed within the broader cultural regions of North and South (or of New England, Middle Atlantic, and South) as well as within more particular subregions such as Chesapeake Bay, the Berkshire hills, or the Carolina piedmont.[21] Rural towns maintained varying relationships with cities and external markets, and agriculture itself varied significantly according to region, age of local settlement, and local peculiarities of soil and terrain. Still, the limits of generalization from a town such as Kingston need not be tightly drawn. Although the particular traditions of the Dutch Hudson Valley will enter our interpretation of the effects of growth on the rural community, it is probably more significant to note that Kingston was a northern town, sharing in no small measure the culture and the social forms of towns stretching, at the beginning of this period, from Maine to Ohio.[22] Economically, it is true, its fully developed farms and its access to water transportation made Kingston more typical of the older, nonfrontier sections of this northern cultural belt, whereas its continued reliance on successful commercial agriculture made it more typical of the rural towns of New York, New Jersey, Pennsylvania, Delaware, and Maryland than of the diversifying towns of New England.[23] Yet these are still wide areas of a nation that had only recently penetrated the Alleghenies.

As Kingston grew it became representative of a different set of communities, fewer in number, perhaps, but wider in geographic spread and closer to the mainstreams of social change. Kingston was, as we have already noted, one of sixty-eight smaller cities whose populations in 1860 ranged between 10,000 and 25,000. Another 136 varied in size between 5,000 and 10,000, and, since most of these were growing towns, they too may be placed on or near the urban threshold. Of the sixty-eight towns closest in population to Kingston in 1860 (Kingston ranked twenty-first among them), forty-three were in New England and the mid-Atlantic states, thirteen were spread across the Midwest from Ohio to Minnesota, one was in California, and eleven were in the Southwest and the southern portions of the Ohio and Mississippi Valleys.[24] Thus, Kingston's location was fairly central for both the overall spread and the greatest concentration of these small cities, twenty-two of which were east of it in New England, and eight of which were within or quite near the Hudson Valley in New York and New Jersey. Most of these towns, moreover, shared with Kingston the characteristic of having recently grown out of rural villages.

To treat Kingston as only a sample of the larger society, as a convenient locale for the study of social change, is, however, to risk losing sight of the community itself. Communities are not merely archives, offering in varying degrees the specific phenomena the political, economic, or social historian happens to be looking for. They are themselves phenomena, shaping (and shaped by) the lives of those who reside within them, and interacting in various ways with other forms of social organization lying partly or wholly outside them. These are not, of course, contradictory or even incompatible points of departure for the study of specific places. Indeed, once the researcher recognizes the distinction and determines to focus at least some of his energy on the structure of the community itself, the town he has chosen becomes both "community" and "archive," or, echoing Conrad Arensberg, "object" and "sample."[25] Unfortunately, this distinction, simple though it may be, is too often not made. It does inform such studies as Michael H. Frisch's *Town into City* and Kenneth A. Lockridge's *A New England Town*,[26] but it is absent from, say, Page Smith's *As a City upon a Hill*, which Frisch describes as "excellent social history, but ... much less satisfactory as an interpretation of the town as an institution, concentrating instead on the many aspects of life within towns."[27] I will, of course, deal with many aspects of life within Kingston. At the same time, I will attempt to organize the various comings and goings of antebellum Kingstonians into a coherent analysis of the town as a community.[28]

Two disclaimers should be entered at the outset. First, it is not my purpose here to derive new definitions of such terms as "city," "urban," and "urbanism." I continue to find Louis Wirth's bare-bones, relativistic definition of the city as "a relatively large, dense, and permanent settlement of socially heterogeneous individuals"[29] more than adequate to the task, precisely because it is in essence a rejection of the notion that the real business of the student of urban life is the making of such definitions and classifications. By going no further than the specification of size, density, and heterogeneity as the fundamental attributes that make one permanent locality more or less urban than another, Wirth *invites* rather than forecloses analysis of what the significance of those attributes may be to the urban "way of life." (And if Wirth's own acceptance of this invitation a few pages later is less than fully satisfactory, his definition of "city" is no less useful for that.)[30] The relativism of his definition, moreover, implies a continuum of real localities rather than a set or pair of abstract categories (e.g., "city" and "noncity") into which these localities must be placed. This leads to a second disclaimer, namely, that it is not my primary purpose to determine whether or not Kingston, with its 1860 population of 16,640, should be categorized as a "city."[31] And despite the fact that the term "urban threshold" is intended to mean a particular stage of local growth—a stage during which a previously rural community can no longer be considered as rural—it is not my intention to offer a new category for the classification of communities. How, then, can I claim that Kingston's growth during this period did carry the town over this "threshold"—that it was rural in 1820 and urban in 1860? A concession to classification does seem necessary on this point. I submit, therefore, that Kingston was rural in 1820 because a large majority of its families resided on farms, because an even larger majority of its work force was engaged in agriculture, and because even the nonagricultural institutions of the town, particularly its stores and workshops, were structured to serve the farm and farm family. It lost this rural character when most of its people came to reside in densely settled villages, when all but a small proportion of its work force engaged in commerce, manufacturing, and finance, and when local institutions were reoriented to the needs and opportunities of the village population. In Wirth's words, Kingston had become during this period a "relatively large, dense, and permanent settlement of socially heterogeneous individuals."

My purpose, then, is not to classify but to understand, in comprehensive terms, the process and consequences of growth in this one American country town, and to focus particular attention on the question of how that growth affected the community's social and cultural integration. The period examined here was, as we have seen, an era of rapid social change, the earliest years of sustained economic development and urban growth in America.[32] Perhaps, too, it was a period in which those communities that participated most directly in this revolution of economy and environment were altered no less dramatically in their basic structure and meaning. Kingston, then, is my laboratory for the study of social change in antebellum America and for the study of the effects of economic development and urban growth on the life of the previously rural American community.

A community is not, of course, a laboratory to those who live in it, and the historian who treats one as such does so at his own risk. In the pages that follow, therefore, I have attempted to depict, as far as surviving sources permit, the *texture* of daily life in this one antebellum American town. What was it like to live in Kingston during the age of Franklin Pierce and P. T. Barnum? To answer this question, perhaps the most difficult of all, I have preserved many of the details that might otherwise have been compressed. Moreover, I have called on some of the inhabitants of antebellum Kingston to assist me. I have held no seances in local churchyards (although the thought often occurred to me). Rather, I have frequently quoted at some length the written descriptions, opinions, and observations of men who lived in the Kingston of that era. It is these men, after all, who knew firsthand the life of the town we must now work to reconstruct.

A Country Town

If you had been in New York City in the spring of 1820 and had wished to travel to Kingston, you would probably have booked passage on one of the steamboats which left New York at 4:00 P.M. on Mondays, Wednesdays, Thursdays, and Saturdays for Albany.[1] None of these boats actually landed at Kingston, however, so you would have had to consider the inconvenience of being transferred to a small boat in midriver for your landing at Kingston Point. But if you were in no hurry, preferred a lower fare, or just did not like changing boats in midriver, you might have waited for one of the two Hudson River sloops which left New York for Kingston every Friday.[2] Your voyage, especially aboard the more leisurely sloop, would have been a beautiful one—the Palisades, Tappan Zee, and Highlands thrilled even Mrs. Trollope,[3] and the human landscape of villages, manor houses, and the fortress of West Point was only slightly less beautiful. The river itself was clean then, and it presented a picturesque traffic of sloops, fishing boats, and an occasional steamboat.

About ninety miles north of New York the west bank of the Hudson gives way to the broad mouth of Rondout Creek, the north shore of which juts out into the river to form Kingston Point. Here your journey by boat would have ended, either at the point or, if you had chosen the sloop, about a half a mile up the creek at Kingston Landing. But in neither case would your journey have been quite finished. The village of Kingston lay not on the river but on a plain about three miles west of the point and about two miles northwest of the landing. Indeed, your first contact with the town of Kingston might well have made you wonder why you had come so far. At the point, according to Marius Schoonmaker, Kingston's major historian, "there were only to be found some seven or eight stone houses, at least one half of them unoccupied and falling in

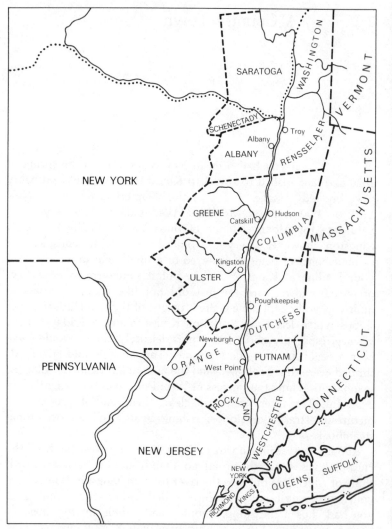

Fig. 1   The Hudson Valley, 1820

ruins, besides two dilapidated frame storehouses unoccupied on the dock."[4] Kingston Landing, or the Strand, was slightly more pretentious—three dwellings, three storehouses, an inn, and a flour mill, all apparently in active use.[5] The point would change but little between that day and this. The landing would have a different history, as we will presently see.

As the hill is steep and the roads were unpaved, the wagon ride to the village would have been slow and uncomfortable. But after the greater part of an hour, or more if the roads were muddy, you would finally have reached your destination, a charming country village with about eleven hundred inhabitants. Your journey could have taken from thirteen hours to three days—the distance traveled would have been under one hundred miles.

One stranger who actually made this journey was a Pennsylvania-born surveyor and geographer named William Darby, who visited Kingston in 1816 and found it a "romantic village," a "little, but interesting town," in which an occasional blackened stone wall "recals [sic] to mind some memorable events of the revolutionary war." The reference is to the burning of the entire village (except one house) in 1777 by the British, in retribution for Kingston's having served as the first seat of New York's revolutionary government. The village had been rebuilt, however, and the Revolution was receding into Kingston's past:

> Time and energy have here effaced the ravages of war. Few, if any villages in the United States, present at this moment, an air of more domestic comfort, plenty and ease, than does Kingston. The houses are scattered, and generally built after the old Dutch taste, low, with few windows, and those small. Some more modern dwellings, are exceptions to the common mode, being constructed with an elegance and convenience equal to the houses of any of our country towns....
>
> In making a tour of this part of the United States, no traveller ought to pass without visiting Kingston, and every stranger will be pleased with the soft beauty of its scenery, with its retired situation, and with the plain but affable manners of its inhabitants.[6]

Darby's advice was probably ignored by most travelers through the Hudson Valley, but his description of Kingston village may be taken as accurate. The homes and shops of Kingston's eleven hundred inhabitants were spread over a fairly large number of streets, and the ample spaces between them were filled with trees, gardens, and lawns. Of course, most properties contained barns and other outbuildings, and in the absence of a functioning village pound there must have been no small number of swine roaming the village's barnyards and unpaved streets. But these additions to the townscape were less offensive to early nineteenth-century eyes and noses than they would be to ours and only heightened the village's country character. The nearby peaks of the Catskill Mountains, plainly visible to the north and west, added to the village's beauty.

This is a quaint picture, but while it is accurate it is also incomplete. For one thing, the "plain but affable" residents of the town were not all alike in wealth and status. Some were slaves, others hired hands or journeymen, still others slave-owning pro-prietors of substantial farms. For another, Kingston's "retired situation" did not isolate the town from the rest of the world, did not produce a set of localized institutions expressing a rich and particular community life, and did not cause the residents of the town to enclose their minds within the daily round of local life. Like most of the rural communities of the Middle Atlantic states and New England, Kingston combined its rustic atmosphere with a series of regular commercial, institutional, and personal links to the complex world beyond its boundaries. Partly, this reflected Kings-ton's status as a modest-sized "central place," performing eco-nomic, political, educational, and religious functions for the farm-dwelling families of nearby townships. For despite Kingston's size and rural character, it was still the largest and most important village on the west shore of the mid–Hudson Valley. Mostly, it reflected the fact that the ordinary farmer of the northeastern states was an active participant in national and even international markets. "His position was neither isolated nor independent. The call of warring Europe sounded in his grainfields."[7]

The economy of the village and town probably best illustrates the nature of the forces—traditional and modern, local and non-local—in Kingston's life. It was, of course, dominated by agricul-ture. In 1820 Kingston was a town of farmers, and it is apparent that even most of those who lived within the village earned all or part of their livelihoods from nearby farms, though a few of these were actually worked by slaves while their owners followed professional or commercial careers.[8] Marius Schoonmaker's de-scription of this village of more than three hundred adult males includes only some sixty businesses, most of which were run by individuals or families. Although much of this disparity is explained by slaves, employees, retirees, and a probable understatement of the number of businesses, it is evident that the commercial traders, professionals, and artisans of the village were outnumbered by its farmers. Furthermore, the businesses themselves were of a country character. Retail stores, for example, nearly all sold general merchandise rather than specializing in particular goods. J. Goodwin, a "druggist and grocer," actually sold drugs and medicines, dye wools and dye stuffs, spices, paints, oil, groceries, liquor, china and earthenware, and even millinery, all at "New York prices."[9] Edward O'Neal, another "druggist and grocer," sold dry goods, hardware, earthenware, drugs and medicines, paints and oil, dye stuffs, and more.[10] Moreover, grain was freely accepted by local storekeepers in payment for merchandise; indeed, such barter seems to have been the rule rather than the exception.[11]

"Manufacturing" bore the rural stamp even more clearly. Of the twenty-five or so established village artisans, at least seven were blacksmiths, two of whom specialized in the manufacturing of plows.[12] Two saddlers and harness makers, a wagonmaker, and a cider miller also catered to a predominantly rural clientele. But even more telling was the backwardness of the crafts. According to Schoonmaker, shoemaking and tailoring were still itinerant trades, with work performed in the home of the customer rather than in a shop.[13] Butchering was strictly a seasonal affair and is described by Schoonmaker in a tone nostalgic for the rural:

> The never-omitted killing time in the fall filled the corn-beef and pork-barrels in the cellar, and after the chopping-knife music, which at that season of the year was to be heard in every part of the village, the pendant sticks in the garret were filled with sausages, and the smoke-house at the same time with hams and other meats. Such preparations, together with a well-stocked turkey and chicken roost in the barn, left no need or occasion for draughts on the market in winter.[14]

Much of this butchering must have been done in the home by family members and by others who became professional butchers for the season. In fact, a substantial portion of the village's manufacturing was still done in the home. Families still spun their own flax and wool and still made some of their own clothing from them; only the weaving was done professionally.[15] Merchants sold cloth alongside clothing, and one of the local shoemakers, "having just returned from New York," offered his customers both shoes and sole-leather skins.[16] Indeed, most of the established tradesmen performed services which had never been performed in the home, for example, the four watchmakers, the two hatters (there were also two milliners), and the gunsmith.

The rural character of Kingston's economy was reflected in the physical structure of the village itself, particularly in the way the villagers distributed their homes and shops. As the above discussion seems to indicate, most of Kingston's storekeepers, craftsmen, and professionals continued the traditional practice of combining home and business on the same property. On the accompanying map of the village of Kingston (figure 2), there are sixty-four shops and stores, of which thirty-three—just over half—are also identifiable as the homes of their proprietors.[17] The true proportion is undoubtedly higher, since surviving sources are vague about some of the buildings near the periphery of the village, and several Kingstonians who seemingly separated their homes and shops really only crossed the street to get to work each day. Thus, commerce, manufacturing, and domestic life were still closely intermingled in Kingston and did not yet constitute separate spheres of existence for the men, women, or even children of the village.[18] Ironically, the only commuters in pre-canal Kingston were some of its village-dwelling farmers.

Although Kingston was a rural town with an agricultural economy in 1820, this does not mean that the town and its citizens were economically self-enclosed. On the contrary, as early as 1679 the Esopus Valley, of which the then stockaded village was the center, was described as "very beautiful and fertile wheatland, which here grows so abundantly, that this Esopus is the granary of the whole New Netherlands, and the adjacent places."[19] A similar but perhaps more modest statement could have been made in 1820. Kingston was still a "granary" for the Hudson Valley and a few "adjacent places," and wheat was still its principal crop, though supplemented by rye, corn, flax, and hay.[20] Interestingly, most Kingston grain seems to have gone not to New York City but to New England ports. According to Robert G. Albion, Boston in particular had begun a lively direct trade in grain with the Hudson Valley in order to compensate for its ever-growing local deficit in

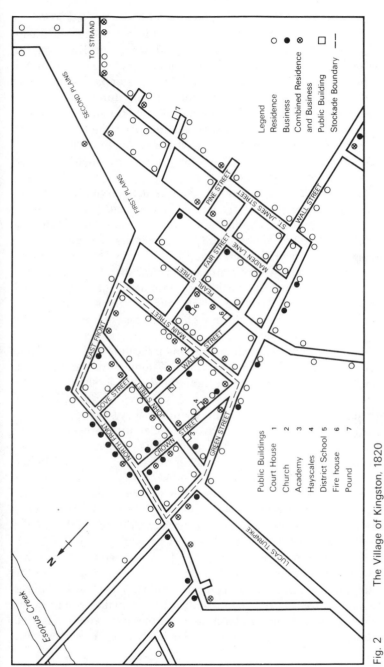

Fig. 2   The Village of Kingston, 1820

flour without paying for an expensive stopover in New York. In 1835, by no means the first year of this trade, thirty-nine shipments of grain, totaling approximately 4,500 tons, left Kingston for Boston.[21] While Albion does not supply equivalent figures for shipments from Kingston to other ports, it is apparent that these thirty-nine shipments were the bulk of Kingston's export. This would account for the otherwise inexplicable statement by a New York merchant (to Schoonmaker, decades after the fact) that the entire Kingston trade to New York was carried in four small sloops, that most of it was firewood and hoop poles, and that "very little grain was sent to New York."[22]

Kingston's local economy also had its more sophisticated side. Six establishments variously labeled hotels, inns, coffee houses, and taverns reflected the village's status as county seat, as did the fact that all three of the county's newspapers (Federalist, Clintonian, and Bucktail) were published there. The newspapers, incidentally, were general merchants in their own way, selling not only subscriptions but also books, stationery, job printing, and even elixir.[23] There were also at least four lawyers, several doctors, and a branch office of the Poughkeepsie-based Middle District Bank.

As the presence of such institutions indicates, and as we have already noted, Kingston performed a number of central place functions for the west shore hinterland. Yet it should not be assumed that the village was the only source of nonagricultural services for the farmers of the Esopus Valley. For example, an analysis of 112 mortgages entered in the County Mortgage Register indicates the degree to which long-term financing in Ulster County focused on Kingston. Of the 112 mortgagors, 104 lived in the county (13 in Kingston and 91 in other towns). And of these 91 rural borrowers, 41, or 45%, were able to locate funds within their own townships, while another 32, or 35%, went beyond the county to New York City (21%) and a variety of other places in the Hudson Valley (11%), Long Island (2%), and New Jersey (1%). This leaves 18 mortgagors, or 20%, who borrowed money in other towns within the county; and of these only 6, less than 7% of the total, came to Kingston for financial support.[24] It is true that this is the highest total in the county, but it hardly makes Kingston the center of long-term local capital.[25] Those who could not find capital in their own towns were more likely to go to surrounding towns than to Kingston—and more likely still to go all the way to New York. Kingston even failed to supply its own long-term capital needs; 5 of 13 mortgagors went outside the town for funds, 2 to other nearby towns.

Kingston's role in the county mortgage market underscores its more general economic status in both the county and the region. Here too, this one-time "granary of the whole New Netherlands" had slipped to a position of only moderate importance. I am not saying that Kingston had become indistinguishable from any other town. It was still the major outlet for the grain and lumber products of the immediate hinterland, even if that hinterland had shrunk considerably with the rise of other river towns north and south of Kingston, particularly Catskill and Newburgh. Kingston also remained the center of a lively shad and herring trade, although the market for this was not New York City or New England but the inland farmer himself, who came to Kingston from as far as fifty miles away for his yearly supply of salted and smoked fish.[26] Finally, Kingston was the source of New York goods for that large number of farmers and villagers who could not make the journey to the city themselves or could acquire the necessary credit only from more familiar local merchants. Still, Kingston maintained its commercial influence over a steadily diminishing area, so that by 1820 it was one of a half-dozen or so competing river towns rather than the most important town between New York and Albany. The role it had once played for the entire mid–Hudson Valley it now played for Ulster County alone.

Kingstonians realized that a continuation of this trend would result in a catastrophe far worse than that of 1777, one that could be prevented only by tapping the lumber and farming regions in and beyond the Catskill Mountains before their products were all drawn to Catskill and Newburgh. In 1802 they had acquired a charter from the state legislature for the Ulster and Delaware Turnpike Road, an ambitious project aimed at restoring Kingston's prominence as a trade center. The turnpike was to have two sections, one extending westward and beyond the mountains, over the Delaware River, through Delaware County, and into the heart of Chenango County, 104 miles away, and the other extending eastward from Rhinebeck on the opposite shore of the Hudson to the boundary of Connecticut.[27] Excitement about the prospects of the road ran high. The trustees bought one hundred shares on behalf of the village, and the incorporators were careful to limit annual dividends to ten per cent.[28] Moses Cantine, who owned Kingston Point (the projected terminus of the road), had the entire point surveyed and laid out in city lots, built himself a large stone mansion, and sold a number of lots to others who built houses in anticipation of the coming boom.[29]

The ruins we noticed on the point at the beginning of this chapter have already informed us of the fate of the Ulster and Delaware Turnpike Road. The eastern section was never begun. The western section was begun and went from Kingston Point through the village and into the mountains, but at a cost which made its completion impossible and its operation unprofitable. "Eventually, after much struggling, it was nearly all sold, surrendered, and districted."[30]

Other roads were attempted with the same result.[31] By 1820, therefore, Kingston was still without an effective and profitable route to the interior and knew of no prospects for obtaining one. When a few years later an interior route actually was accomplished, it resulted from initiatives taken far from Kingston, absorbed much greater sums than could ever have been raised at home, and tapped a hinterland undreamed of by the investors in the Ulster and Delaware Turnpike Road. But this is the story of another chapter.

In sum, the individual economic activities of the Kingstonians form a pattern that is at once rustic and cosmopolitan. The same may be said of the more explicitly communal institutions of government and politics. It is interesting, in light of the reluctance with which the original village was constructed, that the earliest settlers of Esopus erected no local government at all, not even after they came together within the stockade. The first local government was not established until 1661, eight or nine years after the original settlement, when Stuyvesant, acting under orders from Holland, created the municipality of Wiltwyck. The residents themselves seem to have had little to do with the creation of this government, which in turn had very little autonomy or authority.[32] A somewhat expanded local government was instituted by the British in 1669 (at which time Wiltwyck was renamed Kingston).[33] However, true local government did not arrive in the Esopus Valley until 1687, when Governor Dongan incorporated the Trustees of the Freeholders and Commonality of the Town of Kingston.[34] The new corporation could hold common land and sue and be sued as an entity. Its officers—twelve trustees, three assessors, and three constables—were all popularly elected and constituted the effective civil and judicial government of the town. Unlike its predecessors, the corporation enjoyed a long career, surviving the Revolution, accommodating itself to the incorporation of Kingston village in 1805, and finally succumbing in 1816, after a five-year legal battle with the New York State Legislature, which in 1811 had divided it into three ordinary towns (Kingston, Saugerties, and Esopus) with none of the special powers or privileges of the Dongan charter.[35] Also unlike its predecessors, the corporation that ruled Kingston for 129 years does seem to have been rather active and may well have helped generate a sense of communal membership among the Esopus Valley Dutch.[36] But there is reason to believe that during the last years of the eighteenth century, paralleling the general decline of the regional significance of Kingston, the corporation itself lost its impetus. Indeed, by 1805 (the year of the incorporation of the village of Kingston), it had weakened to a point where its very existence could be sacrificed to political warfare. In 1803, the trustees had sold the last remnants of Kingston's common lands and in the process built up a handsome treasury of some £6,000. This Federalist board was defeated in 1804 by the Republicans, who in turn foresaw their own defeat in the election of 1805. A few days before the election, therefore, they gave away almost the entire treasury to the three Dutch Reformed churches within the bounds of the corporation, "so that the interest arising from the same be appropriated toward paying the salary of a minister or ministers in the several aforesaid churches." The generous, saintly (Jeffersonian!) Republicans were defeated, and the incoming Federalist board faced a depleted treasury.[37] Interestingly, they did not attempt to nullify the gift or even alter its terms so that the church would apply the money to a corporation function (e.g., care of the poor). The 1811 act of the state legislature, therefore, was clearly no more than a *coup de grâce*.

In any case, local government in Kingston in 1820 consisted of an incorporated village, a much reduced township, and a county which itself had shrunk considerably since its creation in 1683.[38] The township and county were rather remote and diverse structures, consisting of courts, highway supervisors, commissioners of the poor, and the like, all performing their separate functions as separate bodies. In contrast, the village government was a tangible institution, composed of a single body of men who acted upon the particular problems of the more densely settled community. The village government was, therefore, most easily perceived by the villagers as their own community institution.

This is not to say that the village government was active in a large number of areas. On the contrary, one of the most striking features of the early village government was its inactivity. Its legal range of powers was fairly broad, extending to the regulation of "public markets, the assize of bread, town watch, lighting of streets, slaughter houses, public nuisances, fire companies, drainage, disorderly or tipling [sic] houses, restraining geese or swine, and the use of weights and measures."[39] But its actual operations were much more limited than this suggests. In its infancy it was even rather timid, as in the attempt of the first directors to organize a night watch, "to sustain the dignity of the village in its new position."[40] No funds yet existed in the village treasury, of course, and to arrange for a regular, official watch it would have been necessary either to levy a tax or to impose the obligation of serving on the inhabitants themselves. Fearing a tax so early in the game, the directors chose the latter course and divided the able-bodied, male householders into twenty citizens' watches, six men to each watch. The system took effect in June, failed to obtain the cooperation of the householders, and lasted until the middle of October. It was never revived.[41]

An analysis of the minutes of the board of directors in 1820–21 reveals not only the limited role the village government played in village life but also the informal manner in which its affairs were conducted.[42] The board met only twenty-two times during the year. During these meetings, it considered only thirty-five items of business, many of which were really old items carried over from previous meetings. Five of the meetings (accounting for sixteen of the thirty-five items) were held in the first two months of the board's existence, April and May. These meetings were devoted largely to setting things up for the year—choosing the president and clerk, appointing the village clock tender, establishing the assizes of bread and flour, and appointing new fire wardens to replace those who had been elected but refused to serve. Once the government had been properly established there was little left to do. The board met twice during the summer, then became only slightly more active in September when four meetings were held, two of which were immediately adjourned for lack of business. The other two were devoted to the village plains, two privately owned fields on the edge of the village that occasionally served as a ground for musters and other village events. On September 2, the board resolved to buy the plains for the use of the village, indicating the existence of at least some local sentiment for a genuine village common. On the following week, however, the board's offer of $200 was rejected, and the village remained, for a time at least, with a "common" it did not own.

Between late October and early January the board of directors met four times to consider only one matter, the village hayscales. On January 2 it confirmed an arrangement with Tunis Swart, himself a director, whereby he was to charge 25¢ for each load weighed and surrender one-third of the profits to the village. This arrangement was then scrapped on March 20, when Swart was charged a flat 9¢ per load and given this apparently lucrative concession for a full eight years. Perhaps it was on this day that Kingston's urban political life began.

What emerges most clearly from all this is the minor presence of the village government in Kingston's daily life. The board met irregularly and infrequently, first at the house of Henry Tucker, later at the house of the clerk and treasurer, Solomon Hasbrouck, and once at the house of Simon Mullen, for there was not even a village hall. The hayscales were an important element of the harvest season, but they were not run by the village. Only one nuisance (a defective chimney) was complained of and corrected during the year. There was no village watch. The only continuous physical presence of the village government was the two fire companies, and in fact much of the board's attention was given to their operation. They alone reminded the villagers each day that there was a public entity to which they and they alone belonged.

It is also evident that, unlike the earlier and much larger corporation, the village government had little or nothing to do with politics. Politics were very much alive in Kingston, but they existed only at higher levels. Of the three party newspapers published in Kingston, only the Bucktail Republican paper (the *Craftsman*) survives, but this paper clearly shows that the impetus, organization, and operation of party politics in New York State had very little to do with the local community as such.

Newspapers were, in the early nineteenth century, not community papers but organs of particular political parties or factions. Editors were often local party regulars but were, perhaps, even more frequently imported from other towns. In either case, the purpose of each paper was to spread the party gospel, attack the opposition, proclaim victory, explain away defeat, and, perhaps most important of all, serve as the medium through which the party communicated both doctrine and the schedules of party activity—nomination meetings, conventions, rallies, and elections—to its members. This is not to say that the content of the paper was entirely political, since both politics and business required as wide a circulation as possible. Therefore, much of each paper was given over to other things which could help the paper sell—advertisements, lists of prices and bank note markets, foreign news, fiction—anything which did not interfere with the paper's primary political mission. It is interesting that affairs of the village government (and, for that matter, of the village generally) did not meet either criterion. Political parties were obviously not interested in the annual "charter election"; there was no attempt to organize a ticket or a campaign through the pages of the paper. And the community itself demanded no information about its government; there was no mention in the news columns of the election results or of any other act of the village. Indeed, the village government got into the local press only by paying for it, that is, by advertising the annual treasurer's report or the time and place of a coming election.[43]

It is possible to make too much of the absence of village news. The village was small and the papers were published only once a week, so they could not possibly have competed with the backyard fence as a news medium. It is conceivable, therefore, that there was a lively interest in such things as village elections but no demand that they be reported in the local press. In this sense, the increasing attention given to local affairs in the following decades may say more about the village as a communications network than about the importance of local institutions. Nevertheless, the inattention of the local press (and particularly of the political parties) to village affairs seems to be consistent with our judgment that the village government played a small role in the life of the community.

At the same time that the political parties and their presses were failing to direct the attention of the community inward on itself, they were, of course, directing it outward to the state, the nation, and the world. The news printed in each paper was, as we have seen, almost entirely of a nonlocal character. Thus, in 1826 the editor of the *Ulster Sentinel* (successor to the *Craftsman*) complained:

> Alas! what are we poor editors, who live upon the marvellous, to do? The curtain has dropt upon the Kentucky Tragedy—there are no legislative bodies in session—The Panama Mission sleeps sweetly like moonlight upon a bank—The poor Greeks are down for the present; wars and rumours of wars have ceased in Europe—and as to local topics, the *State Road* has been served up in such a variety of ways, that we fear the public appetite is well nigh palled with it.[44]

The fact that the article that then follows is the first local item of a significant length to appear in the surviving issues of Kingston's press (except for descriptions of July Fourth celebrations) reinforces the point. In other words, only the paucity of state, national, and international news could justify turning the villagers' attention to local affairs. And note, in the above lament, that the word "local" refers to an issue on the state rather than on the community level.

More important than news, probably, were the activities of the parties themselves. For here a large portion of the adult male villagers and townsmen were thrust, in varying degrees, into a system of action that pyramided quite clearly to the state and, more sporadically, to the nation. Parties were organized, far more decisively than today, on the state level, and newspapers were organs of state rather than of national or local factions.[45] In 1820, although elections were held at all levels of government, the *Craftsman* devoted almost all its editorial attention to the gubernatorial race between De Witt Clinton and Daniel Tompkins. The rise of national electoral politics in the presidential campaign of 1828 removed politics one further step from the community. In 1827, the *Ulster Sentinel*, following the Albany Regency (Bucktail) decision to support Andrew Jackson, turned its attention increasingly to the national scene, specifically to the glorification of Jackson and the vilification of John Quincy Adams. All elections, state and local, were now conducted on the national "issues" of Jackson's abuse of military authority and Adams's "corrupt bargain" with Henry Clay, and all tickets, even in the town election, consisted of "Jackson men" and "Adams men."[46] The state parties were still the basic units of political organization, and the *Sentinel* was still a Bucktail rather than a Jacksonian paper. But the significant point is not the primacy of the state over the nation but the primacy of both over the community. In both issues and party organization, politics in Kingston were simply a local manifestation of a system whose center of authority lay well beyond the borders of the town.

Of course, the question of the importance of this system in the lives of the members of the community is a real one. Its importance to candidates, newspaper editors, recipients of patronage, and other party regulars may be taken for granted. But what of the population as a whole? How many Kingstonians actually read the local papers? How many responded in some significant way to this cosmopolitan political system? How many voted? Schoonmaker is one of many who mentions the "extremely bitter and personal" party feuds of the earliest years of the nineteenth century. "Many a fight was the result of a canvass, and the Court House yard and the street . . . were witnesses of many a bitter fray and pitched battle."[47] Alvin Kass has noted the practice of several Federalist banks in Albany and New York that refused credit to Republicans; a Federalist woolen mill in Trenton Falls that sold stock only to party faithfuls; and even a Federalist Catholic priest in Rhinebeck who christened a child with the name of John Adams though his Republican parents had chosen to name their son after Thomas Jefferson![48] Voter turnout in Kingston is simply not available for most elections, but in the gubernatorial election of 1826, which was not at all closely contested, it appears that some 70% to 75% of the electorate actually cast ballots.[49] More substantial evidence of the importance of politics in Kingston is lacking, but I think it is safe to say that politics did engage the minds and arouse the passions of a substantial portion of the community, at least during the autumn campaign.

For those who did participate in it, the political system, potentially one of the most powerful devices for emphasizing both the distinctiveness of the locality and the common life of those who lived there, served instead to emphasize membership in larger, nonlocal systems such as the state and the political party, to supply continuous news of the world at large, and to prevent communal action in a single unified body. On the other hand, politics also energized life in the public sector, and even though Kingstonians may have fought bitterly among themselves over issues that were entirely external to the community, they did experience through politics an intense *group* life that was, after all, acted out on the local level. In short, parties served to combine as well as to divide individuals. It may well be that cooperation within each party constituted the most significant incidence of communal activity and identity to be found in the locality, even if that cooperation was directed toward and by forces outside the locality itself.

Besides the local government, the only other formally organized institution in Kingston which was meant to embody the entire community was the Dutch Reformed Church. In view of the obvious unimportance of the local government, it is tempting to assume that the church was the true locus of community integration and control. Such an assumption would, after all, square with common notions concerning the role of the church in preindustrial, rural communities, and for empirical support we have already noticed the rather extraordinary gift to the church of the entire corporation treasury in 1805. There is, furthermore, much more evidence of the power of the church in Kingston. For example, there are other instances of public support, sometimes in the form of land grants, sometimes in the form of cash, as when the corporation paid one-half of the price of a new church bell in 1724.[50] "The trustees," according to Schoonmaker, "consisting, as they generally did, of the most prominent inhabitants, always exhibited great liberality to the church."[51]

The role of the church in the affairs of Kingston Academy is even more striking. The academy, founded in 1774, was directed by the trustees of the town corporation until 1795, when it became a corporation with its own board of trustees, one of whom was the Reverend George J. L. Doll, pastor of the Kingston church.[52] But the influence of the church did not derive solely from the Reverend Doll's trusteeship. From the beginning, academy students were required to attend public worship and were given a special section in the church gallery.[53] Each day's exercise during the all-important spring examinations were closed with a "declamation" in the church.[54] Of far greater importance, however, was the common assumption that the academy was a special protectorate of the church and that the ministers and church elders (who in fact dominated the academy board) should govern its activities. As we will see in another chapter, only in the 1850s, after more than a dozen different churches had been founded in Kingston, would the control of the academy by the Dutch Reformed Church be openly questioned.

Church attendance, according to Schoonmaker, "was very general on the part of old and young."[55] One of the very few local news items to appear in the Kingston press in the 1820s was an announcement of the annual "Thanksgiving Sermon for the abundant harvest."[56] Finally, the church was the center of two other institutions, both founded in 1816 by the Reverend John Gosman—a Sabbath school created "to teach the people of color to read the Bible" in anticipation of the emancipation of slaves in New York State, and the Ulster County Bible Society, the first of Kingston's voluntary reform societies.[57]

Undoubtedly, the church was important in Kingston. But there is a real danger, I believe, of assuming its role in village life to have been greater than it was. Besides our own prejudices about small-town life in the nineteenth century, the local historians themselves may well have written of the church more out of an arms-length respect than from a considered evaluation of its real influence. Actual membership in the church seems to have been rather small (judging from the surviving records of a slightly later date), and it is likely that the church's influence over noncommunicants was not so great as it was over full members. When Schoonmaker writes of the dances held in the village of his youth, he does so with great nostalgia and all but states that they were very well attended. Yet, "Church members seldom, if ever, attended the dance—it was not considered the proper place for them."[58] Did the members, then, form a respected but generally isolated segment of the community? Was the church an institution "belonging" to its limited membership and not to the community as a whole?

These questions become more significant when we consider the church not as a divine or even moral institution but as the tangible center of ethnic consciousness for the Dutch inhabitants of the village. The Dutch hegemony in Kingston is manifested everywhere in surviving documents. According to Schoonmaker, "The Dutch element was then largely in the ascendant, the Dutch language was the predominant language at the fireside, and Dutch customs prevailed in social intercourse."[59] The most interesting evidence of it comes from the *Ulster Sentinel*, the Bucktail paper founded in

1826 by a local boy, Charles G. De Witt. De Witt's paper was filled with ethnic material. Beginning on October 4, 1826, the masthead was graced with a woodcut of "the celebrated *Antony Van Corlaer*, seated near a tankard of racy *October*, enjoying his comfortable pipe over a sheet of the latest news," along with an appropriate slogan written in Dutch.[60] The premier local article to which we alluded earlier is entitled "The Church Bell." It is a long, humorous piece, detailing the complicated story of the acquisition of the latest church bell from Amsterdam, and filled with thoughtful Dutchmen smoking "several pipes" over each decision.[61] Two other long articles in the vein of Diedrich Knickerbocker followed, and constituted almost the entirety of locally oriented journalism.[62]

But the appearance of such ethnic material in the newspapers of the 1820s may be a sign of the decline of Dutch influence rather than of its survival. There is a distinctly antiquarian tone to these articles, and, perhaps significantly, all the Dutch words are translated into English. This latter point takes us back to the church, for the question of whether to continue the use of Dutch in church services and church records came to a head in 1808, at the beginning of the ministry of the Reverend Gosman. The Reverend Doll had preached occasionally in English; when he retired, the consistory decided that English should become the official language of the church. This precipitated a controversy that apparently, and understandably, was along generational lines. The older members demanded at least some Dutch preaching but were refused, and English became the sole language used within the Kingston church.[63] It is interesting that the lay leadership, not rebellious youth, were responsible for the change, and that only the very oldest members fought the decision. Obviously, the use of the Dutch language had declined markedly in Kingston by the turn of the century, contrary to Schoonmaker's recollection. We may speculate, therefore, that Dutch ethnic consciousness had also declined, and that the church served to focus this ethnic consciousness for a steadily declining proportion of the community.

Still, we must admit that there is simply no firm basis for evaluating the effect of the church on the cohesiveness of the community. Nor can we form a very clear picture of the degree to which the church functioned as a local institution free from external influence. The Kingston church originated within the synodical structure of the Dutch Reformed Church, but a dispute during the eighteenth century left it independent of any extracommunity ecclesiastical connection after 1775.[64] It remained so until the critical year of 1808, when, along with officially adopting the English language, the Kingston church joined the General Synod of the Protestant Dutch Church in North America, fitting into the hierarchy under the Particular Synod of Albany and, more specifically, the Classis of Ulster.[65] In other words, the Kingston church moved from independence to dependence during the early nineteenth century, at precisely the time when it may have weakened as an institution of the entire community. Whether this new structural linkage with the outside world actually changed the way in which the church functioned in the community is, of course, the real question. Consistory minutes, available only after 1841, are devoted largely to local administrative and judicial matters but also include lengthy annual reports to the Classis of Ulster, detailing such things as the general peace and prosperity of the church, the progress of auxiliary activities, and the statistics of membership, communion, baptism, and Sabbath school attendance.[66] But the accountability of the local church to the classis does not automatically translate into the loss of local control over church affairs. Nor does it tell us whether the sense of belonging to a unique and tangible local institution was altered by a new identification with the more general, abstract, and nonlocal denomination. We can note the existence of the new denominational tie, but we can do little more than guess at its significance.

The remainder of Kingston's formal organizations may be reviewed rather quickly. The academy has already entered our survey and will do so once again in the next chapter. Here we should note only that the academy did play a significant role in Kingston's communal life, not because the children of the town went to school there (most did not), but because of the seasonal ceremonies associated with it.[67] The semiannual examinations were public affairs of great importance—perhaps to the entire community and most certainly to those who considered themselves its elite. According to Schoonmaker, at any rate, "Every house was thrown open for the reception and entertainment of strangers and visitors, who flocked to the village on these occasions."[68] The day began with a procession of students and trustees and the ringing of the church bells. The examinations occupied the entire day and were followed by a public dinner and literary exercises, the church "decla-mation" (in the spring), and still more exercises (in the fall). The day was then topped off with a formal commencement ball that was un-doubtedly the biggest social event of the season. To some extent the ritual reflected the academy's excellent reputation in the state; it con-tracted somewhat as the academy declined during the early years of the nineteenth century. But the importance of the examination days in the social calendar of the 1820s cannot be doubted.[69]

All other local organizations were explicitly exclusive in mem-bership, though some were intended to serve the general com-munity. Freemasonry was apparently quite strong in Kingston before the Morgan affair, and each June 24 brought a celebration of the Masonic patron saint, St. John the Evangelist, complete with procession, church service, dinner, and toasts.[70] The two fire companies absorbed some of the energies of at least thirty of the village's young men.[71] New York State law required that all men between the ages of eighteen and forty-five be organized into militia companies, although Kingston could muster only nonuni-formed companies until some time during the early 1820s, when the Ulster Greys were organized.[72] There was also a Kingston Band organized in 1826, apparently from a preexisting, informal associa-tion.[73] The Kingston Society Library advertised in 1821 that stockholder arrearages might force a sale of books, and the Ulster County Bible Society, which we have already noticed, advertised its annual meeting in 1820.[74] There were only two organizations based on occupation, the Ulster County Medical Society and the Ulster County Agricultural Society, and these were divisions of state organizations that were really initiated by the state legisla-ture.[75] Finally, the most exciting local organization seems to have been the Kingston and Hurley Horse Thief Association, formed in 1828 not to steal horses but to protect them.[76]

One important dimension of local organizational life was the contribution that several of the village associations made to the village calendar. In addition to political elections, academy exami-nation days, and Masonic celebrations, there were the obvious church festivals and militia musters, and the annual county fair. But apart from the various organization-related events, there was one annual celebration that had an organizational life of its own, beginning perhaps as early as May and ending with the celebration itself on the Fourth of July. It is not clear when the practice began, but by 1820 the celebration of Independence Day had acquired a distinct pattern and a firm place in the village calendar. What is interesting about it is that it was an explicitly communal celebration, completely outside and above any of the "sectors" of the community. In this sense, it was analogous to the saints' days and other annual festivals of villages and towns all over the world. The analogy fails, of course, in another, equally important sense, in that Kingston's "saints" were national rather than local and were being celebrated simultaneously in other towns across the country. But the affair itself was strictly local in structure, and even though there must have been a great deal of borrowing between one town and another, it seems reasonable to treat this midsummer celebration as an important manifestation of the local culture.

Ostensibly, the Fourth of July celebration was an affair of the entire community. The machinery would be set in motion each year by an unsigned advertisement in the local press, addressed to "The Citizens of Kingston, who are desirous of celebrating the approaching *Anniversary of our National Independence*, without distinction of party,"[77] calling them to a meeting to begin the planning process. Just who placed the ad is a mystery, but it does not seem to have been written by the editor himself. The meeting would do no more than appoint a "committee of arrangements," which would in the following weeks actually plan the celebration and select the orator, the reader of the Declaration of Independence, the marshal, the assistant marshals, and anyone else to be connected with the affair in some official capacity. Then, several weeks before the Fourth, the newspapers would proclaim the Order of the Day (again as an advertisement), which, with some allowance for year-to-year variation, can be summarized as follows: the firing of cannons and ringing of bells at dawn; a procession formed at 11:30 A.M. at the courthouse (consisting of the first marshal, the Kingston Band, several militia officers, the orator and reader, the reverend clergy, the county judges, the second marshal, Captain Roosa's Uniform Company, "citizens generally," more military, survivors of the Revolution, directors of the village, and the committee of arrangements itself); exercises at the church (consisting of an "Address to the Throne of Grace" by the Reverend Gosman, the reading of the Declaration of Independence, and the oration, all interspersed with music); another procession; the official closing of the day with cannon and bells; and, in the evening, "a display of Rockets and other Fire-works" on the plains. Citizens of the village, the town, and neighboring towns were specifically invited.[78]

In addition to the official celebration, one or two (never more) of the village innkeepers would offer a public dinner. Here the burghers and gentry would gather not only to eat but also to offer several dozen prepared and volunteer toasts, usually to the nation's founders, to appropriate national symbols, and to ideological abstractions. Interestingly, very few of these gentlemen felt it appropriate to toast Kingston itself. In 1826, for example, there were thirteen prepared and twelve volunteer toasts—not one of which referred to a local group or institution, or to Kingston, Ulster County, the Hudson Valley, or even New York State.[79] Other years produced an occasional reference to the county or state, and in 1821 there was even a toast offered to "the inhabitants of Kingston"[80] but these were exceptional. Of course, the holiday itself was national, and it is not surprising that Kingston's men should reveal such a cosmopolitan frame of reference on this occasion. On the other hand, in another chapter we will see that even a unique event of great local importance evoked no more localized sentiment than did the Fourth of July.

Of greater significance is the way the Fourth of July celebration itself was planned and executed. Although there was much talk of the "citizens generally," it is clear that the general citizenry had little to do with it. The day was planned by a small committee of leading citizens, and the ceremonies themselves emphasized and rewarded, both in the procession and in the church exercises, the positions of local eminence. The focus of the exercises was the oration and reading, and these were clearly intended as honors bestowed on leading citizens. The dinner provided an opportunity for a small number of gentlemen to persuade one another, at their own expense, of their patriotism and eloquence, with the assurance that the subsequent newspaper article would list the name of each volunteer along with his toast. Only the fireworks seem to have been intended sheerly for the enjoyment of the entire community.

There is little in this description of pre-canal Kingston to suggest that its institutions functioned in ways that were unique to the town or to its more narrowly defined region, the Hudson Valley. Perhaps there are some clues (the inactive village board, the absence of a town meeting, the noncongregational structure of the local church, the organization of the celebration of the Fourth of July) that point to a community that was a less clearly defined and less potent force in the lives of its inhabitants than we might have found, for example, a few miles to the east in New England.[81] But we are obviously not yet in a position to compare Kingston in holistic terms with the communities of New England or anywhere else. Before we do, we must first come to grips with less tangible phenomena—with social classes, with day-to-day relationships, and with attitudes, expressed or implied, toward the community itself.

3   Class and Community
    in the Country Town

Although the white population of the Esopus Valley
was originally drawn from many parts of Western Europe, its
outstanding characteristic in the early nineteenth-century town of
Kingston was ethnic homogeneity. Generations of life and inter-
marriage with the predominating Dutch, and of worship in the
Dutch Reformed Church, had brought French Huguenot families
such as Dubois, German families such as Schoonmaker, and
English families such as Brodhead well within and even to the fore-
front of a community which was, by 1800, as Dutch as Diedrich
Knickerbocker.

The only significant exceptions to this ethnic uniformity were the
black slaves and freedmen, whose positions were rather clearly
fixed at the bottom of the social order. In 1820 about 10% of the
population of the town of Kingston consisted of black slaves, while
another 2% were freedmen, recently liberated in anticipation of the
general emancipation scheduled for 1827 in New York State.[1] The
inferior status of black Kingstonians is illustrated by the *Ulster
Sentinel*'s observation that most freedmen wasted little time in
leaving the community entirely:

> A few of this ill-fated race, more wise and faithful than the rest,
> still remain in their old chimney corners to spend their days in
> comfort; but the wicked ones, the thieves, the drunkards, and the
> bullies, are all gone to that paradise of negroes, *the City of New
> York!* There let them stay, a curse or blessing to those who made
> themselves so busy in their behalf.[2]

Even more revealing is a list of criminal convictions in Ulster
County in 1827, which includes sentences ranging from seven to
fourteen years for counterfeiting, three months for assault and
battery, three years for assault and battery with intent to kill, and,
among these others, a sentence meted out to "a coloured boy" for
burglary—life![3] In the decades that followed, Kingston would

provide very little support for the Free-Soil and abolitionist movements, and the blacks who remained in the town would also remain
at the bottom of the social ladder. By 1860, they constituted less
than 2% of the local population.[4]

The status of blacks in rural Kingston is far clearer than are the
distinctions of wealth, power, and prestige among the white
majority. The problem, of course, is one of data. The United States
census of 1820 is barely more than an enumeration of households,
and the New York State census of 1825 for Ulster County does not
even survive. There are no local tax records or parish registers,
practically no local reportage in the press, and no gossip-filled
diaries. There is only the inevitable Schoonmaker, a diary kept by
one Henry Vanderlyn—an out-migrant who recalls his Kingston
youth—and a random item or two from the press. From this we
must reconstruct a social structure!

Schoonmaker, with memory to serve him, is less timid:

> Although the social manners and customs of those days were
> simple, and not burdened with the formalities of the present
> fashionable life, still there were castes and grades in society as
> strongly marked and as rigidly observed in social intercourse, if
> not more so, than at the present time.[5]

Although this hardly suffices as proof of a highly stratified
community, it is perhaps made more interesting by the strong
impression one gets from the rest of Schoonmaker's history that he
would have liked to have concluded otherwise. The writing of local
history, especially of one's own hometown, is often motivated by
nostalgia for what is remembered as a simpler and purer past.
Furthermore, the "good old days" syndrome generally includes a
conception of the community as a closely knit and unstratified
whole. Schoonmaker is not exempt from this. His comment on
"castes and grades" is sandwiched between discussions of quilting
bees, apple cuts, and Christmas celebrations. His entire presentation of local customs makes no reference to class distinctions, while
another passage, many pages removed from his comment on social
stratification, implies that there were no extremes in the distribution of wealth:

> Their habits were thus at that time simple and plain. Not accus-
> tomed to the luxuries of the city and fashionable society, their
> wants were few and moderate. A man then worth fifteen or

twenty thousand dollars was considered wealthy, and as independent as one who can in these days count his hundreds of thousands.[6]

Wide differences in individual or family fortunes are not, of course, necessary for the existence of a rigid and pronounced social hierarchy. It is thus quite possible that Kingston maintained its "castes and grades" on rather small differences in property and income, especially in the presence of other criteria such as "breeding," church membership, public office holding, and venerable ancestry. Evidence of how these sorts of distinctions operated is, unfortunately, extremely hard to acquire, but we can obtain at least a glimpse of Kingston's early nineteenth-century "aristocracy" from the diary of another youthful participant, Henry Vanderlyn. Vanderlyn was born into an old, "respectable" Kingston family in 1782. His father was a physician and his uncle, the painter John Vanderlyn, was Kingston's most famous son.[7] Henry attended Kingston Academy and Union College and then, after four years of legal study in Kingston and New York, left in 1806 for Oxford, Chenango County, about a hundred miles west of Kingston. There he lived out his long life as a bachelor, wealthy lawyer, and squire, returning to Kingston only once or twice, the last time in 1826. Inspired, perhaps, by the combination of recently won success and his visit to his boyhood home, Vanderlyn began a diary in 1827 that he maintained faithfully for thirty years. It begins with remembrances of his Kingston youth.

Only a small portion of these recollections concern the ordinary small-town pastimes of playing ball, flying kites, and picking berries.[8] Mostly, they are devoted to the author's preparations for life, preparations that the young Henry seems to have enjoyed to an inordinate degree. The academy in particular looms large in his memory:

> I recollect with some pride & pleasure my Youthful studies, to which I then devoted for my age, great application. To be first in my class, & to speak the best speech in public, were the objects of my constant Ambition. I remember, well, sitting on my father's lap, in the morning before school commenced, repeating my latin lessons, & receiving his instruction. He took great pains in preparing my speeches which were delivered in church or court House at the annual fall commencements. I was then much dis-

tinguished in the Academy for my public speaking, and was considered one of the best speakers and scholars.[9]

One can easily imagine this eager young fellow, twenty or thirty years later, rising with complete confidence on the Fourth of July to offer a volunteer toast, perhaps partly in Latin, even without his father there to write it for him.

But the nurture of children like Henry Vanderlyn was not trusted entirely to Kingston Academy or even to the various English schoolmasters to whom they were also sent:

> I was sent to Dancing school in the summer time at deWalls dancing room, when I was in the Academy. The boys & girls of Kingston were here first bro't together to study grace, politeness & the art of pleasing. We had a fine school, and I was fond of the amusement.[10]

Upon graduation from the academy, Vanderlyn attended Union College. Of three other classmates who are remembered in his diary, Christopher Tappen, Jr., went on to Yale, Severyn Bruyn attended Princeton, and Lewis Bevier returned to his native Marbletown to become a "wealthy and respectable" farmer.[11]

It is clear that the education described here was far from a casual affair. Vanderlyn, Tappen, Bruyn, and even Bevier were not pulled out of school for the spring planting or the summer harvest. Neither were they given the rudiments of literacy and arithmetic and then packed off to an apprenticeship. Undoubtedly, their education in the classics and in "grace, politeness & the art of pleasing" was intended to set them off in skill, outlook, and manners from the vast majority of their young townsmen, who probably attended only the district school in the back room of the village gunsmith's shop. "To have said that the early academy was aristocratic," writes one local historian, "would have described it accurately."[12] Higher education has, of course, always served in part and in most places as a training ground for social elites. Our only surprise, if any, should lie in the discovery that it may have played the same role in this small American country town.

On the other hand, Vanderlyn's recollections of Kingston are not all on such a lofty plane. Indeed, one of the most interesting features of his diary is the amount of space he devotes to describing lost fortunes, such as that of "Jacob Tremper (youngest son of old Jacob Tremper a rich man), [who] is now so poor, that he works at day labour, chopping wood, for his support."[13] Vanderlyn's own father died a bankrupt in 1802, which was a great shock to the young law clerk, who had assumed his family to be prosperous.[14] Vanderlyn more than rebuilt his fortune in Oxford, but he was apparently left with a deep impression of the transiency of fortune and status. Imagine his delight when

> On the 13 June 1806, my friend and schoolfellow, Ch. Tappen, Jr. wrote me a letter from Kingston, informing me inter alia that my Brother Peter's nuptials with the $25 thousand dollar prize Miss Bauman of N York was this afternoon solemnized at the Revd. Mr. Doll's.[15]

In general, the limited sources at our disposal suggest a social order in which money combined with breeding and race to divide Kingstonians into at least three and perhaps four fairly tangible strata. At the bottom were the slaves, the freedmen who "still remain in their old chimney corners," and perhaps a few poor whites, lost to our view. A step higher were the white hired hands and village workers who, we shall see later, may have constituted a much larger proportion of the population than both our sources and our prejudices would have us believe. Above these non-proprietary whites (from whom we should probably exclude sons of prosperous citizens, and other young men who were expected to rise in the world in the course of time) were the town's farmers, storekeepers, master craftsmen, professionals, officials, and comfortable retirees, who constituted the "respectable" portion of the community—indeed, in their own eyes, probably constituted the community itself. And within this group, property, polish, and high public office seem to have set off a certain number of men and families as a community elite. Or is the term too strong? Were the "gentlemen" who toasted "the Heroes and Sages of the Revolution" and sent their children to Kingston Academy and Union College really that restricted a group? Perhaps more important, were they a secure and impermeable group, a stable collection of men, perhaps bearing venerable Esopus Valley names, who had little reason to share Henry Vanderlyn's sense of the transiency of fortune and status?

Some sense of the size and stability of Kingston's "elite" may be gained from Schoonmaker's compilation of the names and dates of service of the trustees of the old corporation from 1688 to 1816.[16]

This list may be analyzed in terms of the pervasiveness and continuity of particular family names, provided we bear in mind certain limitations. First, it is possible that there were two or more entirely separate lineages with the same family name. Second, it is also possible that the community itself did not define "family" according to strict kinship lines, as in the case of feuding brothers whose families grow further apart with each generation while continuing to bear the same name. Both these factors warn us that we will overstate family continuity through the mere use of surnames. On the other hand, families may be based as much on maternal as on paternal lineage, especially in the prevailing generation, so the use of surnames will also understate the influence of particular families. Our errors, therefore, will be to some extent self-compensating, although this does not mean that the following analysis of surnames is more than a crude way of analyzing the political influence of actual families. Finally, the list itself refers to the holding of political position, not to membership in a social elite. We can only assume that there was a strong relationship between the two; a better assumption, I think, for the old corporation than for the less active local governments that succeeded it.

Leaving aside the few who Schoonmaker claims were lost because of incomplete records, we find that there were 262 men who served a total of 1,426 terms as trustees of the corporation between 1688 and 1816, an average of over 5 terms per man. These men, in turn, represented 102 surnames, for an average of 2.6 men and just under 14 annual terms for each surname represented. Since we do not know how many different surnames there were in Kingston during this period, it is difficult to estimate the exclusiveness of this list. The United States census of 1790 lists 534 separate households that were headed by men and women bearing 197 different surnames, but there is no way of knowing the number of other names that had been present before that time.[17] Patricia Bonomi, in a similar analysis, finds that 41% of the freeholders (61 of 148) living in Kingston in 1728 served at some time during their lives as trustees. She also suggests, on the other hand, that this proportion dropped as the town grew and aged, with the dozen annually elected trustees drawn from a gradually growing pool of possible candidates, and, more important, with a noticeable increase after 1730 in the numbers of trustees serving multiple terms.[18]

The trusteeships indicated on the Schoonmaker list were not, of course, distributed evenly among all 102 family names. In fact, the concentration of office holding is quite pronounced. Only 27 names provided the corporation with 4 or more trustees, led by De Witt with 10, Elmendorph and Sleght with 9, Dumond with 8, and Dubois and Delamater with 7. At the other extreme there are 51 names, exactly half the total number, that account for only 1 trustee each. In all, 153 of the 262 trustees are accounted for by the leading 27 names. A slightly different "top 27" is achieved by comparing the total number of terms served by men with different surnames, but the concentration is no less pronounced. At one end there are the Sleghts, Wynkoops, and De Witts, each of which accounted for more than 60 terms, while at the other there are 60 surnames that accounted for fewer than 10. If we combine the criteria of number of men and number of terms, we can reasonably construct a list of 32 family names that clearly dominated the old corporation.

What is most interesting about these names is that they are by no means offstage by 1820. Indeed, the continuity between office holding in the old corporation and in the new village and town is remarkable. For example, of the eighteen town officers elected in 1820, ten bore the names of the leading 32 corporation "families," four bore names from the rest of the list of 102, and four were not present at all in the records of the corporation. Remarkably, seven names can be traced back to trusteeships of the seventeenth century! As for the four upstarts, all bore names that were to remain prominent in Kingston's political life for at least the next forty years.

The leadership of the village is every bit as striking. Of the thirteen officers elected in 1820, eight were from the "top 32" surnames, two were on the rest of the corporation list, and three were newcomers. Four of the five directors of the village bore names from the "top 32," all five could trace their names in the corporation trustee list at least as far back as 1727, and three could trace their names to 1695 and beyond. The shortest span of corporation service for the apparent forebears of the village board was by the Swarts, who served over a span of 89 years. (Perhaps the hayscales concession was an inducement to settle down.) Finally, all three of the newcomers in the local government were fire wardens, then the lowest office in the village.

However, even if we accept these figures as evidence of a remarkable continuity of local political leadership in rural Kingston over a span of more than 130 years, we cannot claim to have established the existence of a narrowly restricted community elite. Indeed, we may prefer to regard the thirty-two leading surnames as a fairly broad segment of this moderately sized town, ruling (to borrow Mack Walker's charming phrase) as "a regime of uncles."[19] Bonomi's analysis points up the middling occupational status of many of Kingston's eighteenth-century trustees and reminds us that the economic differences among the white householders of the town—the "respectable" portion of the community—were not that great.[20] Continuity of the castes and grades of this conservative little Dutch community may well have been much greater than in other American settings, but the term "aristocracy," though useful, was used in Kingston only as a metaphor.

The structure of classes, in any event, does not by itself inform us of the texture and tone of local life. How friendly and informal were Kingstonians with one another? To what extent did each interact in the same way with each of his fellow villagers and townsmen? What did each resident expect from his neighbors and expect to give in return? With these questions, of course, we reach that dimension of community life that is most often invoked when an attempt is made to define the small town as something quite different from larger places.

The difficulty of using Schoonmaker's history of Kingston in this connection rises not from his avoidance of the issue but from the problem of separating accurate observation from nostalgic invention. Actually, his comments about the nature of interactions in the village are quite lengthy. We have already seen (and questioned) his statement about the retention of the Dutch language in the home and on the streets, as well as his statement that relationships, though structured along social class lines, were quite informal. But there is much more, all in the same vein of small-town informality and, we may add, communality:

> The social gatherings were usually confined to neighborly afternoon visits, in which the whole afternoon, until an early tea, was passed in social chat, while the knitting needle was industriously plied in preparing comfortable coverings for the feet. Large evening parties were not common.... Quilting bees were frequent, when, after spending the afternoon at that work, the quilt

and frame would be removed, tea discussed and after tea the young men would come in to have a jolly time with the girls.[21]

Quiet ruled this little community on the Sabbath, according to Schoonmaker, and violators of the Sabbath were displayed as such in the courthouse yard stocks. Funerals, "although simple and inexpensive," involved the distribution of gifts of tobacco, pipes, and gin to the friends who attended.[22] As for the extensiveness of friendship, or at least of acquaintance, Schoonmaker claims that he knew every inhabitant of the village, young and old.[23] The farmers of the community turned their friendships into action at harvest time through husking bees, "enlivened with songs and stories, and not infrequently followed by a hot pot-pie supper at midnight."[24]

There was also a somewhat more formal side to social life. Evening tea parties were organized by giving oral invitations on the previous day. Winter and commencement balls were more elaborate, involving printed invitations and hired sleighs but usually stopping short of either a full orchestra or a full dinner.[25] To this we may add Henry Vanderlyn's observation of the social role once played by Marius Schoonmaker's own mother:

Immediately over the way lived Miss Cornelia Morris, daughter of Peter Marius Groen: an amiable girl, with an inviting kindness in her air & manner: & who had the happy art, of making her house an agreeable rendezvous, for the young ladies & gentlemen of K.[26]

It is immediately apparent that all these characterizations suffer not only from nostalgia but, even more important, from the special perspectives of class. Both Schoonmaker and Vanderlyn are describing not Kingston but Kingston's polite society. When we turn to the local newspapers for a more general view we get only a little help. The idea of the informality of village life is buttressed slightly by one editorial in the *Craftsman* that attacks the county clerk for insisting on keeping his office open only according to regular hours.[27] But this is a political attack; the county clerk was the brother of the editor of the rival *Plebeian*. Somewhat more revealing is the following threat of public ridicule which appeared in the *Ulster Sentinel* in 1827:

The person residing at Eddyville [a small hamlet about three miles from the village], who on Friday night last, carried away from the Store of the subscriber a valuable Book, is requested forthwith to return it, or he will be called upon in his proper name.[28]

The ad appeared but once.

A community where acquaintanceship is universal, and where shoplifters are effectively intimidated by threats of public exposure, is not necessarily a community that evokes a strong sense of local identity and commitment. What, then, shall we make of the fact that virtually the only written local commentaries that survive from this period of Kingston's history are a few humorous, mildly satirical articles in the *Ulster Sentinel* and some disdainful remarks about the town in the diary of an apostate son? What shall we make of the failure of gentlemen assembled at public dinners to toast the town, its colorful history, its people, or any of its institutions? Was Kingston important to its inhabitants only as the immediate locale of social life, as a collection of specific individuals, relationships, and recurring activities? Or was its significance as a locus of cultural identity and citizenship so great and so clear that it required no comment? These questions are answerable, if at all, only by reference to those dimensions of the community's life that we have already surveyed. That is, while we may never be able to interpret confidently the silence of rural Kingstonians on the subject of their community, we can at least characterize the social context of that silence and from that context, perhaps, suggest the superiority of one interpretation over another. To Sherlock Holmes, who knew all about such matters, the fact that the dog did *not* bark was even more significant than if he had:

> "Is there any point to which you would wish to draw my attention?"
> "To the curious incident of the dog in the night-time."
> "The dog did nothing in the night-time."
> "That was the curious incident," remarked Sherlock Holmes.[29]

Let us note first that rural Kingston was anything but an isolated, self-sufficient community. What Roland Warren has called the "vertical pattern" of the community, "the structural and functional relation of its various social units and subsystems to extracommunity systems,"[30] was strong, complex, and in some respects reached back to the earliest settlement of the Esopus Valley. Of the various components of Kingston's vertical pattern, the most important, and the most visible, were the economic relationships with New York City and New England and the political relationships with the state government in Albany and with the state's political parties. But nearly all of Kingston's "voluntary" organizations, including the church, the Masons, the professional societies, and the militia, were linked in varying degrees with larger organizations, usually on the state level. And there were significant extralocal relationships of a nonorganizational character. Local residents maintained ties, through correspondence and travel, with friends and kin living elsewhere. Local storekeepers urged their customers to shop in Kingston rather than New York, and, although this may be less significant for the question at hand, there was apparently a certain amount of travel, to New York and elsewhere, for the sheer pleasure of seeing other places. Charles G. De Witt, the young, native-born editor of the *Ulster Sentinel*, writes of the "patriarchs among us who knit their brows and knock the ashes out of their pipes, when we speak of going to New York twice a year"[31] and of "The *Second Crop*, (as they call us youngsters,) who have been taught Latin and Greek and once or twice had the immortal honour of a walk in Broadway."[32] Henry Vanderlyn's diary (written, remember, in Oxford, New York) is filled with references to correspondence, to long-range visits between friends and family, and to pleasure journeys to such places as New York, Niagara Falls, and Saratoga Springs, although the latter really do not begin until the 1830s. On October 24, 1820, Kingston's delinquent firemen appeared before the village board to offer their excuses. Of the sixteen delinquents, eight reported that they had been out of town—four to New York, one to Albany, two "to the westward," and one simply "from home."[33] Finally, we should recall the cosmopolitan influence of the local newspapers, not simply in their political function but also as bearers of news from Albany, Washington, and far beyond.

Contact with the outside world was probably not distributed evenly across all segments of the community, although the sources here are as elusive as those relating to social stratification. Vanderlyn's diary presents a fascinating picture of travel in which each small party of travelers, cooped up together for hours, quickly turns its small stagecoach into a salon of polite conversation, the conversation itself often turning on the discovery of mutual acquaintances in various towns. Never does there appear to be a

simple yeoman or mechanic to intrude on the affair. The cosmopolitan organizations were probably led by and sometimes even
restricted to the well-to-do, and it is likely that these organizations—political parties, professional societies, militia units, and the
like—were critical to the creation and maintenance of what one is
tempted to call a regional elite community.[34] Commerce was, of
course, the most important link between members of different
localities and may well have shaped extralocal organizational life.
Finally, I have already indicated that education in academies and
colleges was primarily an elite phenomenon. I may add the
suggestion that many of the relationships constituting the "regional
elite community" were formed at the few educational centers to
which the wealthy sent their children.

On the other hand, it is far less certain that nonlocal social life
was restricted exclusively to the rich. Vanderlyn's travel descriptions surely reflect his own class-bound perceptions as faithfully as
they do the actual composition of the traveling population, and
there were, besides, many ways for even the poor to travel other
than in stagecoaches. Migration, a phenomenon more characteristic of poor and middling folk than of the wealthy, is travel of a
different sort, but it too may break down social parochialism,
particularly when kin are left behind. The degree and pattern of
travel and of extralocal social relations by ordinary people in the
prerailroad age are extremely difficult subjects to speculate about,
and so is their participation in cosmopolitan organizations. How
many ordinary citizens participated actively in political party
mechanisms? To what extent did this participation actually expand
their associations and social frames of reference to levels beyond
and larger than the community? These questions and others like
them must be answered before we can assume that the wealthy
were more cosmopolitan than their less comfortable neighbors.[35]

Warren's concept of the community's vertical pattern is primarily intended to help identify and interpret the sources of community weakness and is set against the parallel concept of the community's "horizontal pattern, . . . the structural and functional
relation of its various social units and subsystems *to each other.*"[36]
The two sets of orientations are intended to appear as competitors, so that the most significant fact of community life in
contemporary America may be seen to be "the increasing orientation of local community units toward extracommunity systems of

which they are a part, with a *corresponding* decline in community cohesion and autonomy."[37] But this formulation seems to ignore an equally imposing threat to community cohesion from "below." Cannot a community consist of essentially autonomous households, joined to one another by little more than physical proximity? Cannot the community's horizontal pattern suffer from the self-sufficiency of local units as well as from their orientation to extracommunity systems?

Rural Kingston does seem to have been weakened from both above and below. Consider, for example, certain aspects of its economic life. Warren's conception of the community system includes the performance of five "locality-relevant functions," one of which is "production-distribution-consumption."[38] His assumption is that this function will be integrated locally through the exchange of goods and services within the community and nonlocally through the numerous economic relationships that local retailers, wholesalers, manufacturers, banks, and consumers maintain with the outside world. Kingston's residents, as we have seen, bought consumer goods in Kingston itself and in New York City, and the town's agricultural products were sold both locally and in wider markets. But the balance of these horizontal and vertical transactions does not fully account for the performance of this local function. Much was done in the household itself, in isolation or near-isolation from other local institutions. Kingston's farmers, along with their families and slaves, grew much of their own food and manufactured clothing and a wide range of household articles, with only a moderate amount of interaction with other households or with stores. Corn was shucked by the farmer and his friends, but the land was sown and the harvest gathered by individual households (including slaves and hired hands). Kingston maintained a professional weaver or two, and both cloth and clothing could be purchased locally (or in New York), but much of the clothing worn in the village and on the farm was made in the home, some of it from homegrown flax. Shoes and hides could also be purchased, but the butchering season yielded leather as well as meat, and the months that followed left plenty of time for tanning and leatherwork.

The general weakness and inactivity of Kingston's formal organizations (for example, the village government and the fire and militia companies) and the paucity of communal events on the village calendar may well reflect the orientations of many of her residents to systems both above and below the community. In any case, the horizontal pattern of rural Kingston appears to have been weaker, perhaps much weaker, than the sociologists of the twentieth-century community and the historians of the New England town would lead us to expect. Early nineteenth-century Kingstonians, at least, seem to have preserved the anticommunitarian social tendencies of their not so remote ancestors, the first settlers of the Esopus Valley.

Given this social context, the silence of Kingstonians on the subject of Kingston strongly suggests a culture in which the abstract ideal of "community," and the rather more concrete ideal of membership in *this* community, were of minor significance. Moreover, we should note that this interpretation coincides with those of the few scholars who have inquired into the culture of the Hudson Valley Dutch. "The individualism of the [early] Dutch was in strong contrast to the social spirit shown in the English towns," comments Albert E. McKinley in an article published at the turn of this century. "They had no common interest in the land, no local political powers, and ... but scant opportunity, perhaps little desire, for common religious worship."[39] Dixon Ryan Fox cites McKinley in his fascinating account of some two centuries of border and culture conflict between communal "Yankees" and individualistic "Yorkers,"[40] and Lee Benson, in his study of Jacksonian politics in New York State, finds Fox's distinction useful for explaining political behavior as late as the election of 1844.[41] The American Dutch are probably better known for their resistance to change than for their individualism, but in the studies of Fox and Benson we find evidence of a great deal of both.

In the diary of Henry Vanderlyn there exists a charming little sketch of one of Kingston's early nineteenth-century residents:

> Opposite to us, lived David Delamater, a farmer, whose peaceable life, passed on without a struggle. He was every day seen smoking his pipe, and lived in ignorance of the common events of the world: His only employment was to smoke and light his pipe.[42]

It has been the argument of this chapter, in effect, that David Delamater was not typical of his fellow villagers and townsmen.

Kingston was not an isolated, tightly knit "folk" or "peasant" community in 1820. Its economy was agricultural, but it was also commercial. Kingston's "formal" institutions were not bureaucratically organized, but they did pyramid upward to rather modern extracommunity systems such as state legislatures and political parties. Its residents shared one another's acquaintance, but they seem to have recognized no special common bonds beyond that of "neighbor" and were probably more likely to identify themselves as Americans, Yorkers, Republicans, or Van Keurens than as Kingstonians. But by describing rural Kingston as both cosmopolitan and individualistic, we have not reduced the significance of the change the town would experience in the decades of growth that would follow the opening of the Delaware and Hudson Canal. Rather, we have only removed one possible misconception about the nature of the rural town that is our baseline. Let us turn, then, to that sequence of events and developments that made even David Delamater knock the ashes out of his pipe.

4   The Canal and the Economy

On the twenty-fifth day of November, 1826, an
unusual celebration took place in the valley of Rondout Creek, not
far from the junction of the Rondout with the Hudson River. At
about 10:30 A.M. the *Morning-Star*, carrying the members of the
local lodges of the Masonic fraternity, the Kingston Band, and
other citizens, left the dock at Wilbur and headed, not downstream
toward Kingston Landing, Poughkeepsie, Newburgh, or New
York, but upstream toward the falls at Eddyville less than a mile
away. A large crowd had already assembled at Eddyville to await
the *Morning-Star* and to watch her strange voyage—around the
falls of the Rondout and back into the creek above the falls—
inaugurating and dedicating the brand-new canal lock that made
this feat possible.

The celebration itself was, in country terms, splendid. Cannons
roared and the band played when the *Morning-Star* "locked
through" to waters never before navigated by craft larger than
Indian canoes. Freemasons performed the impressive ritual of
"laying the perfect ashlar," and the Reverend Gosman offered a
prayer "to the Throne of Grace." Then the *Morning-Star*, drawn by
a pair of "gorgeously caparisoned" horses, went for a short voyage
up the Rondout:

> Every where the old and the young, the mother and the
> daughter, the husband and the wife, hurried forward to witness
> the sight. They smiled, they shouted, they shrugged their shoul-
> ders and stared with open mouths at the magic scene which the
> *Yankees* had conjured up.[1]

At the end of this ride another Masonic procession led to a
farmhouse where Radcliff, the Kingston innkeeper, had prepared a
dinner. The dinner and the day were concluded, like a Fourth of
July, with a series of toasts—to the canal, the canal company, the

officers and stockholders, the engineers and contractors, the *Morning-Star*, the Masons, internal improvements, "American Enterprize," De Witt Clinton, and so on. Characteristically, not one glass was raised to Kingston, to Ulster County, or to the Rondout or Hudson Valleys.[2]

But even though the assembled dignitaries failed to turn the occasion toward the glorification of Kingston and the Rondout Valley, they did understand its importance to the area's economy. For the tiny stretch of canal dedicated on November 25, 1826 was soon to become the tidewater lock of the 108-mile, 110-lock Delaware and Hudson Canal, which in less than two years would join the Hudson River to the anthracite mines of northeastern Pennsylvania and cause a substantial portion of their vast mineral wealth to flow through the Rondout Valley on its way to New York City and other ports. Moreover (though the Kingstonians did not know this yet), the Van Gaasbeck farm at Kingston Landing would be transformed into the tidewater coal depot of the Delaware and Hudson Canal Company. It little mattered that Kingston itself had played no part in the acquisition of the canal or that the canal's operation lay in the hands of businessmen from New York and Philadelphia. Nor did it particularly matter that the profits from the coal trade would line few local pockets. The canal was significant to the men who celebrated the Eddyville lock because it would turn substantial amounts of New York forest and farmland into a hinterland of Kingston rather than of Newburgh or some other river town. Farm produce, lumber, tanning bark, tanned hides, and other country products that might have gone elsewhere would now flow through Kingston on their way to New York and New England, often under the control of Kingston merchants. The profits to be gained would inspire other enterprises as yet unvisualized by local entrepreneurs; these, in turn, would spur still others. Perhaps more important, Kingston would grow and in the process provide an expanding local market. The decision to build the D & H Canal through the Rondout Valley, made by men who knew and cared little about its towns, was indeed "the turning point in the prosperity of Kingston."[3]

It was to prove that and much more. The most frequently recalled event in the history of Kingston is unquestionably the burning of the village in 1777. But in the years after the British had done their day's work the village was rebuilt to almost exactly its old form and appearance, and although individual fortunes were dramatically changed, the catastrophe of 1777 did not permanently alter the life of rural Kingston. The very opposite is true of the invasion of more peaceful and more welcome outsiders in the 1820s. The construction of the D & H Canal set in motion a virtual transformation of this old country town—its economy, its population, its physical form, its institutions, its social relationships, and even its meaning as a community to those who lived there in that first post-canal generation. For about seven generations Kingston had been rural, with a slowly growing village and an economy based squarely on agriculture. In the next generation it would become a small commercial city. This transformation, from rural to urban and from agricultural to commercial, is, of course, the subject of this and all the chapters that follow.

It is here, however, in the examination of the changing economy of post-canal Kingston, that we can see most clearly the significance of the canal in dislodging the town from its rural past.

The anthracite trade itself was, first of all, an enormous new input into Kingston's rural economy, increasing from 7,000 tons during the first full year of operations to a million tons and more during each of the nine years preceding the Civil War.[4] Even though there were few local owners of D & H stock, a large number of Kingstonians found other ways of participating in this trade.[5] Some purchased canalboats or became wage earners in the company's employ. Others made livings by selling groceries, liquor, and dry goods to boatmen and laborers on the company's docks. Still others joined in the carrying of coal *away* from Kingston to other ports in the valley. (In September, 1833, a little past the midpoint of a season that would yield only 111,333 tons of coal, the *Ulster Republican* reported the following vessels cleared since April 1: 56 barges, 11 brigs, 166 schooners, 372 sloops, and 42 canalboats—almost 650 vessels, all bearing Lackawanna "stone coal."[6]) Still, the direct benefits of the coal trade were overshadowed by the canal itself and the opportunities it now gave to Kingston-based traders in country produce. The hinterland trade never rivaled the anthracite trade in volume, of course, but it did increase substantially—from just under 33,000 tons in 1831 (itself a substantial increase over prior years, no doubt) to over 83,000 tons by 1850 and fully 150,000 tons by 1860 (see table 1). In 1834, a group of Kingston businessmen and politicians interested in creat-

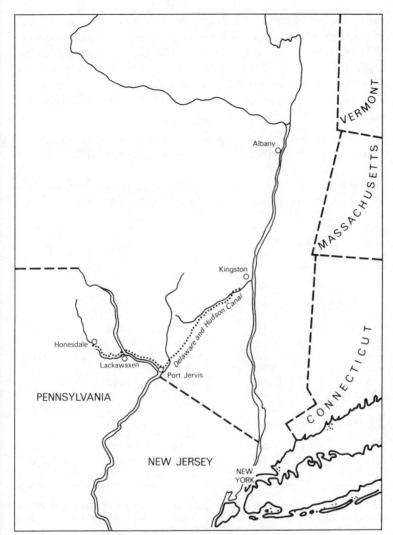

Fig. 3   Route of the Delaware and Hudson Canal

ing a new local bank could already point to an impressive increase in dockside activity, for there were now four steamboats and from thirty to forty sloops engaging in regular trade between Kingston and other ports.[7] And this, of course, was only the beginning, the first five years of Kingston's canal era. By 1850 a local merchant, after reading a steamboat advertisement from the year 1815, could reflect:

> What a change: now we have 7 or 8 steamboats of double the tonnage each ... from the village of Rondout alone! Instead of 4

Table 1   Freight Tonnage (Excluding Anthracite) on the Delaware and Hudson Canal, 1831, 1840, 1850, and 1860.

	1831	1840	1850	1860
Merchandise and provisions	5,193	6,978	18,029	15,542
Cement and cement stone	2,941	11,440	23,298	57,846
Stone, brick, and lime	537	1,009	3,624	3,423
Lumber[a]	5,045	11,059	16,954	41,984
Firewood[b]	15,928	17,954	1,092	12,156
Other wood and wood products[c]	2,217	3,519	6,702	6,178
Leather and hides	—	686	4,962	7,299
Other[d]	1,042	2,826	8,593	5,644
Total tonnage	32,903	55,471	83,254	150,072

SOURCE: *Annual Report of the Board of Managers of the Delaware and Hudson Canal Co. to the Stockholders* ... (New York, 1832, 1841, 1851, 1861).

[a] Calculated at .00175 tons per board foot.

[b] Calculated at 2 tons per cord.

[c] Includes shingles, tanning bark, charcoal, ship timber, railroad ties, barrel staves, hoop poles, and miscellaneous wood manufactures. Shingles calculated at .25 tons per 1,000. Ship timber and railroad ties calculated at .024 tons per cubic foot.

[d] Includes iron, tools, plaster, millstones, glass and glassware, lead ore, and others.

trips per week from Albany and New York we have 2 boats per day from our creek—those from the two great cities are beyond mental enumeration.[8]

The "Rondout" to which this statement refers was the bustling new village that had grown up around the docks at Kingston Landing. Its growth was itself indicative of the increase in trade after the opening of the canal. But not all of Kingston's (and Rondout's) new trade came through the Rondout Valley. Inspired by the canal, Kingston's merchants quickly rekindled the movement for improved overland linkage with the western hinterland, for the southwesterly course of the canal meant that Kingston still did not effectively tap the forests and farmlands that lay directly to the west. Delaware County logs, for example, were still run down the Delaware River on spring freshets, avoiding the Hudson Valley entirely. Around 1830, the old scheme of constructing a turnpike from Kingston to Delaware County was revived by local entrepreneurs, who secured the incorporation of the Kingston and Middletown Turnpike Road Company.[9] This time the project succeeded. Whether local capital was by then sufficient to the task, or whether outside funds were drawn to Kingston by its favorable prospects, is impossible to discover. In any event, stock in the company was adequately subscribed and directors were chosen in 1831.[10] Construction was apparently begun immediately, for on June 26, 1833 the *Ulster Palladium* reported the road to be nearing completion. By 1838 the *Ulster Republican* could boast of large quantities of produce being brought to Kingston from both Delaware and Greene counties,[11] and connections with Greene County were improved five years later with a branch road called the Prattsville Turnpike.[12] By the early 1850s the Kingston and Middletown Turnpike had become the Ulster and Delaware Plank Road and had been connected with another plank road which ran through the village of Kingston to the docks at both Roundout and the adjoining hamlet of Wilbur.[13]

Much of Kingston's new business, of course, was simply an expansion of a very old trade in the products of farm and forest. At least two major developments, however, must have been entirely unforeseen before the opening of the canal. Kingstonians had long been aware of the usefulness of the stone that lay beneath their feet, and for several generations they had been building substantial homes out of locally quarried limestone. Before the canal, however, there appears to have been no sustained attempt to turn this local resource into a commercial enterprise. After the canal had been built (the excavations themselves uncovered important new deposits), the limestone and cement trade developed, gradually at first, then very rapidly under the spur of demand created by the construction of the Croton Aqueduct.[14] After a temporary peak in 1839 the trade leveled off and even declined for a few years, but by the late 1840s it provided the most important article of general commerce on the D & H Canal, rivaled only by lumber and provisions. By 1860 it was the clear leader, accounting for more than a third of the noncoal tonnage clearing the Eddyville lock. And this tells only a part of the story, for a number of quarries and plants had appeared below the tidewater lock. The largest of these was a quarry belonging to the Newark Lime and Cement Company, opened in 1844 on a steep hill next to the village of Rondout.[15] By 1851 a cement plant had been added to the quarry, and processed cement joined limestone as a major item of export from the new village.[16]

In 1836, inspired no doubt by the success of the cement trade, Kingstonians began turning to a similar resource—a variety of sandstone called bluestone—that would ultimately give Kingston a certain measure of economic fame. The rapid growth of America's cities, particularly the one at the mouth of the Hudson, was creating an immense demand for construction materials. One special need was for a flagstone for sidewalks, crosswalks, outdoor stairs, and the like that would not become smooth and slippery under continual wear. Bluestone, as it happened, met this criterion,[17] and soon a lively trade was developed between Kingston and New York. The first shipment was made by one Philip Lockwood in 1837, from a quarry he had opened the previous year.[18] In 1839, William and Simeon Fitch entered the bluestone trade and soon became the largest of the local exporters. Their yard, like most of the bluestone yards, was located in Wilbur; their stone was brought to the Wilbur docks by wagons that passed through the village of Kingston and down the steep, mile-long Wilbur Road. The trade soon became extensive enough to dominate village traffic. In 1850 one local paper noted the arrival of 180 "stone teams" in one day at Fitch's dock alone.[19] Three years later the *Ulster Republican*, tabulating the January sleighing traffic in the village, counted some 190 flagstone loads each day for a week and estimated their daily value at more than $2,000.[20]

Although we cannot measure the growth of the trade that passed through Kingston in the decades following the completion of the canal, there can be no question about Kingston's emergence as a commercial center for a large portion of the countryside that stretched back from the west bank of the Hudson River. Indicative of this development are some of the listings in the *Kingston and Rondout Directory* of 1858—for example, eleven flour and grain dealers, sixteen hotels (several of which advertised in the local newspapers), and two "Forwarding and Transportation" firms.[21] Even more indicative, however, was the increase in such critical ancillary activities as banking and insurance. In 1820 the only banking facility in Kingston was a local branch of the Pough-keepsie-based Middle District Bank. But this bank went out of business in 1829—ironically, at the very moment that Kingston's prospects for economic development were assured. Accordingly, it was with no great difficulty that Kingston acquired a charter for the Bank of Ulster County, which opened its doors in 1832.[22] The next bank, however, was the significant one, for its possession was hotly contested by the town of Saugerties. Kingstonians argued that the canal made their town the most convenient location for serving the capital needs of the county.[23] Saugerties, ten miles to the north at the falls of Esopus Creek, claimed that the falls provided her with manufacturing advantages that Kingston did not have and that it would be unfair to locate both the county's banks in one town. Saugerties's arguments were accurate and fair, but Kingston was awarded the new bank.[24] Thereafter, owing to the easing of the banking law by the legislature, banks and other financial institutions were founded whenever and wherever the local means and will existed. By 1860 Kingston could boast of five such facilities—four commercial banks and the Ulster County Savings Institution[25]—as well as two fire insurance and two accident insurance companies,[26] all products of this era of rapid commercial development.

That Kingston's financial institutions were intended to serve commerce rather than the capital needs of farmers and household-ers is indicated by their minimal involvement in the mortgage market. A sample of 137 mortgages entered in the Ulster County Mortgage Register between 1858 and 1860 includes only 12 in which the mortgagee is specified as a Kingston financial institution, and 11 of these specify the Ulster County Savings Institution.[27] Interestingly, however, there does appear to have been a modest increase in the concentration of the county's long-term, secured capital in Kingston, even though this sort of borrowing remained in private hands. In 1820 there had been no such concentration. Mortgagors tended to find capital in their own towns, and, when they did look elsewhere, they were more likely to find it in New York City than in Kingston. By 1860 they were still likely to borrow money in their own towns; 55 of 91 mortgagors who lived in Ulster County towns other than Kingston contracted with mortgagees from the same town. But now Kingston was the most important "external" source of secured loans. Of the remaining 36 borrowers residing in other towns, 15 secured funds in Kingston, compared with 11 mortgagees from all other Ulster County towns, 7 from nearby counties, 1 from Cayuga County, and, most surprising of all, only 2 from New York City. On the other hand, Kingston borrowers still did not contract more than 21 of 36 mortgages with fellow townsmen.[28] The change after 1820, in sum, was modest, but when we combine it with the increase in local banking facilities, we can sense the degree to which Kingston's commercial development was paralleled by an increasing concentration there of commercial and noncommercial capital.

Kingston, in short, had come to acquire most of the economic institutions characteristic of the mid-nineteenth-century commercial city. Its major new transportation facility, the D & H Canal, was somewhat uncharacteristic for a New York canal in that it was built by a private company for the movement of its own goods; it was the only major canal in the state that did not connect with the great spinal system that centered on the Erie. It was, however, open to general merchandise, and it played the same role in Kingston that all the trunk and feeder canals played for their terminal cities. The more important local industries stimulated by the canal were also a bit unusual but had the same vitalizing effect on the economy that they would have had if they had been cotton mills or machine shops. And there was nothing unique in Kingston's new financial facilities, or its port, or its new wholesalers and hotels. These were the same institutions that were appearing in all the cities that had recently become breakpoints and termini on the nation's new transportation system. Kingston's history in these respects was repeated wherever this system turned little villages into the collecting points of American abundance.[29]

The same was true of the manner in which old facilities and practices were transformed by expanding commerce. The dominant commercial enterprise in pre-canal Kingston, as in any rural village of that era, was the general store; and the most obvious characteristic of merchandising, even by those who identified themselves with a particular product, was the absence or near-absence of specialization. Second, a cash economy undoubtedly did exist, but it was probably less important than the exchange of consumer goods for country produce. Finally, many of the items sold in Kingston's stores were the materials for home manufactures—cloth, leather, and the like—rather than finished goods.[30]

All this changed dramatically in succeeding decades. The newspaper advertisements of the 1850s reveal at a glance as well as on deeper examination a local commercial structure that can no longer be called rural. Those of the 1830s and 1840s allow us to follow the course and sense the pace of that structure's evolution. For example, the advertisements in the *Ulster Palladium* of 1831 differ from those of 1820 only in an increased emphasis on the willingness of local merchants to accept country produce and wood in exchange for merchandise, reflecting, no doubt, the recent upsurge in trade. Joseph S. Smith's Ulster County Store, for instance, advertised the usual country assortment: dry goods, flannels, plaids, broadcloths, calicoes, silks, muslins, handkerchiefs, cravats, thread, linens, gloves and mittens, hose, hairbrushes, combs, umbrellas, groceries, spirits, tea, sugar, molasses, fish, goose feathers, flour, candles, iron, nails, crockery, mirrors, window glass, Shaker brushes and brooms, churns, paints, oils, putty, axes, powder and shot, cheese, butter, and seed. Moreover, Smith was willing to receive, in exchange or for cash, farm and forest goods: wheat, corn, rye, oats, buckwheat, beans, peas, dried peaches and apples, hemlock shingles and joists, and hemlock and chestnut boards. Interestingly, a "card" offers the hope that the state legislature will charter a local bank and a turnpike from Kingston to Delaware County, and praises the hard work and other attributes of the farmer.[31]

General stores like the Ulster County Store still dominated the advertising columns in the early 1830s. Furthermore, more specialized tradesmen such as tailors and metalworkers continued to produce goods largely or even entirely on order, and, along with the general merchants, still offered materials for home manufacture. Like the general merchant, the more specialized craftsman or storekeeper continued to accept produce and other goods in exchange—for example, William Hall's Copper, Tin, and Sheet Iron Manufactory accepted country produce, old pewter, lead, and rags.[32]

In 1840 the structure of local commerce was still much the same as it had been for longer than two decades. But the advertisements in the *Ulster Republican* of that year reveal some interesting new developments. First, though general merchandising was still the rule, there was a slight trend toward specialization, both in the number of stores that were identified with specific products and in the range of products actually carried in each store. More important, there was the beginning of a trend toward cash payment. J. H. Eamon, for example, advertised a "cash dry goods store" as a new enterprise that would coexist with his old, traditionally operated store in the same line.[33] Jacob W. Dillon, a general merchant, advised customers that he had just adopted the "new method" of buying and selling for cash, "on principle of the nimble sixpence."[34] On the other hand, many ads continued to emphasize that farm and forest products would be accepted as payment for merchandise. Third, there is something quite new in the advertising columns of this period—the patent medicine ad. At least seven of them appeared in the *Ulster Republican* in 1840, each listing a local agent who was sometimes, but not always, a druggist. Thus, while Harrison's Specific Ointment was available at Clay's drugstore to sufferers from swelling, tumors, ulcers, sore legs, and "other external diseases," Dr. Taylor's Balsam of Liverwort could be purchased at J. W. Baldwin's general store, and Morrison's Genuine Hygaean Universal Medicine was sold at Chipp's bookstore.[35]

These new elements, barely visible in 1840, were highly developed by 1860. Specialization was now the rule rather than the exception; only one true general store, Langworthy's Emporium, was discernible out of more than eighty local advertisements.[36] Now there were stores that sold only boots and shoes; stores that sold only fur hats, coats, and gloves; and stores that sold only hardware. Grocers sold only groceries (and sometimes only liquor), and even dry goods stores tended to restrict themselves to dry goods. There were also a photographer, a hairdresser and perfumer, a piano store, a tree nursery, and a gas fitter—none of whom sold flour, fish, crockery, or even patent medicine. More than one ad indicates that specialization was not only continuing but was becoming a selling point as well; for example, H. R. Romeyn advertised his desire to sell out his dry goods so that he could concentrate exclusively on groceries.[37] Romeyn, incidentally, was the last Kingston merchant whose ad in the *Republican* showed him combining these two branches of retailing. The *Kingston and Rondout Directory*, which appeared for the second time in 1858, used 87 different headings in that year to classify some 450 businesses and professionals.[38]

Still, the trend toward specialization was not complete and may have been less fully developed for the town as a whole than for those stores which advertised in the newspapers. In the Rondout *Courier* of August 28, 1857, there is a letter complaining that Rondout merchants are too generalized ("toothbrushes and No. 3 Mackeral, . . . Rancid Lard, Wagon Grease and Fancy Letter Paper") and are, therefore, inexpert in any one line of goods.[39] But this letter may say more about the acceptance of specialization as a virtue than about the actual structure of local retailing. Three years later, the *Courier* described at great length the emergence of sophisticated (i.e., specialized) merchandising in Rondout since the "primitive days" of ten years earlier: "Hardware refuses a longer alliance with groceries, or even stoves and tin ware. . . . Hats and caps will no longer keep company with boots and shoes. . . . Dry goods . . . have actually divided upon themselves and split into the purely useful and the purely ornamental departments."[40]

By 1860 most if not all goods were sold for cash or cash-based credit. Not one advertisement indicates that country produce would be taken in exchange, and only one storekeeper (a jeweler who needed old gold and silver) advertised exchange of any kind. Several ads mention cash specifically, but most are silent on the subject, indicating, perhaps, that the "new system" of 1840 was taken for granted by 1860. The cash system, after all, is but an extension of commercial specialization, and farm and forest products were probably being shipped almost exclusively by men who specialized in wholesaling country produce.

The advertisements of 1860 clearly indicate that home manufacturing was no longer significant in Kingston. In the place of the cloth and leather that once formed a large portion of imported merchandise, local merchants now sold a wide variety of clothing, hats, gloves, and shoes. Furthermore, many of these items were ready-made, although custom craftsmanship had by no means entirely disappeared. Most often, a local shop would offer a variety of ready-made articles and add at the bottom of the list the fact that goods would also be made to order. It is impossible to determine the proportion of local craftsmanship to the sum of finished products sold locally, but it is fair to estimate that it was rather small, at least for those products that had formerly been made in the home. Corroboration for the disappearance of home production, moreover, may be gained from the 1855 state census schedules, which describe the production of each local farm. Domestic manufacturing is indicated for only twelve of 157 farms listed in Kingston, and these produced a total of 359 yards of cloth and no other products. The 1835 census had recorded 7,687 yards produced "in the domestic way," which means that the home manufacture of cloth had declined by more than 95% in twenty years.[41]

In other ways, too, the advertising columns of the 1850s suggest a new kind of economy. There had always been two or three ads from nonlocal businesses, usually from New York City. As late as 1840 there were only three, plus the seven quasi-local patent medicine ads we have already noted. Shortly thereafter, the number of nonlocal ads began to grow substantially. In 1845, the *Ulster Republican* created a short-lived special section of some two columns for the ads of over sixty New York City wholesalers and manufacturers whose attention had been drawn to the growing town up the river.[42] This was exceptional, however, and probably resulted from a special solicitation by the newspaper itself. Still, the number of ads placed by New York manufacturers, wholesalers, and retailers did grow steadily from the earlier base. By 1860 there were at least 20. In addition, there were at least 6 advertisements by big-city publishers of books and magazines, and no fewer than 27 ads for patent medicines and other medical marvels. (One, perhaps more candid than the rest, advertised: "Tastes like Bourbon whiskey").[43] Many of the medicines, incidentally, were no longer sold through local agents but could be ordered only through the mail.

On balance, the proliferation of local stores was probably more important than the increase in nonlocal and mail-order advertising. Kingston's merchants had for years implored their townsmen not to go to New York to shop; now, for the first time, they could offer them the opportunity to meet almost all their needs locally. Undoubtedly, there was a per capita increase in both local and nonlocal consuming as more and more Kingstonians involved themselves with the marketplace generally. But the more significant development seems to have been local consuming, and at least a portion of the increase in local retailing, especially in such lines as furs and fancy dry goods, must have been achieved at the expense of New York. It would be a mistake, therefore, to emphasize only those ways in which Kingston's post-canal economic development brought it increasingly within the orbit of New York City. In some respects its effect was just the opposite, for the population growth that attended economic development had provided the basis for expanded, more sophisticated local institutions. Though more closely integrated into a regional and perhaps national economy, Kingston was at the same time capable of providing local services that it could not have provided in its rural past; and its residents looked to the town for some of the things they had found previously only in larger, distant places. Just as Kingston expanded the scope and range of its "central place functions" for the farmers, loggers, and tanners of the mid–Hudson Valley, it found the means to perform "locality-relevant functions" better for its own citizens.[44] The point, obviously, has wider application than to retailing alone or even than to the economy as a whole. We will return to it in subsequent chapters.

It must not be assumed that Kingston's economy developed equally in all sectors. On the contrary, the concept of specialization is even more strongly applicable to the town as a whole than to its retail stores. Kingston developed, specifically, as a regional entrepôt and a local retail center. With the exception of the processing of lime and cement, its manufacturing remained largely undeveloped, differing from that of the pre-canal town primarily in that very little manufacturing was performed in the home in 1860. The number of producing shops grew with the population, of course, and some shops grew in size; but most remained small, and much of the transfer of production from home to shop was accomplished by transferring production to other localities, particularly New York City. Several documents of the 1850s permit an unusually close view of these developments.[45] The manuscript schedules of the New York State census of 1855, for example, detail the industrial firms of each census tract. The itemizations are far

Table 2   Kingston's Ten Leading Industrial Firms, 1855

Name	Product	Capital	Value of Annual Product	Average Employment
Newark Lime & Cement Co.	cement	$85,000	$156,000	204
Lawrence Cement Co.	cement	80,000	100,000	64
Baldwin & Co.	machinery	22,000	70,000	?
Alexander Schufeldt	cement	17,000	50,000	60
Langworthy & Dillon	iron castings	20,000	32,000	34
Brown's Lime Mfry.	lime	7,000	31,500	48
Hermance & Brigham	carriages	3,000	28,500	30
Stirling Smith & Co.	wire, etc.	6,600	20,850	27
Nathaniel Bruce	lime	9,000	20,000	28
Spears & Briggs	lime	8,000	19,700	23
Total		$257,600	$528,550	

Source: Manuscript census schedules, 1855.

from perfect (a number of small shops are missing, while several entries refer to nonindustrial firms), but they do include most if not all of the larger companies. Of twenty-nine entries which may be said to be industrial, only nine indicate an average employment of more than twenty hands, although Baldwin & Co., whose employment figures are not listed, probably employed at least twice that number. Six of these ten firms were lime or cement manufacturers, led by the industrial giant of Kingston, the Newark Lime and Cement Company, which employed two hundred men and four boys to process $156,000 worth of cement each year. No other lime or cement company besides these six appears in the schedules, indicating that this particular industry consisted entirely of fairly large units. Similarly, there are only two iron foundries listed in the 1855 census, and both of these were among the largest ten firms. The remaining two were the carriage shop of Hermance and Brigham and a manufacturer of wire and other metal products (including dog muzzles) named Sterling Smith & Company. If the census tract had been drawn a bit differently, the list would probably have included the lager beer brewery of George F. Von Beck. Von Beck's brewery, located across Rondout Creek in South Rondout, seems to have been the nation's largest, although we should quickly note that lager (as opposed to ale or porter) brewing was in its infancy in America in 1855, and Von Beck's firm was probably not very large.[46]

Even with the brewery included, the list of Kingston's leading producers is not very impressive either in its length or in the size of most of its units. The remaining entries in the 1855 census, furthermore, demonstrate even more clearly the continued domination of the small shop. Four cabinetmakers, for example, employed a *total* of fifteen men and three boys. Two carriage makers besides Hermance and Brigham employed six hands apiece. The town's only tannery employed five men, the only listed baker employed six, and the chandler employed three. There were also cigar makers, carpenters, a confectioner, a spoke maker, a dyewood manufacturer, and several others. Only one of these others employed as many as a dozen men (the Rondout and Kingston Gas Light Company, which should not really be considered industrial), and most of them employed fewer than six. As for the producers who were not included in the survey, we may safely assume that these were generally even smaller.

The editors of the papers of both Kingston and the new village of Rondout were sensitive to Kingston's industrial backwardness. In the 1850s, with increasing frequency, the Rondout *Courier* and the *Ulster Republican* urged the development of local manufacturers so that Kingston might become something more than a village of stores. The local banks were lending much of their capital to outsiders such as the Hudson River Railroad, the Erie Railroad, the Delaware and Lackawanna Mining Company, and even "some Pennsylvania land speculators," none of whom intended to help develop and diversify the local economy. More of this capital, argued the *Republican*, should be used for the development of industrial firms such as Baldwin's foundry.[47] The Rondout *Courier* was even more insistent on the development of local manufacturing and less particular about its source. Outsiders should not be discouraged but encouraged, particularly if they could bring to the area industries which were presently lacking, such as wool and cotton manufacture.[48]

The local editors might have shown a little less enthusiasm for the development of local manufacturing if they had reflected on its implications for the organization of labor. As things stood, there was very little organization among the wage earners of Kingston and Rondout and a very short history of labor agitation, at least according to surviving documents. In 1836, a year in which trade unionism was nearing a temporary peak in America, the *Ulster Republican* reported a "mechanics' meeting," called "to take into consideration the propriety of establishing some general regulations for their respective branches of business, and adopt measures to prevent the merchants interfering with their rights."[49] A committee of fifteen was appointed to confer with the merchants, and the proceedings of the meeting were submitted to "all the papers in the county willing to publish them."[50] This is all that remains from the first decade of post-canal growth. There is not even a follow-up article on the meeting with the merchants.

There is more to be learned from this one item, however, than that overt conflict between capital and labor was infrequent. The fact that the adversary relationship was between mechanics (undifferentiated as to masters and journeymen) and merchants suggests that industrial production was evolving much more slowly in Kingston than in larger cities. In the latter, the "merchant-capitalist stage" of production—that is, the emergence of large shops or many small shops under the control of exporting merchants—had severed the old guildlike ties between master and journeyman. In New York, Philadelphia, and other cities, associations closed to master craftsmen were becoming vehicles for pressing the rights and expressing the grievances of journeymen, and the master was increasingly identified with the large capitalist as the enemy of wage labor. The master, caught between the price he could get from a more powerful merchant-capitalist and the wages he paid to his journeymen, formed organizations of his own or continued those being abandoned by journeymen.[51] In short, that series of complex, intricate, and rapid changes usually labeled the Industrial Revolution was occurring in and around American cities at precisely the time that Kingston's mechanics were sitting down with local merchants to discuss their grievances. But the structure of this meeting, and the ad hoc character of the mechanics' meeting which preceded it, indicate that these dramatic changes in the structure of industry and of the relationship between labor and capital had not yet affected the few little shops of this Hudson Valley town. Rather, what seems to have happened was that local merchants were beginning to ship goods made by local artisans into the hinterland, creating, for the first time, a contractual relationship between producers and distributors. Whether this relationship had provoked any significant antagonisms between artisans and merchants before August, 1836 is a matter on which we can only speculate.

With the exception of the report on a meeting held in 1841 to elect delegates to a state convention protesting the use of state prisoners for cheap labor,[52] there is not a hint in the local press of further labor unrest or organization in Kingston until 1850. Even then there was nothing which could be called a labor movement. On March 29, 1850, for example, the Rondout *Courier* carried a paid notice of a meeting of journeymen ship carpenters and caulkers, which included a resolution of *individual* resistance to an uncompensated lengthening of the work day by the Delaware and Hudson Canal Company.[53] Sixty signatures were claimed in the ad, but as with the mechanics' confrontation with the merchants fourteen years earlier, there is no indication of the outcome.

Not until 1854, apparently, did Kingston actually experience a strike. Then on April 11 some three or four hundred laborers struck the D & H for higher wages and a ten-hour day. The precipitating factor was a raise in pay from 75¢ to 87½¢ per day, with a promise of another raise to $1 in two weeks. The workers had expected an immediate raise to $1, and, with the first coal of the season coming down the canal, walked off the job.[54] On April 12, the striking workers met at the Rondout Village Hall, where they resolved to demand an immediate raise to $1 along with a ten-hour day, heard the company manager reject their demands, and listened to a Catholic priest and one Bernard Quinn urge them to return to work. On the next night the striking workers resolved to form a "Laborers' Protective Union."[55] The Rondout press disapproved of the whole affair. The nonpartisan (but Whiggish) *Courier*, while admitting that "a dollar a day is little enough for any laborer," lectured the strikers that "there is always a right and wrong way of getting at amended conditions between employers and employed." The laborers had chosen the wrong way: "Had they simply and temperately stated their wants, in all probability the Company would have met them on a fair compromise."[56]

In any case, the company won, simply by reoffering the raise to $1 after the date originally intended for that raise arrived. The strikers went back to work on April 24, without their ten-hour day and under the threat that anyone remaining out on strike would be fired.[57] No further record exists of the Laborers' Protective Union "founded" on April 12. During the following season, while the price of food rose substantially, the D & H laborers' wages fell back to 87½¢ without incident.[58] An attempt to strike in 1856 was ignored by the D & H and broke during the first day. The *Courier* gloated, "'sivin shillins' sure, was better than whistling for a dollar."[59]

Other incidents may have occurred without having been reported in the local press. Nathaniel Booth, the Wilbur diarist whom we caught marveling at the improvement in steamboat service, mentions in his entry of July 18, 1854, an "Exodus" of bluestone quarrymen which he attributes to the low price of stone and the high price of food.[60] Booth also recorded, on January 3, 1853, the rather mysterious entry:

> The insidious remarks of our neighbors in the same [bluestone] trade, places us in a dilemma. . . . The workmen on the quarries have been tampered with and refuse to acknowledge any right on our part to the stone or the land they work on—they number about 120 men and will probably give us trouble.[61]

Whether any questions more fundamental than that of Booth's legal title to the quarry are involved here is impossible to say. In any case, exactly one week later his diary relates the end of the difficulty.[62]

If there were any other incidents of conflict between labor and capital in Kingston before the Civil War, there is no surviving record of them. Nor is there any sign of labor organization except, perhaps, for something called the Hudson River Health Association, identified in the *Ulster Republican* as an "association of working men and others," founded to provide accident insurance for its members,[63] and a similar association called the Rondout Laborers' Benevolent Association, founded by George F. Von Beck and other prosperous, German-born Rondouters.[64] Records of subscriptions to and payments by these two organizations do not exist, but one suspects that the "others" were more important to their operations than were the "working men."

The virtual absence of an organized labor movement in antebellum Kingston reflects its emergent industrial structure. There were, first of all, relatively few manufacturing firms. Second, most of those that did exist were small and rather varied, so that there were seldom more than a few journeymen who shared the same grievances at the same time. But the relative backwardness of Kingston's industry does not mean that its wage-earning class was insignificant or that there were no large units in the local economy. On the contrary, we have seen that several companies involved primarily in *extractive* processes and commerce gave the town both an identifiable proletariat and a significant element of large-scale economic organization. The fact that the employees of the canal company, the lime and cement companies, and the bluestone quarries were mostly unskilled and semiskilled (and, we may add, mostly recent emigrants from Ireland and Germany) meant only that they were less able to organize successfully into effective unions. The Newark Lime and Cement Company, let us recall, employed over 200 hands. The Delaware and Hudson Canal Company employed approximately 800, according to the state census of 1855, although it is possible that this figure includes men employed elsewhere. The same source attributes over 350 employees to the steamboat company of Thomas Cornell of Rondout. The average monthly wage paid to male employees of these three companies was almost the same—$26 by the canal and cement companies and $25 by Cornell, just about the level of unskilled labor. The bluestone quarries were small businesses, but they supplied between them another 200 to 300 unskilled and semiskilled jobs plus many more in adjoining townships, mostly to Irish and German immigrants, and generally paying about a dollar per day.[65] According to the population schedules of the New York State census of 1855 and the United States census of 1860, approximately 45% of the male population over fifteen years old in Kingston were employed in unskilled and semiskilled jobs.[66]

Both of these elements—a very large wage-earning class and several fairly large economic organizations—were absent from the country town we surveyed in the previous two chapters. They constitute, in themselves, rather dramatic evidence of change in the structure of Kingston's economic life after the construction of the canal. Insurance companies, banks, savings institutions, fancy shops, plank roads, quarries, cement plants, a busy harbor—these too had made their appearance in the decades immediately following the first shipments of coal through the Rondout Valley. In the visible structures of economic life, therefore, Kingston had changed enormously since the construction of the Delaware and Hudson Canal. But the specification of structural changes such as these only begins to answer the general question of how the transportation revolution affected the people who lived in antebellum Kingston. Gaining some understanding of how these structures operated goes somewhat further. However, there are many questions that remain. How did other local institutions develop in response to, or at least in association with, the changes we have surveyed? Can we locate any significant changes in the local population, and if so can we relate these in some meaningful way to economic change? How did all these structural changes affect the network and tone of social life? Did they affect the ways in which decisions of collective importance were made in the community? How did they affect the institutional and cultural linkages between the community and the rest of the world? In what ways did they affect the local culture itself, particularly the manner in which the residents of Kingston conceived of their town as an entity? The attempt to answer these questions belongs, as I have said before, to later chapters. Before we conclude this one, however, there is at least one other dimension of local economic life that merits observation.

Just as there is a rhythm to rural life, a series of recurring variations in the pattern of social and individual activity, there is a rhythm to life in more densely settled communities. This would hardly need to be stated, except that, obvious as it may be, the study of urbanization has seldom if ever been explicitly directed toward comparing the rhythms of rural and urban life or toward the changing rhythms of particular places as they grow from villages into cities. The reason may lie in a general tendency to focus on different rhythms in town and country—on the daily patterns of commutation and work in the former and on seasonal patterns in the latter—in such a way that an explicit comparison is seldom suggested. Or it may be the elusiveness of the task, for, especially in past communities, it is extremely difficult to document the day-to-day social relations of a particular place—much less to place a great number of them within a minutely defined time dimension. For antebellum Kingston, we can document only the broadest (but surely one of the most interesting) rhythms of social life—the seasonal. And since the seasonal cycle of social life is not entirely economic, we can properly do but part of the job in this chapter.

Appropriately, this brings us back to the canal itself, for the economic activity of Kingston varied above all around the openings and closings of the D & H Canal. The basic pattern is described most effectively by the Rondout *Courier* in 1854 in an article well worth quoting at length:

> With the cold winds and freezing point of November, the last canal boats of the season come slowly in, and are filed in an amicable sort of way, side by side, for their winter's rest. The men too, either lose their long-shore appearance, and merge into quiet citizenship, or disappear mysteriously to enjoy the fruits of their summer's labors. . . . Through the winter months, a long unbroken silence reigns over the whole canal interest. But with the warm sunny days of April, comes an influx of men, boys and horses. Up the dock you will see the men overhauling their cabins, furbishing ancient stoves, disposing bundles of straw in curiously contrived bunks, chaffering with dealers for the various articles needed in their outfit, whilst the gurgling noise of pumps is incessant. . . . Meanwhile the crowd of men, boys and horses, waxes in size each day. We meet them at every turn, and narrowly escape being trampled upon by some young Jehu at every crossing. One day word comes that the first boat has been "locked" through. The steam tug goes slowly up the creek, with long strings of boats in her wake. Squadrons of mounted boys file rapidly up the road, and for two weeks an unusual quiet is manifest "up the Company's dock."[67]

The quiet lasted only long enough for the boats to make the trip to Honesdale and return with the first loads of coal. Then the business season began in earnest, not merely for the Delaware and Hudson Canal Company but also for the entire town. The infusion of several thousand laborers who had left the town at the close of the previous season (a phenomenon we will observe more closely in other contexts) meant that local retailing picked up dramatically after a period of relative dormancy. The diary of Nathaniel Booth is particularly useful in revealing this ebb and flow of local commerce. Before entering the bluestone trade, Booth maintained a grocery and dry goods store at Wilbur (which understandably retained the general country store a good deal longer than the two incorporated villages). Each year he made a number of journeys to New York to order merchandise, and each year these journeys would occur between early March and early December. Each year his diary records the opening of the canal, the increase of business, and the general quickening of the local pace. Each year his entries are turned to matters of business in the spring and to matters of leisure and social life in the winter.

The Rondout *Courier* reflects the seasonal cycle even more clearly. The article quoted above is but one of a number of pieces which appeared every spring, each with the same theme of the reawakening of business. The opening of the canal and the river and the arrival of the first canalboats and steamboats are all carefully recorded, as are the construction projects begun in the village, the health of the village (cholera was an occasional visitor to Rondout), and any signs of what the business prospects were for the year. But the *Courier* went well beyond mere reportage. For many years it ran a spring series on the businesses of Rondout, proclaiming and philosophizing upon the astonishing growth of commerce, and enumerating a seemingly endless list of local heroes:

> The dingy office of Sleight & Co. has undergone various mutilations, until it shines with light and beams with business.... Sims has not only enlarged his bowels but his conceptions, and has given us an idea of the handsomest Dry Goods store in Ulster county.... North has declared that he must trim and paint, and now since Steffens & Co. have made such improvements underneath him it would seem that his ideas are just and proper.[68]

The pace of business activity was apparently maintained as long as the canal remained open. In 1849, when the governor proclaimed an unusually early Thanksgiving (it was usually observed in December), the local celebration of it was a failure. Only "the more pious sex," complained the *Courier*, had time to pause to give thanks:

> The major part of the people have been shovelling coal, loading and unloading vessels, hoisting and lowering sail, getting up and blowing off steam, and driving all the multifarious business of our busy place.[69]

Of course, business did not entirely cease in the winter. Besides the continued (but probably reduced) demand for goods by the permanent residents of Kingston, teamsters continued to bring down bluestone that had been quarried during the previous season. In addition, there was the ice business. For a few weeks, at least, local workers could find employment on the Hudson River and Rondout Creek. By the end of our period this business seems to have become rather large, for in 1859 the *Courier* reports that the Knickerbocker Ice Company was using 750 men (at $.88 per day) and 150 horses to fill their icehouses with 80,000 tons. A new company, with only a slightly smaller capacity, was also on the river.[70] But these figures may have been unusual, and, in any case, the work lasted but a few weeks.

Obviously, the significance of this seasonal rhythm for our understanding of change in Kingston does not derive from its timing, for its ebb and flow is almost precisely that of the agricultural year. Nor is this coincidental. The canal, the quarries, the water-driven mills, and the docks of Rondout and Wilbur all awaited the same spring thaw that had signaled the beginning of the year to the Dutch farmers of seventeenth-century Esopus. Only in the larger towns of antebellum America and only later for the nation generally would economic complexity and an advancing technology cause the agricultural year to become overlaid with many rhythms that were truly different or that echoed the old rhythm by reversing it (so that for most of us today—students, teachers, television viewers, theatergoers, and even many business-men and workers—the year begins rather than ends at harvest time). Rather, the significant change in post-canal Kingston lay in the instruments on which the seasonal rhythm was played. By the 1850s, the editor of the Rondout *Courier*, the young merchant-diarist of Wilbur, and an undeterminable number of their townsmen greeted the spring with thoughts of docks and stores rather than fields, of canalboats rather than plows, of coal and dry goods rather than wheat. Perhaps, too, they differed from their predecessors by framing their hopes for the season in the abstract terminology of profit and loss rather than by the traditional and concrete notion of "a good harvest." That it was still the spring that they greeted as the time of reawakening should not obscure the fact that the content of the seasons had changed dramatically. The agricultural year had been *usurped* by commerce rather than destroyed by it. There may be no better way of describing the first step away from rural life.

New People

Of all the changes associated with the development
of Kingston's economy in the decades following the construction of
the Delaware and Hudson Canal, none was more dramatic or more
basic to the social life of the community than the growth and
transformation of its population. Kingston did not, of course,
become a great or even a medium-sized city, and it will not be
possible to match in these pages the astounding statistics of growth
which appear in the histories of such cities as Chicago, Rochester,
and Cincinnati. But the fivefold increase in its population, from
just under 3,000 in 1820 to 16,640 in 1860, was more than enough to
destroy the town's rural character. For nearly two centuries
Kingston was a country town, a collection of farms and farmers,
with a village that never contained more than one-third of the
town's total population. In the generation following the opening
of the canal, however, thousands of new residents, very few
of them farmers, moved into the town to help run Kingston's
new economy. Most, of course, settled near the canal, in and
around the old village of Kingston, and, most striking of all, in the
new village that was growing up around the D & H docks at
Kingston Landing. By 1860, eight of every nine Kingstonians lived
in this small corner of the town and passed their days and nights on
thickly settled village streets rather than on empty fields and isolated
farmsteads. The farms remained, of course, but no longer were
they more than a minor element of local life, an economic and
social periphery to Kingston's new urban center.[1]
The village of Kingston, which in 1820 had contained 1,100
residents, expanded steadily during these years. By 1840 it had
doubled in population to 2,220, and by 1860 it had doubled again
to 4,610. Much more impressive, however, was the growth of the
village of Rondout. In 1820, as we have seen, the site of this village
was called Kingston Landing, or the Strand, and consisted of no

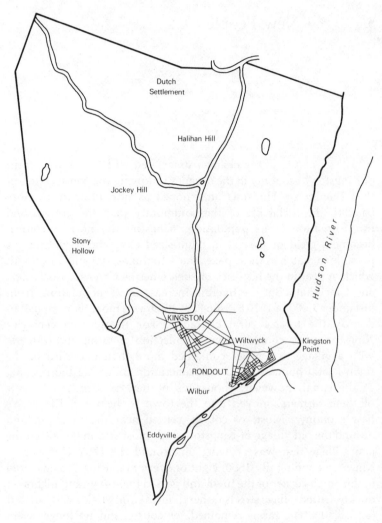

Fig. 4   The Town of Kingston, 1858

more than a dock, a handful of buildings, and two farms. One of these farms had come up for sale just when the Delaware and Hudson Canal Company was seeking a tidewater depot for its new canal, with the result that Kingston Landing became the real terminus of the D & H. This one real estate transaction shifted the entire pattern of Kingston's growth. As soon as the company's docks were established at the landing, the shanties of the unskilled, mostly Irish dock workers grew up on the hillside, earning for this portion of the old Van Gaasbeck farm the informal name, "New Dublin."[2] Other buildings, commercial and residential, also quickly appeared with the general growth of trade, and it was generally assumed that a new and permanent village had taken root. There was even a dispute over its name. Kingston Landing would no longer do, for this had ceased to be its primary function. Neither would so unprogressive a name as Strand. The new president of the company, John Bolton, tried to name the hamlet after himself, but Abraham Hasbrouck, the owner of the remaining farm, refused to permit it. Even though Hasbrouck soon sold out to local developers, the impasse continued until 1831, when Bolton left the presidency of the D & H and, by means that are apparently lost to history, all sides agreed on the name Rondout.[3]

The new village grew rapidly. By 1840, according to a state gazetteer, it contained some 1,500 inhabitants, 200 dwellings, a Catholic church and a Presbyterian church, six hotels and taverns, twenty-five stores, three freighting establishments, a tobacco factory, a gristmill, four boatyards, two dry docks, and, of course, the office and dock of the Delaware and Hudson Canal Company.[4] In a dozen years, therefore, it had outstripped the older village's growth of a century and three-quarters. By 1850 Rondout had probably passed the old village in population and had, in the previous year, received its own village charter. The editor of the Rondout *Courier*, in that first year of the village's incorporated life, wrote offhandedly of the inevitable day "when we get our city charter."[5] By 1857 he could describe Rondout as a "bustling, energetic, and thrifty 'little city.' "[6] And why not? By that date it was considerably larger than the village of Kingston, having surpassed 6,000 in population in time for the state census of 1855, while Kingston village had not yet reached 4,000. According to the state, Rondout had more than tripled its already respectable population of 1845 and was almost as large as the city of Hudson, which had received its city charter years earlier.

The growth of both villages caused each to spill over its boundaries until the usable space between and around them began to disappear. This does not mean that the two villages were entirely eclipsed by a new physical entity, even after both villages, along with Wilbur, Wiltwyck, and other unincorporated neighborhoods, were all enclosed within the city of Kingston after 1872. Each village maintained its separate institutions until 1872. Each has maintained a distinguishable physical identity to the present, to some extent because of physical factors, such as the hilly terrain of Rondout, which caused its early growth to spread along the river rather than behind it toward Kingston village, and the rough intermediate wilderness of Jacob's Valley, which was suitable only for rural cemeteries and Romantic fancy. Of greater significance, however, is the fact that Kingston never did become a large city; the two villages, growing toward each other from centers two miles apart, could do no more than join outskirt to outskirt. They did, however, achieve this much by 1860. Joined by the heavily traveled Union Plank Road and the unincorporated village of Wiltwyck (naming things "Wiltwyck" had become fashionable in post-Dutch Kingston), the lower portion of the township did achieve a measure of physical and social unity. To that extent we may speak of the residents of Kingston, Rondout, Wilbur, Wiltwyck, and adjacent areas as a single population aggregate comprising more than 14,000 individuals in 1860. This was the urban or urbanizing population of the town, as distinct from the 2,000 or so who continued to work the farms and quarries of the town's more remote corners and who experienced the growth of the congested portion on less than a day-to-day basis.

Far more dramatic than the growth of the town, however, were the changes in the *content* of its population. In 1820 Kingston was a relatively homogeneous community of native-born Protestants, many of whom could trace their ancestry back to the Netherlands, and most of whom made their livings primarily or exclusively in agriculture. As the town grew and diversified economically, the old Protestant Dutch hegemony gave way to a population of great ethnic, religious, and occupational diversity. This, of course, is hardly surprising. That occupational diversity should accompany economic development is almost tautological, and the association of ethnic diversity with urban growth is so common that it has become almost an axiom of the theory of urbanization.[7] Nor is it surprising that old-stock Kingstonians should have treated the infusion of many new types of people into their midst as one of the most significant elements of their own collective experience. As we will see, one of the dominant themes of the surviving documents of antebellum Kingston is the problem of achieving orderly progress in a community with so many disparate elements that its very social boundaries had become unclear. The preoccupation with this problem is clearest in the politics of the community, which were increasingly reoriented during this period from the promotion of local growth to the establishment and maintenance of social order. We will have ample opportunity to probe this phenomenon, as well as the entire question of community self-definition, in later chapters. Before we do, however, it will be necessary to look more closely at the population itself, for the response to diversity cannot be fully understood until the extent and shape of that diversity have been established. Besides, there *are* a few surprises.

The structure of Kingston's population can be examined in great detail for only the final decade of our period, as the major historical sources—the population schedules of the federal and state censuses—are relatively useless for the time before 1850.[8] Other public and church records, moreover, are fragmentary and unreliable, while newspapers can hardly be expected to serve as comprehensive repositories of social and demographic data. Newspapers do indicate in one or two places (as in the reference to New Dublin) that unskilled Irish laborers began moving into Kingston, and particularly into Rondout, with the very first activities on the canal. Undoubtedly many of Rondout's early residents had worked on the construction of the canal and simply remained to work on the company's docks once the canal had been completed. In 1833 the *Ulster Republican* complained of an (unspecified) "infamous insult offered in the last Sentinel to the whole class of voters in the enterprising village of Rondout," indicating perhaps that the Irish had already become something of a local political issue, and it reported an "infamous" brawl between three Irishmen in Kingston village in 1836.[9] On the other hand, the real significance of such items may well be in their scarcity. Compared with subsequent decades, native Kingstonians seem to have paid little attention to the Irish, even though to some the presence of this Catholic proletariat must have been a somewhat uncomfortable novelty. Apparently, the numbers of Irish were still small—the 1835 census lists only 71 male aliens in the town, as compared with 279 in Saugerties.[10] More important, as residents of the new village of Rondout, they were physically removed from most of the older townsmen. And it may be significant that it had been their hard work that had dug the precious canal, and it was still their work that was helping the canal turn Kingston into a boomtown.

Although Kingston's population must have diversified further between 1835 and 1845, it was the next decade that witnessed the most profound changes. This was, of course, a period of enormous immigration into America from Ireland and Germany and of extremely rapid economic development in Kingston, particularly in those industries (coal, bluestone, lime, and cement) that offered the sorts of jobs that uprooted immigrants could expect to fill. Accordingly, several thousand recently arrived immigrants came up from New York to Kingston between 1845 and 1855, mainly to work the docks and quarries, to serve as domestics in middle-class homes, and, of course, to swell the local population. By 1855, despite an impressive in-migration of native-born Americans from nearby counties and towns, fully half Kingston's people were foreign-born. Approximately one-third were Irish, 88% of whom had arrived in Kingston within the previous ten years. Another one-sixth were Germans, 40% of whom had arrived within two years. Other immigrants constituted only 3% or so of the total population, but these equaled in number those residents born in other states and in the western counties of New York. At the end of its most significant decade of growth, therefore, Kingston's population was almost evenly split between natives of the Hudson Valley and emigrants from Ireland and Germany.[11]

The proportion of immigrants in Kingston's population was relatively high, even in comparison with some of the great port cities. Boston, for example, was about 60% native in 1855, and though most of its immigrants were Irish, the proportion of Boston's Irish-born residents was slightly lower (29%) than the proportion of Irish in Kingston.[12] Philadelphia was 70% native-born in 1860, with only some 17% of its population born in Ireland, and 8% born in Germany.[13] But Kingston's immigrant communities were not so large as some (Buffalo was more than three-fourths immigrant, and in Hamilton, Ontario, less than one resident in ten was a native of Canada).[14] They were quite in line,

Table 3 Place of Birth by Years of Residence in Kingston, Adult Males, 1855

Years of Residence	Ulster County	Other New York	New England	Mid-Atlantic	Other U.S.	Canada	England, Scotland	Ireland	Germany	Other Europe	Other	Total
0–2	10.5%	29.4%	32.1%	32.1%	—	—	25.3%	24.3%	40.7%	—	—	23.8%
3–5	8.1	20.6	22.7	13.2	—	—	24.2	39.3	31.1	—	—	25.1
6–10	10.5	19.5	13.4	26.4	—	—	28.6	24.5	19.2	—	—	18.5
11–20	20.8	19.2	18.7	20.8	—	—	15.4	10.3	7.5	—	—	14.5
21 +	50.1	11.3	13.3	7.5	—	—	6.6	1.7	1.2	—	—	18.1
Total	100.0%	100.0%	100.0%	100.0%	—	—	100.1%	100.0%	99.7%	—	—	100.0%
N	1,282	530	75	53	5	9	91	1,438	667	28	13	4,191
Percentage of Population	30.6%	12.6%	1.8%	1.3%	0.1%	0.2%	2.2%	34.3%	15.9%	0.7%	0.3%	100.0%

SOURCE: Manuscript census schedules, 1855.

proportionately, with those of other cities in the Hudson Valley. For example, Poughkeepsie's foreign-born inhabitants constituted more than 40% of the local population in 1860,[15] while Troy's immigrant proportion, 49%, was almost the same as Kingston's.[16] Troy's Irish-born proportion, 36%, was slightly higher. The reason for this rather high concentration of immigrants in the Hudson Valley is not hard to discern: the valley's outlet to the world, New York City, had become the leading immigrant port on the entire eastern seaboard. "Increasingly," writes Marcus Lee Hansen, "those in Europe had no idea in mind but to get to New York, which they knew bore some sort of relationship to the rest of America."[17] Of course, New York City's most proximate relationship was with the towns of the Hudson Valley; and as the numbers of immigrants disembarking in New York rose, so too did the number who found their way out of the city into its most immediate hinterland. Kingston's ethnic diversity is therefore a reflection of factors operating on three levels: the national upsurge in foreign immigration, the town's own economic development, and the growing influence of New York on its emerging metropolitan region.

In a sense, however, nativity is too conservative a yardstick for the measurement of ethnic diversity, for its use assumes that the members of a particular nativity group perceive and act on a bond coextensive with the entire group. Now while this may be a fairly good assumption for emigrants from Ireland, almost all of whom were Catholic, it is likely to obscure real differences among Catholic, Protestant, and Jewish Germans, or among members of that strange "ethnic" group generally labeled "native." It may be instructive, therefore, to look briefly at the increasing diversity of Kingston's churches. In 1820, as we have seen, there was only one church in Kingston, an institution which over the generations had helped mold Netherlanders, French Huguenots, Englishmen, and anyone else who happened along into the "Dutchmen" for which the region was famous. The monopoly of the Dutch Reformed Church ended in Kingston, however, when a Methodist church was founded shortly before the opening of the canal.[18] This was followed by Baptist and Episcopal churches in the early 1830s and by a Presbyterian church in Rondout in 1835.[19] The year 1835 also saw the founding of the Roman Catholic Church of St. Mary, which received its first resident pastor at the close of the decade and acquired a church building in 1849.[20] For some years St. Mary's served all the Catholics in Rondout, Kingston, and the surrounding countryside. Most of its parishioners were, of course, Irish, and it is interesting that when a second Catholic church was built in 1856 (St. Peter's), it was intended specifically for Germans.[21] Meanwhile, other Germans had founded the German Evangelical Lutheran Trinity Church of Rondout, the Congregation of Israel in the village of Kingston, and the Emanuel Congregation in the town of Kingston.[22] By 1860 Kingston and Rondout contained no fewer than nineteen churches and synagogues, and even the once unchallenged Dutch Reformed Church had split into three congregations.[23]

Increasing ethnic heterogeneity was accompanied in Kingston by a growing diversity of occupations. Economic development naturally introduced many new occupations to the town and drastically reduced the proportion of the local work force devoted to agriculture. Over 150 distinct occupations are listed on the manuscript schedules of the 1860 census, while those men listed as farmers or farm laborers constituted only 10% of the adult male work force. Moreover, the numerically dominant occupations in 1860 were, for the most part, the newest ones, those brought to Kingston by the canal and the quarries. Unskilled laborers, most of whom were coal heavers on the D & H docks, were by far the most numerous, followed by boatmen who worked on the canal itself. Quarrymen constituted the sixth largest occupational group (behind farm laborers, farmers, and the clerks of Kingston's expanded commercial sector), and these were closely followed by the coopers, stonecutters, and teamsters, most of whom worked in the bluestone and lime and cement trades. But note that the preponderance of these new occupations suggests an overall occupational structure quite unlike that in larger cities in either the extent of its diversity or the character of its work. Only six occupations accounted for half the adult male work force; and of these six, only the clerks and perhaps the laborers can be considered "urban." About 90% of Kingston's men worked in fewer than fifty occupations in 1860, and although this represents a considerable departure from the conditions prevailing in the country town of 1820, it does not put Kingston in the same league as the great coastal cities.

The fact that so many of Kingston's new workers were unskilled or semiskilled (we have earlier estimated them at being nearly half

Table 4   The Twenty Most Frequently Listed
               Occupations, All Adult Males, 1860

Rank	Occupation	Number	Percentage of Male Work Force	Cumulative Percentage
1	Laborer	1,026	21.8%	21.8%
2	Boatman	511	10.9	32.7
3	Farm laborer	253	5.4	38.1
4	Farmer	220	4.7	42.8
5	Clerk	190	4.0	46.8
6	Quarryman	182	3.9	50.7
7	Carpenter	139	3.0	53.7
8	Cooper	117	2.5	56.2
9.5	Stonecutter	105	2.2	58.4
9.5	Teamster	105	2.2	60.6
11	Blacksmith	102	2.2	62.8
12	Shipwright	91	1.9	64.7
13	Shoemaker	90	1.9	66.6
14	Grocer	85	1.8	68.4
15	Mason	81	1.7	70.1
16	Brickmaker	78	1.7	71.8
17	Merchant	75	1.6	73.4
18	Painter	61	1.3	74.7
19	Tailor	55	1.2	75.9
20	Innkeeper	49	1.0	76.9

SOURCE: Manuscript census schedules, 1860.

of the adult male work force) suggests that Kingston did develop a
class structure quite similar to that in the larger, more diverse cities.
It is difficult to estimate, however, just how much more stratified
Kingston had become during these years, for we lack comparable
information for the pre-canal town. In 1860, two men (Jacob A.
Burhans and Thomas Cornell) reported individual fortunes of
$100,000 to the federal census marshal, while forty men and two
women claimed fortunes exceeding $25,000. According to Schoon-
maker—and my own best judgment—these were values unheard of
in the pre-canal town. Nor is it likely that the wealthiest 10% of the
householders of pre-canal Kingston owned 74% of the town's
wealth—a proportion that did obtain in 1860. In Marlborough, a
predominantly rural township a few miles below Kingston on the

Hudson, the wealthiest 10% owned 58% of the total real and personal property reported to the census marshals in 1860, while in Troy, a larger city than Kingston, the equivalent proportion was 82%.[24] In Philadelphia, the nation's second largest city, the wealthiest 10% owned 89% of the city's total wealth.[25] But if these figures suggest a direct relationship between urbanization and increasing inequality,[26] they do not reveal the course of stratification over time in a given locality. Marlborough in 1860 was not necessarily the same sort of place that Kingston was in 1820, for it too had participated in the valley's economic development between 1820 and 1860.[27] In all likelihood Marlborough in 1860 was *more* stratified than Kingston had been in 1820, and if this were so, it means that economic inequality had advanced considerably in Kingston since the construction of the canal. Even then, however, we could not simply assume that the laborers, quarrymen, and "canawlers" of 1860 were poorer or proportionately more numerous than the slaves, freedmen, and hired hands of 1820, for the increasing share of wealth owned by the wealthiest 10% may have been entirely the result of the increasing size of their personal fortunes. There were probably not more than 250 farms, shops, and stores in the town of Kingston in 1820, and even if we double this number to account for resident adult sons, retired fathers, and skilled workers, we account for only a small majority of the 900 men who lived in the town at that date. Were the remaining 45% hired hands and laborers? (In rural Marlborough in 1860, exactly 44% of the adult males were employed in unskilled jobs.) Were the native farmhands of the 1820s any less poor than the Irish dock workers and German quarrymen of the 1850s? Unfortunately, we have only our prejudices (and a few clues to the contrary) to tell us whether poverty was more widespread in the small commercial city than in the country town of 1820.

We can, however, confidently specify at least one significant difference between the workers of rural and urban Kingston. In 1820, most workers, whether they were slaves, hired farmhands, or journeymen, were members of the households of their employers. Only in backwoods portions of the town, therefore, where subsistence farmers might have lived, could there have been poor neighborhoods, and these, almost by definition, were of no consequence to the good order and appearance of the town. Kingston's workers, in other words, were physically separated from one another and lived under the close surveillance of their middle-class employers. A far different situation prevailed in the post-canal town. By 1860, most of Kingston's unskilled and semiskilled workers were employees of large companies and formed their own households in closely packed neighborhoods in the village of Rondout. This made them more visible as a group to a middle class already nervous about the idea of a significant Irish Catholic presence in the town and, what was more important, made these workers less susceptible to traditional means of social control. The physical relocation of Kingston's "dollar-a-day" workers, in short, may have been as significant to the life of the town as any absolute or relative increase in their numbers.

It seems also to have sensitized local commentators to the fact that the new workers were quite transient. In observing the near-emptiness of Rondout during midwinter, the editor of the *Courier* remarked: "Many of the coal laborers leave here in the fall in search of winter employ, and scores of boatmen and other employees of the summer migrate when winter closes around us."[28] The floating population of Rondout was certainly very large, and its apparent rootlessness gave more settled residents yet another cause for alarm.[29] But if they thought that each new business season brought an entirely new horde of strangers to the town, they were mistaken. Of 1,687 unskilled and semiskilled male workers listed on the 1855 state census for the town of Kingston, only 91 claimed less than one year of local residence. Yet the census was collected only three or four months after the canal was opened for the year. Apparently, the movements of the floating population were cyclical as well as seasonal. When the canal closed for the year and the number of jobs was drastically reduced, many of Rondout's workers left town to find employment for the winter (I suspect a large number went into the nearby Catskills to cut timber), only to return the following spring. It is doubtful that very many kept up this cycle for more than a few years, for a majority of the town's workers were in fact relative newcomers. But the work force of Rondout was not replaced anew each year. Indeed, the workers on the docks and canalboats simply continued a seasonal pattern of short migrations that was no doubt begun by the agricultural workers who had preceded them.

Even granting these probable continuities with the rural past, we must still recognize that the population of Kingston had changed enormously in the generation following the construction of the canal. What remains to be determined, however, is how the major elements of Kingston's new diversity—ethnicity, occupations, property, and even residential tenure—were related to one another. To what extent did Kingston's new ethnic minorities constitute a separate and distinct class of poor and near-poor workers? To what degree could wealthy and middle-class natives realistically focus their fears for the peace and good order of the community on a floating population of Irishmen and Germans? We may probe the first of these questions by turning again to the manuscript schedules of the federal and state censuses. In table 5, for example, Kingston's adult white males are classified by place of birth and by functionally defined occupational categories. Place of birth, incidentally, may serve as an acceptable indicator of ethnic group membership, but only because of the happy circumstance that there was not yet a significant second generation of Irish or German adults in Kingston by 1855 or 1860. With very few exceptions, those adults identified by the community as Irish or German were actually born in Ireland or Germany.[30]

Table 5 reveals very striking differences among the occupations held in 1860 by native American, Irish, and German men.[31] Natives were well represented in all types of work, ranging from the professions, which they almost completely dominated, to the unskilled dollar-a-day jobs with which about one-quarter are identified. Farming, unsurprisingly, was almost exclusively the sphere of natives of the state (and, as the 1855 census shows, of those born in the county), while native Americans from other states were more heavily represented in the professions, commerce, and skilled trades. Immigrants from Ireland, on the other hand, were mostly wage earners. Fully 64% worked as day laborers and in other unskilled jobs, while most of the 10% listed as semiskilled in table 5 were quarrymen who should probably be "demoted" to the bottom category. Another 20% are listed in the census as craftsmen, but as is generally true with mid-nineteenth-century occupational data, it is impossible to tell whether these were middle-class master craftsmen who owned their own shops or wage-earning journeymen employed by masters or manufacturers. The facts that the Irish were overrepresented in only two trades, and that both of these—stonemason and stonecutter—were characterized by a comparatively large number of journeymen, suggest the latter. There may even be an important element of deception

Table 5   Place of Birth by Occupational Category, Adult White Males, 1860

	New York State	Other U.S.	Ireland	Germany	Other	Total	N
Professionals	3.5%	7.2%	0.3%	0.6%	1.0%	2.0%	91
Merchants, Manufacturers, and Semiprofessionals	12.6	20.1	3.7	9.1	15.5	9.5	431
Farmers	9.8	2.2	0.6	1.2	0.5	4.9	220
Clerical Workers and Officials	8.6	7.2	1.0	1.5	3.1	4.7	215
Skilled Tradesmen and Workers	31.9	38.9	20.3	40.5	47.7	30.2	1,369
Semiskilled Workers	7.6	4.3	10.0	10.6	10.4	8.9	401
Unskilled Workers	26.0	20.1	64.0	36.5	21.8	39.8	1,802
Total	100.0%	100.0%	99.9%	100.0%	100.0%	100.0%	
N	2,022	139	1,496	679	193		4,529

SOURCE: Manuscript census schedules, 1860

here, with quarrymen elevating themselves to the more skilled occupation of stonecutter. Conceivably, as many as 90% of the Irish adult males in Kingston were wage earners in 1860. Almost none, in any case, were professionals, farmers, or even clerical workers, and very few, under 4%, were merchants, taverners, or storekeepers of any kind.

German immigrants were somewhat better situated. Only 36.5% are listed in unskilled jobs, while the greatest proportion, 40.5%, were skilled workers or proprietors. As with the Irish, German professionals, farmers, and clerks were rare in Kingston in 1860, but there were a fair number, 9.1% of the total group, who kept shops of various kinds, mostly taverns and grocery stores. German skilled craftsmen were, moreover, fairly widely distributed among the various trades. They were heavily overrepresented in shoe-making, tailoring, coopering, brickmaking, butchering, and baking (actually constituting a majority of the local bakers), and well represented in cabinetmaking, wagonmaking, carpentry, ship carpentry, cigar making, and a few smaller trades. Again, however, we must be careful not to assume that all these craftsmen were self-employed.

The occupations of women are harder to survey, as the census marshals were instructed not to make occupational entries for married women. Just under 40% of the unmarried women over the age of 15 are credited with occupations, and most of these were largely or entirely within the acknowledged domain of women—seamstresses, milliners, schoolteachers, and domestic servants. Native women held the greatest variety of jobs, but even they were restricted to no more than a dozen distinct occupations; the four mentioned above accounted for some 97%. Unmarried German-born women are listed mostly as servants, with only a dozen listed in more skilled occupations—seven seamstresses, three milliners, a baker, and a jeweler. The Irish were incredibly restricted—of the 254 Irishwomen for whom occupations are listed, 240 were servants and the other 14 were seamstresses.

The picture that emerges from all this is a familiar one—natives were considerably better off than immigrants, and, among the immigrants, Germans were somewhat better placed than the Irish, largely because a greater number of them brought usable skills with them to America. But these differences should not obscure the important fact that nearly one-third of Kingston's native-born white men were listed as unskilled and semiskilled workers in 1860, or that about 30% of Kingston's unskilled and semiskilled work force was native-born. Of course, we must not rely too heavily on the sometimes ambiguous occupational labels that come down to us through the census. Many of these native "workers," for example, were boatmen and farm laborers, a small portion of whom were actually boat captains and resident sons of substantial farmers. On the other hand, when we turn to the census entries reporting real and personal property, we find, if anything, an even larger proportion of native-born white men at or near the bottom of the economic ladder.

In general, table 6 upholds the pattern observed within the occupational structure. Nearly all the wealthiest men in Kingston were native-born; there were only two immigrants among the 42 householders who listed themselves above $25,000 [32] One of the two was George F. Von Beck, the brewer, hotel owner, and property speculator we met in the previous chapter. Von Beck, a German born in France (presumably Alsace), had come to Rondout in 1835 as an employee of the canal company and had worked his way up to a position of considerable local prominence and substantial wealth. Even after business reverses in the 1850s, he listed his wealth in 1860 as $65,000. The other wealthy immigrant was John O'Reilly, an Irish-born farmer who claimed $30,000 in 1860 and whose residence in Kingston stretched back over more than four decades.

Natives dominate all the higher categories of wealth, accounting for nine of every ten men who reported themselves to be worth between $10,000 and $25,000 and eight of every ten worth between $5,000 and $10,000. Natives even supplied three-quarters of the men reporting between $3,000 and $5,000, a level of solid middle-class comfort but by no means great wealth. Just under one of every four native-born household heads reported property in excess of $3,000, while the comparable proportion for the foreign-born was less than one in twenty. Even at the $1,000–$3,000 level, the native-born exceeded their proportion of the population.

Only at the very bottom of the ladder, among household heads reporting $100 or less in real and personal property, did immigrants outnumber natives. But the proportions were not so different as we might have expected. It is true that a clear majority of immigrant household heads could (or chose to) report no more

Table 6   Place of Birth by Total Real and Personal Property, White Heads of Household, 1860

	New York State	Other U.S.	Ireland	Germany	Other	Total	n	Percentage Native
$25,001 +	2.7%	4.4%	0.1%	—	0.8%	1.4%	42	95.2%
$10,001–25,000	5.1	2.6	0.4	—	3.3	2.5	76	89.5
$5,001–10,000	10.2	7.9	1.9	1.6%	3.3	5.6	170	81.3
$3,001–5,000	7.4	9.6	1.5	2.8	2.5	4.5	138	76.1
$1,001–3,000	15.8	13.2	9.6	10.0	20.5	12.8	389	55.5
$501–1,000	9.5	8.8	10.3	9.6	9.8	9.7	296	45.0
$101–500	16.6	14.9	15.5	22.3	13.1	17.0	516	45.0
$0–100	32.7	38.6	60.7	53.8	46.7	46.5	1,413	34.3
Total	100.0%	100.0%	100.0%	100.0%	100.0%	100.0%	3,040	45.5%
N	1,269	114	1,033	502	122			

SOURCE: Manuscript census schedules, 1860.

than $100 in real and personal property, but the same obtained for more than one-third of the natives. Immigrants, in other words, had no monopoly on poverty in Kingston, and any attempt (by us or by nineteenth-century Kingstonians) to dichotomize the town into comfortable native Americans and poor immigrants is accomplished only by ignoring at least one-third and perhaps one-half of the native population!

Table 7 indicates, furthermore, that native poverty cannot be explained away as a phenomenon peculiar to young men. It is true that native American householders below the age of thirty reveal a much higher proportion of property entries in the $0–$500 range than any other age group, and that this difference between young men and older men is much more striking than it is among immigrants. Still, more than half of those native Americans in their thirties, and just under half of those in their forties and fifties, reported less than $500 worth of property to the census marshal in 1860. Only among the oldest natives does the proportion of low entries dip below 40%, and even some 30% of these men valued their property at no higher than $500.

Table 7   Proportions of Nativity Groups Reporting $0–$500 in Total Property, by Age; Heads of Household, 1860

| Age | Place of Birth | | | |
	United States	Ireland	Germany	Total[a]
20–29	80.3%	85.0%	89.8%	83.6%
30–39	55.5	79.5	76.8	68.8
40–49	43.2	70.5	72.8	57.5
50–59	47.9	70.8	58.5	55.7
60 +	29.4	69.6	63.6	43.1
All Heads	51.1%	76.2%	76.1%	63.9%
N	1,441	1,033	502	3,101

SOURCE: Manuscript census schedules, 1860.

[a]Total column includes 125 household heads born in England, Scotland, and continental European countries other than Germany.

Nor can we explain native poverty as a temporary artifact of rapid in-migration. Earlier we noted that many of Kingston's residents in the 1850s, including many native Americans, were relative newcomers to the town. Perhaps the large numbers of low-status, low-income natives were to be found mostly among the recent in-migrants, while poor foreign immigrants were distributed in more or less equal proportions among newcomers and long-term local residents. Table 8 divides the native, Irish, and German members of the adult male work force of 1855 into categories of residential tenure in Kingston and shows the proportion of men in each category holding unskilled or semiskilled jobs.[33] The results

Table 8   Proportions of Nativity Groups Reporting Unskilled and Semiskilled Occupations, by Years of Residence in Kingston; All Adult Males, 1855

| Years of residence | Place of Birth | | | |
	United States	Ireland	Germany	Total[a]
0–2	24.1%	70.9%	53.3%	48.1%
3–5	25.1	78.5	58.4	59.8
6–10	33.2	74.7	48.7	54.3
11–20	32.4	73.0	49.0	45.2
21 +	24.6	38.1	—	25.6
Total	27.3%	74.4%	53.7%	40.2%
N	1,564	1,224	588	3,500

Source: Manuscript census schedules, 1855.

[a]Total column includes 124 men born in England, Scotland, and continental European countries other than Germany.

are quite striking. Irish and German men living in Kingston longer than a decade were, as hypothesized, just as well represented in poorly paying jobs as those who had just arrived. But the same was true of the natives. If anything, the most recently arrived native American men were a bit underrepresented in unskilled and semi-skilled work. The highest proportion of laborers, quarrymen, and the like were among those who had resided in Kingston between six and twenty years. When age is added as a second control, as in table 9, the proportions become even more evenly distributed among the length-of-residence categories. Clearly, then, the presence in Kingston of large numbers of recently arrived native men does not explain poverty among the American-born, and we can use neither this variable nor age to explain the overlap in the economic statuses of local ethnic groups.

Table 9   Proportions of Nativity Groups Reporting Unskilled and Semiskilled Occupations, by Years of Residence in Kingston; Males Aged 30–39, 1855

	Place of Birth			
Years of residence	United States	Ireland	Germany	Total[a]
0–2	22.1%	71.3%	53.9%	49.4%
3–5	29.8	76.8	55.5	57.3
6–10	22.1	73.0	46.3	51.4
11–20	21.4	73.2	—	44.8
21 +	29.4	—	—	30.6
Total	25.7%	73.4%	51.6%	48.2%
N	385	379	215	1,032

SOURCE: Manuscript census schedules, 1855.

[a]Total column includes 53 men born in England, Scotland, and continental European countries other than Germany.

The experiences of natives and immigrants intersected in other ways, too. For example, there were many boarders in Kingston, a fairly large number of single men, and a very large number of men who seem to have left the town a short time after their arrival. These are phenomena generally associated with in-migration, both by careful scholars and by community residents fearful of a young, unattached, irresponsible floating population.[34] Kingston had, of course, received many in-migrants in the 1840s and 1850s, and these newcomers did in fact account for disproportionate numbers of single men, boarders, and subsequent out-migrants. But not all of those who moved to Kingston during these years were foreign immigrants. As we have just seen, many were native Americans, born in nearby towns, counties, and states, and it is interesting that these more familiar newcomers were not significantly less transient and unattached than their counterparts from Ireland or Germany. In-migrants from other towns within Ulster County, it is true, could be traced much more frequently from the 1855 census to the 1860 census (table 10), but native newcomers from other counties and states "persisted" in Kingston slightly *less* frequently than did the foreign-born. Only among residents of three years and longer, that is, among those no longer counted by the community as members of the floating population, did ethnic differentials in the rate of local persistence become significant. Similarly, the proportion of boarders in the immigrant adult male population (22.4%) was only moderately higher than among non-Ulster, native Americans (17.3%), while the proportion of young migrants (aged 20–29) who were unmarried was about the same (just under 60%) for both natives and foreigners.

Table 10   "Persistence" by Nativity and Years of Residence, 1855–60

	Percentage of 1855 Census Entries Located in the 1860 Census[a]		
Years of Residence in 1855	Ulster County	Other U.S.	Foreign[b]
0–2	45.0%	13.3%	15.0%
3–5	53.3	46.4	24.1
6–10	42.1	50.0	25.3
11 +	53.4	50.0	33.3
N	215	104	374

SOURCE: Manuscript census schedules, 1855 and 1860.

[a]Based on 16.7% interval sample from the 1855 census.

[b]Excludes 11 men born in England and Scotland.

It is difficult to tell whether the more prosperous and more firmly rooted members of the community were sensitive to the ethnic heterogeneity of Kingston's unskilled and semiskilled work force or to other similarities between native and foreign-born in-migrants. Most of their anxiety was directed toward the Irish, who did in fact contribute the greatest number to Kingston's new proletariat of dock laborers, "canawlers," and quarrymen. The Irish, for example, receive a great deal of attention in the diary of the English-born Catholic, Nathaniel Booth, and the theme is almost always the same:

> Today a regular Irish row came off in the cooper's shop the cause of which was some poor devil had the misfortune to be born in Tipperary and the rest considered it sacred duty to half murder him—A great clan fight came off in Rondout on Sunday among the Irish—11 persons engaged were lodged in jail yesterday.[35]

The usual accompaniment to the Irish brawl was, of course, drinking. The Irish, it seems, were always getting drunk, and St. Patrick's Day was "a day of special devotion—to the bottle—a day whose legitimate observance is swilling vast quantities of villainous drink—staggering through the streets—swearing and fighting, in which sacred duty the Wilbur Irish are particularly pious."[36]

Violence and drunkenness—these are the central themes of almost every discussion, in Nathaniel Booth's diary and in the local press, of the Irish of Rondout and Kingston. There were other indictments, of course—Catholicism and susceptibility to political manipulation, to name two of some significance—and a fair amount of sympathetic discussion that focused on low wages and inadequate housing. But none of these themes can compare in importance with the image of the Irish immigrant as a drunken brawler. What is most interesting about this image, however, is that the local Irish were forced on occasion to share it with both the other major nativity groups. The Germans, for one, contributed their share to local drunkenness and disorder and were given occasional credit.[37] (It is perhaps indicative of the extent of the decline of Dutch influence in Kingston that the word "Dutchman," used elsewhere in America as a derisive term meaning "German," was similarly employed in Kingston.) But of far greater significance was the recognized contribution of native Americans, particularly those young, American-born "boys" who organized themselves, after the pattern of similar institutions in larger cities, into anti-Irish gangs.

It is extremely difficult, owing to the variability of newspaper coverage, to assess the amount and types of violence in antebellum Kingston and to attribute that violence to specific individuals or groups. At times small incidents involving no more than personal animosity are covered in great detail, while a number of seemingly large incidents reported in Booth's diary are entirely neglected by the local press.[38] How many are missing from both? Judging from occasional comments about peaceful election days, St. Patrick's Days, July Fourths, and even Sundays, we may guess that violence of some sort was more or less expected on days when men were not at work. In August of 1854, for example, the *Courier* reported that "Sunday last passed without riot or disturbance ... probably the most decorous Sunday enjoyed by Rondout for twenty years."[39] But it is impossible to say just how much violence occurred on other Sundays and what form it took. Nor is there much information about such nighttime phenomena as the "squad of rowdies who make occasional evening progress from Rondout to Kingston."[40] They must have been fairly frequent, for they provoked the good citizens of Rondout into a public meeting and voluntary subscription for the creation of a regular night watch—which, unlike the abortive affair a generation earlier in Kingston village, actually seems to have functioned.[41]

Most probably, the great majority of incidents omitted from the local press (and many of those included) were small fights, assaults, and acts of vandalism. Of those that were reported, only two appear to have been major events. Both were street fights between native and Irish young men, and both occurred on special days that brought Rondouters to Kingston. The first occurred on July 4, 1851, and the second took place during the annual township election in the spring of 1853. Neither would have occurred, probably, if Rondout had held its own July Fourth celebration and had maintained its own township poll.

The July Fourth riot began when two native Americans from Kingston village got into a fight with three Irishmen, the outcome reflecting the odds. The victory seems to have provoked the Irish to hold their own patriotic celebration, "and soon were heard shouts of 'Hurrah for Ould Ireland,' 'Tipperary forever,' 'I can whip any

American be Jabers,' and various other expressions, uttered in the most demoniacal manner."[42] (This quotation is from a Kingston paper which put most of the blame on the Rondout Irish. The Rondout paper blamed Kingston "rowdies.") A second event sparked the riot itself. One of the Irishmen stopped a passing wagon by grabbing the horse's bit and swore that he would allow no American to pass. The driver easily broke through, and as he passed the Irishman tried (unsuccessfully) to grab his female passenger. This "aroused the righteous indignation of many who beheld it, and particularly of an exceedingly nice young man,' who prides himself on being one of the 'Bumble Bee Boys,' of this village," and who quickly gathered his companions.[43] The "Bumble Bee Boys" combined forces with assorted "rowdies" and "loafers" and began to pelt the Irish with stones and brickbats, driving them into a nearby "shabeen shop." The sheriff soon arrived (possibly timing his arrival for the moment when the Irish could be effectively sealed off from the natives by surrounding the building) and was able to restore order. Fifteen arrests were made, and the fighting was not renewed, save for a few fistfights in the evening. The July Fourth fireworks display went off as scheduled.[44]

The election riot of 1853 seems to have been a somewhat bloodier affair, and the papers of both villages and Nathaniel Booth of Wilbur all agree how it started. In the morning, while standing in line at the poll, an Irishman from Rondout stepped on the foot of one Bob Baggs, "a Kingston rowdy of some note,"[45] a leader of the Bumble Bees, a man "notoriously quarrelsome when intoxicated, which he was early in the day, and so continued."[46] The Irishman apologized in vain, and Baggs began to fight. Though he was soon restrained and led away, tensions mounted until the early afternoon, when a small fight (provoked by Baggs and a few friends) triggered a large and furious street battle. A wagon loaded with wood appeared (fortuitously, according to the Rondout paper; as a deliberate maneuver by the Irish, according to the Kingston press), and both sides armed themselves. This time there was no retreat and no easy sealing off of the two sides. The sheriff's men worked without success to restore order and seem to have received the worst beating. Ultimately the village fire bells were rung and the firemen summoned to help. This now turned the tide against the Irish, as the firemen of Kingston village were mostly young natives and many had already been fully involved in the fight before being deputized and armed. (Baggs was himself a Kingston fireman, although possibly not at this time.) The Irish, in other words, now faced an enemy freshly equipped with both bayonets and legal authority. Many fled, and eleven were arrested, while no arrests were made on the other side. Minor rows continued in both villages. Injuries were numerous, and one man was shot.

The names listed in the newspaper reports of the 1853 election riot allow us to probe a little deeper into some of the participants in Kingston's overt ethnic conflict. Six of the eleven Irishmen arrested, and perhaps a seventh, can be identified in the 1855 and 1860 censuses. All were unskilled laborers, and all were fairly young men of around thirty. It is perhaps surprising that they were not younger and that all were married men; at least four had children. Also, none of them had lived in Kingston for less than two years at the time of the riot, and the six who can be confidently identified averaged just under five years of local residence. All six, moreover, can be identified as residents in 1860, seven years after the brawl. In short, at least the majority of the Irishmen who were arrested on March 1, 1853 were neither juveniles nor unattached transients. Though all those identified were at or near the bottom of the economic ladder (they averaged $133 in reported property in 1860), all were family men and all were at least fairly well rooted in the community. It should be noted in this connection that the brawl occurred before the canal had opened for the year, and that the participants were probably year-round residents rather than seasonal migrants.

Only four native rioters, all Bumble Bees, are named in the newspaper accounts, and three of these can be identified in at least the 1855 census. All three were young men at the time of the riot (around 25), all three were married, and two had children. Two were natives of Kingston; the other, a native of Ulster County, had lived in the town for most of his life. On the other hand, two had disappeared by 1860, an interesting contrast to the persistence of the arrested Irishmen. Although only one was listed as a laborer (Bob Baggs was a harness maker and Fred Kent was a printer), it is not likely that they were much better placed than their foes. All lived in multiple-household dwellings (Baggs shared a building with three other households and Kent shared one with two, while Henry Styles, the laborer, shared with one), and all were probably wage earners. Bob Baggs, who remained in Kingston, is the only one for whom we could have had property figures, but by 1860 he was widowed, separated, or divorced, and had moved back to his mother's home (in a two-household dwelling). His mother listed no property.

Such fragments do not, of course, permit generalization about the rioters as a whole. They do seem to hint at the insufficiency of easy interpretations of Kingston's ethnic conflict. The identifiable rioters were not very young, transient, or unattached. The "groups" were neither so different from one another that they represented different classes nor so similar that the newcomers appear to have been an economic threat to the natives. The immigrants may well have been perceived as a threat by the natives themselves, but we have not yet demonstrated anything beyond the fact that on at least two occasions in the early 1850s a significant number of natives and a significant number of Irishmen decided to knock each other's heads in.

The point is that the decision was mutual. If anything, the two riots, and particularly the more severe election riot in 1853, demonstrate a somewhat greater eagerness on the part of the natives. They were surely the better organized, even granting the Irish credit for the wood wagon (which didn't work very well anyway). For nowhere in the newspaper reports or in other discussions of local ethnic violence is there a hint of organized Irish or German gangs such as those that carried the native banner into battle. There were "squads" of Irish, but these seem to have consisted of no more than a handful of "lads" who happened to be together during a particular evening. On the whole, Irish violence in Kingston seems to have been a matter of individual inspiration. The native gangs, on the other hand, seem to have been fairly well organized and may have been a potent force among the young men of Kingston village.

Moreover, native Americans were quite capable of fighting among themselves. The following description of a riot during a local steamboat excursion makes no mention of Irishmen, and in 1850 this could only mean that none was involved:

> On the way up one of the male passengers intruded on the privacy of the ladies apartment and the Captain was obliged to eject him forcibly. This led to a general fight between the crew of the boat and a portion of the passengers in which the Captain got knocked down and 70 hurt. Oars and poles were broken up and

used as clubs—chairs were also used freely—glass was smashed—
blood flew—oaths and yells sounded everywhere. The Rowdy
party came off best—the Captain was demolished—the crew put
"hors du combat"—the chambermaid was choked—two women
passengers severely hurt one being struck in the face with a
chair—one passenger either jumped or was thrown overboard—
others much bruised. The peaceful ones saved themselves by
hiding in the closets, etc. A more disgraceful or bloody affray has
not been witnessed.[47]

In sum, it is difficult to determine whether the Irish were more
quarrelsome and violent than the native-born. Nor, for that matter,
did the Irish monopolize local drinking. The temperance movement
that came to dominate local politics in the 1840s was, as we shall see,
aimed at natives as well as at immigrants. And it could hardly have
been otherwise, for there was a great deal of drinking among all
groups. Even the respectable Nathaniel Booth was capable of an
occasional carouse:

In the evening went to Kearney's. John [illegible] expressed a wish
to renew old times and play a little music. About 11:00 we. . .
started on a serenading trip—awakening from their slumbers
every man woman child dog pig etc. in the village many of which
kindly assisted in the concert. It was near day when we finished—
pretty doings truly.[48]

Evening serenades could be sober affairs in antebellum Kingston,
but this one seems to have been otherwise.

"Respectable" natives did, as we have suggested, recognize the
native contribution to public disorder. The editor of the Rondout
Courier, as spokesman in all but labor disputes for his predominantly immigrant fellow villagers, was particularly outspoken on
the subject of native rowdies, and he was joined occasionally by editors of the Kingston press. It is from the Courier, too, that we learn
of a rather special form of native poverty among the Binnewaters, an
area of depleted woodlots and pickerel-filled ponds to the west of
Kingston village. In a previous era, a nomadic band, consisting of
individuals with varying degrees of black, white, and Indian
ancestry, and informally called "the Schoharies," migrated each
year between the Binnewaters and the northern Catskills. The
Schoharies were basket weavers, broom makers, and berry pickers,
and appeared in the village as street peddlers. By 1850, however, the
nomads had been replaced by permanent squatters, who were

apparently native whites, carried out identical marginal economic functions, and occupied the same status beneath the bottom of the social hierarchy.

> This is a rather singular truth [wrote the *Courier*] when we consider the contiguity of thriving villages and a rich agricultural country, and more especially that these semi-barbarians are hardly out of hearing of a score of church bells, and within the area of the common school system of the state of New York.[49]

But in one sense the appearance of items such as these in the Rondout press only underscores the importance of ethnicity in the local consciousness. For if J. P. Hageman, the Rondout editor, defended his villagers primarily by pointing out native gangs and discovering native poverty, it was only because Rondout was attacked primarily in ethnic terms. And Hageman himself (a native-born Whig) had difficulty in discussing poverty, wages, and housing conditions in Rondout without assuming that the poor, the poorly paid, and the cramped were Irish.[50] To this we may add that for three years the Native American party reigned supreme in Kingston village. Still, the abundant attention paid to the Irish by worried or simply bigoted natives did not preclude a deeper awareness of the changes brought to Kingston by the Delaware and Hudson Canal. If the Irish received too much of the blame, it was because they, far more than any native-born "canawlers" or brawlers, embodied the discomforting diversity of the new town that had grown up around the old country village of Kingston.

There were, of course, other elements to this diversity besides immigrant workers, and one in particular warrants brief review. Many of Kingston's new businesses were owned and operated by men who were themselves newcomers to the town—in-migrants from other counties, other states, and other countries. Though native Kingstonians and others born in Ulster County were over-represented in the professions, commerce, and manufacturing, the majority of the town's professionals and businessmen came to Kingston from outside the county. Nearly a third of the professionals and a quarter of the merchants and manufacturers were in-migrants from other counties in New York State, and in-migrants from other states, though representing only 3% of the adult male population, constituted 6% of the professionals and 8% of the nonmanual businessmen. Although foreigners were greatly under-represented among the professionals and businessmen, they were numerous enough to contribute nearly a fifth of the former and more than a third of the latter. Just as significant, many of the largest and most lucrative enterprises were in the hands of newcomers. Thomas Cornell, the wealthy shipper, was born in Westchester County and came to Kingston in 1843. C. W. Schaffer, whose Exchange was Kingston's largest retail store, arrived in 1845 from Maine. Perhaps the most active of Kingston's entrepreneurs was George F. Von Beck, the German Rondouter who owned a brewery, a hotel, and a good deal of local real estate. Erastus Cooke of Otsego County, and James O. Linderman of Orange, were two of the town's wealthiest and most respected lawyers. The list could be extended much further, and later we will see how easily these wealthy and middle-class newcomers moved into positions of leadership in the community's political, cultural, and social institutions. That they did so without first becoming members of the Dutch Reformed Church, and without marrying the daughters of the Schoonmakers, Tappens, and Bruyns, emphasizes the diversifying effects of commercial and urban growth on the rural community. At the top, as well as at the bottom, Kingston was no longer "Dutch." Whatever the degree of its cultural particularism in previous generations, by the 1850s this old Hudson Valley town had acquired the unsettling complexity of the ordinary American city.

6   New Town

The most obvious of the changes associated with Kingston's post-canal growth is perhaps the least obvious in its significance—the development of a townscape in which fourteen thousand rather than one thousand villagers lived their daily lives. Surely, the physical face of Kingston changed considerably between 1820 and 1860, but what effect, if any, did the new village environments have on the way life was lived in the town? What, if anything, does the particular distribution of homes, stores, and workshops reveal about the kind of community Kingston had become? Does this distribution reveal some underlying pattern, and if so, does this pattern resemble in any way the spatial structures of larger contemporary cities? Did Kingston in the late 1850s *visibly* resemble larger places, and did its inhabitants perceive that something new and tangibly different—perhaps something deserving the name "city"—had emerged on the banks of the Rondout and Esopus creeks?

A glance at figure 5, a map of Kingston and Rondout in 1858, suggests one further question: can the two villages be realistically described as a single locality? Physically, the integrity of each village appears to have remained unimpaired, even though the Union Plank Road, which once served as the road from Kingston to its landing on Rondout Creek, by 1858 had become a busy avenue of traffic between one village and the other. Not only distance but also physical character separated the two villages. Kingston was a spacious village of large blocks and regularly spaced streets, while Rondout was a congested waterfront district, with many more buildings—mostly warehouses, shops, and workers' homes—squeezed into smaller blocks. The new village, moreover, was dominated by two elements that would have been quite out of place in the old village: the quarry of the Newark Lime and Cement Company, and the new island dock belonging to the D & H. The dock was over half a mile long and could be seen, with its huge piles of coal, its swarms of workers, and its surrounding fleet of canalboats, from almost any point in the village. The quarry, which wedged down through the village all the way to the creek, cutting off the central portion from "Ponckhockie" to the east, was perhaps even more conspicuous, for the sounds of blasting and of limestone avalanches were never absent from Rondout while it was in operation.

It would be a mistake, however, to regard the villages of Kingston and Rondout as entirely separate (and therefore smaller and less urban) localities. Indeed, their differing physical characters only point up their interdependence, which in turn may be taken as an index of their conjoined urban development. By the 1850s the two village centers had become rather specialized zones within a larger locality consisting of these and other zones of specialized land use. The central portion of Rondout, for example, was the port of both villages, while Kingston contained most of the town's professionals, financial institutions, fashionable shops, and schools.[1] Imagine, then, a survey of the two villages as distinct entities. Kingston would appear as a lively center of retail trade that somehow managed to import and export every manner of goods with practically no facilities of shipment and storage. Rondout would be credited with an equally remarkable achievement—an extensive commerce, requiring hundreds of ships and barges and more than a mile of docks, but only one bank and two lawyers! Obviously, the economic institutions of both villages were required for a fully articulated, functioning local economy. Their physical separation represents, in slightly exaggerated form, the same sort of specialization of land usage that was developing at the same time in the downtown sections of the nation's largest cities.[2] Thus, the broadest patterns apparent on figure 5 begin to suggest a spatial structure that did resemble larger, more distinctly urban places.

As in the larger cities, specialization was carried even further; specific streets and even blocks were associated with particular trades or types of trade. In Kingston village, where earlier even the busiest of streets had contained an even mixture of shops and homes (see figure 2), the northern half of the old stockade area had become a fully developed and rather differentiated commercial center. North Front and Wall streets constituted the heart of

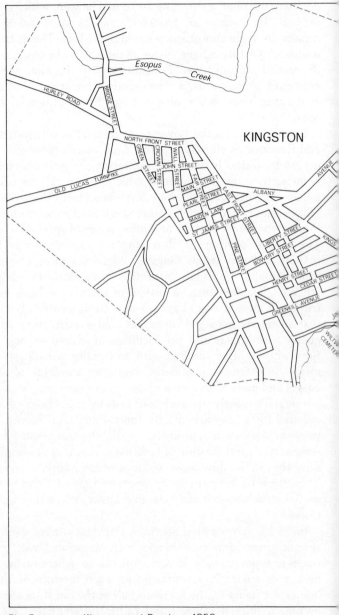

Fig. 5   Kingston and Rondout, 1858

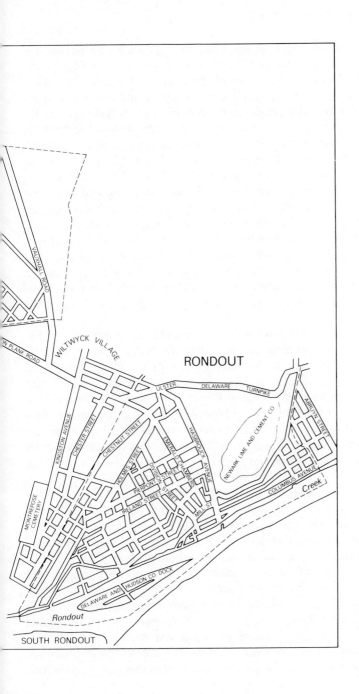

RONDOUT

WILTWYCK VILLAGE

VAUXHALL ROAD

N PLANK ROAD

KINGSTON AVENUE

CHESTER STREET

CHESTNUT STREET

HOLMES STREET

EMERICK STREET

PIERPONT STREET

IRELAND STREET

DIVISION STREET

HASBROUCK AVENUE

UNION STREET

MILL ST.

ABRUYN STREET

NEWARK LIME AND CEMENT CO.

COLUMBUS AVENUE

ULSTER   DELAWARE   TURNPIKE

Creek

MONTREPOSE CEMETERY

DELAWARE AND HUDSON CO DOCK

Rondout

SOUTH RONDOUT

Kingston's retail district and contained almost all its fashionable shops. According to the 1858 business directory, six of eight china and glassware stores, all ten clothing stores, both "fancy goods" stores, all five milliners, all five watchmakers and jewelers, and ten of the nineteen dry goods stores were on these two streets, mostly within a block or so of their intersection. About three blocks south of the retail center, on and around St. James Street, a small industrial center had arisen. It contained, according to the directory, all five carriage makers, both sash and blind makers, the plane and plow manufactories, the coppersmiths and the brass foundry, and Baldwin's iron foundry. A smaller industrial center, occupied mainly by blacksmiths, wheelwrights, coopers, bakers, and tanners, lay just north of the retail center between North Front Street and the bridge over Esopus Creek. There was even a marked clustering of lawyers' offices around the courthouse at the southern edge of the retail center. Not one of the twenty-two law offices listed in the directory was located more than a block from the courthouse.

Rondout, which was itself a specialized area of industry, crafts, wholesaling, and shipping, was also internally differentiated by trade. Lackawanna Street, in the heart of the village, contained nearly all Rondout's clothiers, boot and shoe dealers, and dry goods stores, while nearby Ferry Street was devoted to the shipment of flour and grain. Most of Rondout's blacksmiths were gathered at the foot of Hasbrouck Avenue, a block from the termination of the Union Plank Road, while its four livery stables virtually adjoined one another on the plank road itself. Most of the butchers and fish dealers were gathered, after 1853, into Clinton Market, built near the foot of the plank road by George F. Von Beck.[3] The districts of each village were still very small, of course, but by the 1850s they were sufficiently developed to provide each resident and visitor with the same sort of mental map that guided people from one service to another within a big city.

Even more indicative of urban development in Kingston and Rondout were the broader patterns of specialization, in which commercial and industrial sections were differentiated from areas devoted almost exclusively to residence, and in which residential sections were differentiated from one another in terms of their desirability. The residential sections are not so easily analyzed, incidentally, despite the common association of working-class Irish and German immigrants with Rondout and of the native middle class with Kingston village. Neighborhoods were, of course, smaller than the two villages, and even though no neighborhood overlapped village boundaries, we cannot simply distinguish between Kingston and Rondout as though each was internally homogeneous. We are prevented, furthermore, by the fascinating institution of "moving day," from using the 1858 directory to retrace the steps of the census marshals. Virtually all dwelling leases were written to terminate on the same day, May 1, and vast numbers of those who lived in rented quarters moved to new ones each year rather than renewing their old leases. Moving day existed in both villages.[4] Its effect is captured by Nathaniel Booth:

> Move—move—keep moving—straw—soot—dust and ashes at every step—all confusion—today anything in the shape of a horse is invaluable—hand carts are comfortable property— wheelbarrows a great acquisition—a boat in some cases a treasure and even baskets have risen 25% on their original value.... Everyone has his or her hands and arms full—all are on a trot—it is like the sacking of a city ... but it is like nothing but itself, first of May in New York villages.[5]

Moving day should also warn us that there is a dynamic element in the urban spatial structure that a static description of neighborhoods is likely to miss. If large numbers of lessees did in fact move from one place to another each year, or even every few years, then neighborhoods where rentals were the rule must have had quite different prevailing personal relationships from neighborhoods where most people owned their own homes, even where no other differences, such as class or ethnic background, existed.[6] In other words, we may find real differences between the class and ethnic composition of various neighborhoods, and we may correctly and usefully relate these differences to the question of the specialization of urban land usage. But such information only begins to inform us of the life of each neighborhood and only suggests whether a particular cluster of families and individuals actually functioned as a real and significant social group.

Neighborhood differentiation is, nonetheless, a useful indicator of the extent and nature of urban development, and even though we are prevented from making effective use of the census here we can, to a degree, outline and characterize Kingston's neighborhoods by associating the occupations and residential addresses of those listed in the city directory of 1858. In Kingston village, for example, we find that a large majority of the village's merchants and lawyers resided within the area of the old stockade, and that just under eight out of every ten lived either within or immediately south of this village core. The members of three specific trades (carpenters, shoemakers, and butchers) resided mostly in and beyond the small industrial zone around St. James Street, three or four blocks from the core, with only one of six listing homes within the core itself. Laborers, teamsters, and boatmen lived even further away, with fewer than 4% listed within the core and 80% listed around and beyond St. James Street. Individual streets in different sections of the village display this pattern of residential segregation just as vividly. For example, Fair Street above Maiden Lane contained the homes of six merchants, two lawyers, the cashiers of two of the three village banks, a clergyman, a doctor, two foundry owners (James and Ira Baldwin), three master butchers (proprietors of the same firm), and one milliner (a woman who may or may not have owned her own shop). With the possible exception of the last, all were proprietors or professionals. Further south, St. James Street contained, in addition to the ten foundries and shops we mentioned earlier, fifty-nine residents who also listed occupations. A few of these were professionals, businessmen, and clerks, and one was a farmer. The bulk of the residents, however, were manual tradesmen or workers, forty-one of whom were skilled and eight of whom were unskilled, and their specific occupational designations indicate that almost all the skilled were employees in the nearby shops. Still further south, the character of the neighborhood changed again. Cedar Street, almost a mile from North Front, contained twenty-two listed residents, eleven of whom were unskilled workers and nine of whom were skilled workers, mostly in the construction trades. There was also one farmer, and the one businessman owned the street's liquor store.

The pattern of land use in Kingston village, including the distribution of residential neighborhoods, was far from unique. And if this pattern appears to twentieth-century eyes as a distinctly nonurban distribution of stores, workshops, and homes, it is only because the industrial cities of the present differ in fundamental ways from the cities of the preindustrial and early industrial past. Kingston, in fact, was developing in a physical form that was almost identical to that of America's largest cities and that in turn was representative of what has been referred to generically as the preindustrial city.[7] Before the emergence of large-scale manufacturing and urban mass-transit systems, cities were structured on the simple principle of proximity to the city center. Businessmen located their stores as close as possible to the center of commerce (usually the port) and residents located their homes as close as possible to their businesses. Accordingly, those most capable of buying locational profitability and convenience worked and lived at the center of town, while those of more modest means were generally forced either into less desirable central streets and alleys or outward toward the periphery. The centralized neighborhoods of affluence in turn reinforced the centralization of such urban facilities as retail stores, government buildings, libraries, and theaters. And the appearance of enlarged workshops, mills, and factories on the outskirts of the city, where land was cheap and labor plentiful, derived from and further reinforced the pattern.

Ultimately, these new industrial facilities on the urban periphery would help destroy the physical configuration they initially reinforced. As industry grew, the city itself grew, at its center as well as at its edges. Although railroads had taken over much of the task of shipping goods in and out of the city, the old, centrally located port expanded rather than contracted, as did the traffic from dockside warehouses to factories and stores all over the city. Other central functions, particularly retailing, also expanded, in an absolute if not a relative sense, until congestion destroyed both the elegance and the convenience of life in the old city center, even for those who still made their fortunes from nearby businesses.[8] By this time, of course, the same technology that had transformed the economy of the city had been applied to the movement of its people, so that it was now possible to travel several miles in the same time that it had once taken to walk to work. Wealthy and middle-class residents of the inner city were now able to escape on trains and trolley cars to the suburbs opening up beyond the industrial belt that now completely hemmed in the old city.[9] When the affluent did move away, the resulting vacuum was soon filled by the ever expanding economy and by a new population, usually poor, often of minority ethnic or racial stock, and usually housed in segments of the decaying former homes of the new suburbanites.[10]

In the 1850s, however, this transformation of the preindustrial or commercial city into the industrial city was in only its first stages. Pressure on the inner city was beginning to mount, suburbs were beginning to appear, and urban transit systems were beginning to carry a fair number of people between the two each day. But the basic shape of the city's neighborhoods was still much the same as it had always been, and it was this shape, to return to the matter at hand, that Kingston was assuming. In 1820 there had already existed some hints of a pattern of district and neighborhood differentiation in Kingston village, with some clustering of stores along North Front, Crown, and Wall, and an apparent tendency for families of greater means to live toward the center of the village, while families of lesser means found homes closer to the periphery.[11] But at that early date the village was too small, its householders too alike in wealth and status (recall that most workers still lived in the homes of their middle-class employers), and work too closely associated with residence for there to have existed neighborhoods and districts distinct enough to have had much meaning. By the 1850s, though, all these patterns had emerged with great clarity. The area of the old stockade was now a highly differentiated core of commercial streets and nearby upper- and middle-class neighborhoods, occupied almost exclusively by the merchants and professionals who worked and lived in the core. North and south of the core lay two small industrial sections, in which shops and foundries were intermingled with the homes of skilled workers and others who could not afford to live in the core and whose employment opportunities were increasingly to be found outside the area of the old stockade. Finally, on the southern periphery of the village lay a sparsely settled section occupied almost entirely by unskilled and skilled workers, most of whom probably worked in Rondout as often as they worked in Kingston.

This development along lines similar to those of larger preindustrial cities does not, of course, mean that Kingston village was itself a fully formed city by 1860. If anything, the comparison of this village of fewer than 5,000 inhabitants with cities with populations as large as 800,000 points up the embryonic state of urban development in Kingston. If we could create a scale of spatial development stretching from the village of 1820 (which already revealed a degree of differentiation) to the largest preindustrial American cities, we would certainly place the village of 1860 much closer to the former than to the latter. We would, however, recognize that some urban development had occurred—more, certainly, than we would have recognized if we had conceived of urbanization in terms of the industrial cities of a slightly later era.

The neighborhoods of Rondout developed along lines quite different from those of the older village. Differentiation was just as pronounced, but in Rondout there was no relationship, either direct or inverse, between centrality and wealth. Instead, the core of the village was divided into a commercial center (which contained more residences than did Kingston's) and two distinct neighborhoods, one immediately above the center and occupied almost exclusively by unskilled workers, the other adjoining the first on the west and occupied by most of the village's merchants and professionals. Another neighborhood of workers lay further west, in the vicinity of the old Delaware and Hudson Canal Company dock (and apparently the bridge to the new island dock). Still another, Ponckhockie, housed the employees of the Newark Lime and Cement Company at the eastern edge of the village. Some 84% of the unskilled laborers listed in the 1858 directory resided in these three neighborhoods, along with 71% of the listed members of three specific trades (carpenters, shoemakers, and coopers). The wealthy neighborhood adjoining the commercial core contained 60% of Rondout's merchants and professionals, 15% of its skilled tradesmen and workers, and 6% of its unskilled workers. Those merchants and professionals who did not live in this neighborhood lived in the commercial core itself (two of seven boarded at Von Beck's Mansion House), in the extreme northern portion of the village, or outside Rondout in Wiltwyck, or even in Kingston village. Of the thirty-one Rondout merchants listed in businesses which were probably substantial (flour and feed, stone, hardware, ship stores, etc.), three resided in Wiltwyck and another three commuted all the way from the neighborhood just south of the stockade in Kingston village.

The differing patterns of land use in the two villages reflect their differing histories. Rondout grew quickly in and around a core that had not even existed beforehand and which, therefore, could not influence the pattern of village development. The source of Rondout's growth, furthermore, was commerce and industry of a type that required large numbers of unskilled workers and large segments of village land for docks, warehouses, quarries, and plants. These two factors—the absence of a preexisting commercial, political, and social village core and the industrial and "heavy" commercial character of Rondout's economic development—were critical to the shape of the village's physical growth. The canal company's docks, having no competitors, became the foundation of the emerging village core, and the shanties of "New Dublin" formed its earliest centralized neighborhood. The first stage of Rondout's growth, then, established a pattern opposite to that of Kingston and of commercial cities generally, in which the elements of early growth were merchandise and merchants rather than Lackawanna coal and Irish laborers. By the time Rondout's general commerce and mercantile population emerged, the pattern of centralized working-class neighborhoods and centralized unskilled work was firmly established. This left the merchants the choice of carving a neighborhood for themselves out of the remaining centrally located land or of creating a "suburb" at the top of the hill. It is interesting that they chose the former, near their own docks and stores, but near the workers' homes and the coal docks as well. Apparently, though the merchants of Rondout were given the chance to follow the industrial-urban pattern of suburban residence and commutation to inner-city work, they preferred not to. Proximity to work, it seems, was still an unquestioned asset. The merchants of early Rondout located their homes as close to their businesses as possible, even though by doing so they sacrificed insularity (from both coal workers and coal dust), a fine view, and perhaps the additional prestige of a hilltop neighborhood.[12]

In both villages, indeed, and among all occupational groups, proximity to work was still the rule. Nearly a third of Kingston's merchants continued to combine residence with commerce, while another third walked but a block or two to work. A few traveled as far as five, six, or seven blocks each day, but none, apparently, commuted from Wiltwyck, Rondout, or the countryside. Kingston's lawyers, all of whom kept offices in the core, also lived close to their work. Only one combined his office with his home, but seventeen of the remaining twenty-one walked three blocks or less to work each day. One was a true commuter, traveling between his office on Wall Street and his house on Vauxhall Road more than a mile away. Skilled and unskilled workers seldom listed their places of work, but we have already noted a clustering of the homes of carriage makers, cabinetmakers, metalworkers, and the like near the carriage and cabinetmaking shops and the foundries of St. James Street. In Rondout, too, workers' homes clustered near the loci of employment—the village core, the D & H docks on the west, and the Newark quarry and cement plant on the east. A few of the merchants of Rondout, it is true, commuted from Wiltwyck and Kingston, but most lived within four or five blocks of their stores.

In a strict sense, the separation of work and residence in the settled parts of the town of Kingston had advanced considerably since 1820. Few if any of the large numbers of unskilled and semiskilled workers worked at home, and the skilled workers too (many of whom were in the construction trades or employed in medium-sized shops) most often left home each morning to work elsewhere. A number of proprietors continued to combine commercial and domestic life, but these were now a distinct minority. In another, perhaps more important sense, however, the separation was incomplete. When men left their homes in the morning they did not go very far. Many returned for the midday meal, and, aside from an admittedly large number of island dock workers, quarrymen, and boatmen, most were accessible to wives and children throughout the day. Residential neighborhoods, even those clearly differentiated from commercial areas, were hardly dormitory suburbs belonging during the day to women and children. It is true that the home was no longer a workshop (even domestic manufacturing by women had nearly disappeared) and no longer contained a number of people of both sexes and all ages performing a variety of tasks within a fairly elaborate system of authority. In this sense, at least, the separation of shop and home, even by two blocks, was probably significant. But the incompleteness of the separation, especially when viewed from the perspective of the twentieth-century metropolis, was no less significant, and it may be of some importance to our understanding of the history of this quiet revolution in human relationships. If Kingston is at all typical in this respect, then we would be mistaken to conceive of the separation of work and residence as a dramatic event in which family farms, stores, and shops were suddenly pulled apart and replaced by commutation, dormitory suburbs, remote fathers, thoroughly domesticated homes, and a man's workday into which wife and children never intruded. In Kingston, the segmentation of domestic and economic worlds developed only gradually as the town grew. In larger places, where longer distances and urban transportation systems made a more dramatic separation possible, it is likely that suburbanization was preceded by the sort of moderate separation that occurred in Kingston—in short, that a partial pulling apart of work and family life, permitting a degree of overlap between the two, was characteristic of the early stages of urban growth.[13]

Suburbanization itself was not yet an important element in the changing spatial structures of Kingston and Rondout, and each of the two villages continued to display a physical distinctiveness that belied their social and economic interdependence. During the 1850s, however, there were real signs that suburbanization would soon restructure the local townscape. The most tangible was the unincorporated village of Wiltwyck, named, according to the Rondout *Courier*, for "the post office—when it is got, and the city—when it is built," and to be governed, "by a council of burgomeisters and schepens, the first to do the smoking and joking and the latter the laughing."[14] But the *Courier* would soon learn to take Wiltwyck a little more seriously. By 1852 it noticed that the laying out of new streets in the southern end of Kingston and in the northern portion of Rondout was the beginning of a convergence of the two villages, and that the emergence of a tangible community in Wiltwyck had already destroyed the boundaries between them.[15] The 1858 map, furthermore, contains two large sections, one in each village, clearly intended for imminent suburban development. Neither of these would work directly toward convergence, but both would, in subsequent years, contribute to the weakening of the village cores and the transformation of the plank road from a commercial highway into a central city street. There were even signs that suburbanization might be carried well beyond the boundaries of either village. As early as 1859, the Rondout *Courier* carried an advertisement for "building lots and cottage residences" in Rhinebeck, on the eastern shore of the Hudson River. This remarkable ad features an engraving of a thatched cottage, in front of which sit a young man and his wife, watching their *two* children and the family dog play on a manicured front lawn. Its language would have been appropriate for the advertising pages of New York City:

> To persons doing business in Rondout and vicinity this place is favorably located for residences for their families it being second to none either for health or for purity of air. . . . And favorable arrangements for commuting with the Ferry will be made.[16]

The 1850s also produced an assault on an even more formidable barrier to the emergence of a unified locality, the intervening wilderness known as Jacob's Valley. At the beginning of the decade a local real estate developer named Abijah Smith incorporated a portion of this lovely but seemingly useless acreage into his plan for a fashionable suburb at the southern edge of Kingston village. Just above Jacob's Valley, along Greenkill Avenue and Cedar Street, there was to be a neighborhood of fine homes, a church, a female academy, and flower gardens. A new road would extend from the Rondout road (soon to become the plank road) into the valley, where beautiful pine trees would provide a setting for a large cemetery. Additional acreage would be deeded to the public, after having been groomed with walks, a carriage drive, and even a small artificial lake. Jacob's Valley, in short, would be turned into two of the most modern features of the nineteenth-century cityscape, the "rural" cemetery and the public park. In addition, water from the lake would be pumped up the hill into the homes of Smith's new suburb, and all the way to the center of Kingston village for public use.[17]

Nathaniel Booth visited the site of this ambitious undertaking in June, 1850 and found the carriage road complete, the scenery beautiful, and, what is more important, some four or five hundred people enjoying it with him. But he doubted its success. "Abijah Smith deserves the thanks of the Kingston people for the pains he has taken," Booth wrote in his diary that night, but "this he will get and nothing more—it will not pay."[18] It is difficult to tell whether "Smith's folly" succeeded or not. The lake and the water system seem not to have materialized, and the fashionable suburb became a working-class neighborhood and then, of all things, a railroad right-of-way. But the cemetery did materialize, along with another on the Rondout side of the valley, and both seem to have "prospered."[19] Jacob's Valley was not turned into a full-fledged city park, but a portion of it was turned to what was, after all, an important function in a place of increasing density. Ultimately, other sections would be transformed into house lots, and new roads would link the two villages.

The physical development of Kingston and Rondout cannot be fully appreciated, however, from even a close analysis of the map and the directory, for these documents tell us of but a few of the social consequences of growth and nothing at all of the reactions and accommodations of those who lived there. Indeed, the very closeness of our analysis obscures the deepest significance of the map and directory—that they existed at all. Before 1857 (the date of the first *Kingston and Rondout Directory*), no one bothered to catalogue the streets and locate the stores and inhabitants of the two villages, presumably because the problem of finding one's way had not previously existed. The growth of the post-canal era, however, along with a new economic status that brought numerous strangers to town, finally resulted in a locality that had outgrown effective, word-of-mouth guidance of visitors and perhaps even complete comprehension by its own inhabitants. In 1851, the *Courier* urged that street signs be erected in Rondout, "where all the people move once a year and some of them oftener,"[20] and during the decade the practice of assigning numerical addresses to buildings was instituted on the more important streets in each village.[21] Even more telling, perhaps, is Nathaniel Booth's reaction to what was once an effective use of the public press:

> Hayes and his wife agreed to disagree and they succeeded most admirably. I see he has put an advertisement in the paper asking a suspension of public opinion until next week when he promises a full statement. What do the public care about him or his affairs. . . . I doubt if any beyond his immediate neighborhood has even heard of him.[22]

The streets of Kingston and Rondout changed in character as they increased in number. Before the 1850s they were entirely unpaved, and sidewalks, even in this home of "Kingston bluestone," seem to have depended for their existence and maintenance on private property owners.[23] "As you pass along our side walks and find no flagging," writes one rather cynical correspondent to the *Ulster Republican* in 1851, "you may be sure that the owner of the adjoining land is either rich or determined to become so."[24] The condition of village streets and sidewalks had become an important local issue by the early 1850s, however, and after a brief flurry of bylaws and new village charters, local government was drastically expanded and reoriented toward the grading of streets and the construction of curbs, gutters, crosswalks, and sidewalks. The Rondout *Courier* reports the grading of Kingston's streets in the summer of 1852,[25] and the minutes of the Kingston board of directors after 1853 (the volume covering 1830–53 is missing) are filled with the details of street and sidewalk improvement.[26] Rondout began its campaign somewhat later, but by 1860 the *Courier* was willing to congratulate both boards for their progressive approach to the problem of traffic in the two villages.[27] And in 1854 the old job of the village lamplighter was modernized by the Rondout and Kingston Gas Light Company, which received a franchise from both villages for the laying of gas pipes and the illumination of fifty public streetlamps.[28]

The growth of the two villages and of their interdependence increased the demand for regularized public transportation facilities. Carriages had run from Kingston Landing to the old village long before the Van Gaasbeck farm was turned into a coal dock, but these were occasional affairs, based solely on the arrival and departure of sloops and steamboats. The number of carriages and wagons increased as the boat landings themselves increased, but it was not until 1851 that an urban transit system, based on the clock, arrived in Kingston. In that year Joseph F. Davis began operations with a fourteen-passenger omnibus named *Wiltwyck* (naturally), "to run from a given point in both villages, passing the principal hotels, and not diverging from such route for anybody."[29] The *Union*, bearing on its panels a portrait of the late Abraham Hasbrouck, was added a year later. The two vehicles constituted a line that made hourly trips from one village to the other.[30] By 1854 a competitor had appeared in the person of Jacob Rider, whose *Sopeander* was:

> a beautiful, finely finished vehicle, and has on its sides a likeness of some one we have never seen. It is supposed by some that it is intended for a portrait of John P. Dumond, one of the stage pioneers of this place, but it don't look like him.[31]

At first, Kingston's new urban transit system seems not to have lived up to expectations. In 1857 the *Republican* complained that the "hourlies" were run more like taxis, adhering to neither schedule nor route, waiting in front of private dwellings while passengers endured "the lovely scene of 'kissing goodby,'" and consuming an hour or more for a journey that could be accomplished in twenty minutes.[32] The *Republican's* complaint was a direct appeal to Joseph F. Davis, who had just repurchased the line he had established three years earlier. Whether its deterioration was simply an episode in poor management is not known, but it is perhaps significant that in the year after Davis's return the *Kingston and Rondout Directory* advertised omnibus departures every half-hour from each village.[33]

As the streets of Kingston changed, so did the buildings facing them. The village of Marius Schoonmaker's youth was dominated by the trees, barnyards, and lawns that surrounded virtually every building, including those on North Front Street. By the 1850s, however, a few streets—North Front and the upper portions of Wall

and Crown—were lined with unbroken rows of commercial buildings, while a number of others were more thickly settled than any
had been before the canal. The size of the new stores and homes, it is
true, was no greater than that of an earlier day, and there was no
attempt to celebrate and advance the new urban face of the old
stockade with monumental public architecture. The two largest
buildings in the village were added during this period, but it is
interesting that they were churches rather than secular halls of
government, commerce, or leisure, and that they were built on
foundations of rivalry and exclusiveness rather than of community
pride. The Second Dutch Reformed Church had split off from its
ancient parent in 1849 and set about the task of building its own
church, "a grand affair, far exceeding anything in the country—
throwing the 'first' far into the shade."[34] The members of the original
congregation complained at first that the cost of maintaining the old
church would fall on too few shoulders, but, after discovering that
the second would be the largest in the village, "the 'first' awoke with
a start—the old church so lately large enough for the *whole* was now
discovered to be far too small for the *half*! They too would have a
new church, and having possessed themselves of the plan of the
'second,' laid their plans so as to outshine them!"[35] Of course, the
churches that resulted from this little elite war did display the
newfound wealth of the village, and in this sense fulfilled the
function of monumental urban architecture.

If the Rondout *Courier* could, in 1849, refer to Kingston as "that
village 'of magnificent distances,'" it was partly because Kingston
was just beginning to assume an urban aspect, and partly because
Rondout itself was already quite congested.[36] The doubling of the
population of Rondout over the next decade would cause new
ground to be broken on the periphery, but much of its growth would
be directed inward, so that by 1860 practically the entire village core
was covered with buildings. Some of them were large—George F.
Von Beck's Mansion House, for example, covered an entire block.
Most of the dwellings were small, but many were packed closely
together in or near the village core. And the fact that 63% of them
contained more than one household and 33% contained more than
two only increased the amount of human congestion associated with
each row of homes.

This phenomenon, the appearance of large numbers of multiple-
household dwellings, is one of the most telling indexes of Kingston's

urban character, for it was primarily in the cities that such dwellings were to be found. To indicate how far Kingston had come in this respect, therefore, table 11 compares the town with two Hudson Valley localities mentioned in the previous chapter: Troy, a medium-sized city of just under 40,000 inhabitants in 1860; and Marlborough, a rural township of some 3,000 inhabitants in the southeastern corner of Ulster County. In Troy only a minority of

Table 11   Proportions of Households in Single and Multiple
                  Dwellings; Troy, Kingston, and Marlborough,
                  New York, 1860

	Troy	Kingston	Marlborough
Single-Household Dwellings	36.1%	58.8%	83.3%
Multiple-Household Dwellings			
Two Households	40.4	22.1	13.0
Three Households	14.1	10.0	2.2
Four Households	5.3	4.7	0.7
Five Households	1.4	1.8	—
Six or more Households	1.2	1.8	—
Boarding Houses	1.5	0.6	0.7
Others[a]	—	0.2	—
	100.0%	100.0%	99.9%
Number of Households	(736)[b]	(3,104)	(538)

SOURCE: Manuscript census schedules, 1860.

[a]Consists of six workers' barracks (of brickmakers in a rural portion of the town), and the household of the sheriff, whose quarters adjoined the county jail.

[b]Based on a 10% interval sample.

households (36%) lived in single dwellings, while a smaller but still substantial minority (22%) lived in dwellings containing at least three households. In rural Marlborough, on the other hand, single dwellings were the rule, accounting for five out of every six households, while only 3% lived in buildings that combined more than two households. The town of Kingston, as we may expect, lay between these distinctly urban and rural places. Its overall profile was a bit more like that of Troy, particularly with respect to the proportions of households living in the most complex units. When households outside the urbanized southern portion of Kingston are eliminated, moreover, the proportion of single households drops to almost 50%, a great deal closer to Troy's 36% than to Marlborough's 83%. Marlborough, incidentally, did contain two small incorporated villages. Neither can be identified precisely in the census schedules, but it is instructive that in none of the occupational groups associated with village life was the rate of single-household residences below 75%. The households of Kingston, we may presume, had "urbanized" significantly after the construction of the canal.

Kingston and Rondout not only looked more urban in the 1850s, they sounded and smelled more urban too. A letter in the *Courier* in 1854 is given the heading, "We want quieter Streets," and complains at length of the noise of Rondout, attributing most of it to the availability of whiskey in the village, "day or night, Sabbath or week day."[37] It is unlikely, however, that a dried out Rondout would have been much quieter, for the complicated machine which consisted of blasting powder, picks, shovels, steamboat whistles, carpenters' hammers, horses' hooves, and wagon wheels would have run with or without lubrication. Nor would it have smelled much sweeter. The *Courier* complained often of the filth that was allowed to remain in Rondout's streets and of the resultant "sickening odors and stenches."[38] It complained also of odors attributable to the commerce of the place, particularly the transshipment of hides.[39] But Rondout monopolized neither noise nor unpleasant smells. Wagons loaded with bluestone passed continually through Kingston's streets, and the old-fashioned smell of butchering, once restricted to a week or two in the autumn, now issued from slaughterhouses for much of the summer as well:

> This evil may have been of comparatively little moment a very few years ago. But now, our streets becoming compactly built up, and our bounds extending, preventing the free circulation of air, these places with the best care become great nuisances. . . .[40]

In a number of ways, therefore, the lower portion of the town of Kingston had become something tangibly different from what it had been before the construction of the canal. Its development could be seen, heard, and even smelled. Kingstonians, as we have seen, responded in writing to many of these changes, particularly those that intruded most forcibly upon the senses. But how did they respond to growth itself? Did they perceive the growth of the local population as urbanization? Did they conceive of the lower portion of the town of Kingston as a city, or perhaps as two cities, each with a separate existence and identity? Did they greet the physical development of Kingston and Rondout with enthusiasm or with regret? Of course, each of these questions is unanswerable in that there were but a handful of men who left us their responses to local growth. To the extent that local editors, correspondents, and our diarist were spokesmen for more general opinion, however, we can at least answer the last question rather firmly. Growth was embraced and equated with progress, largely because of its more immediate association with prosperity. This is to be expected. But unlike a slightly earlier period, when editorials promoting growth were balanced by paeans to rural life, there seems to have been little or no ambivalence toward growth among the writers of the 1850s. Nathaniel Booth does complain once of industrial pollution in the Twaalfskill Brook.[41] But beyond this there are few if any qualifications to the attitude that growth is a blessing, either in Booth's diary or in the local papers. There is a great deal of commentary on violence, crime, poor housing, filthy streets, noise, and other problems, of course, but these are seldom associated explicitly with growth, and even when they are, they are presented as soluble problems rather than as evidence of social decay.

It is more difficult to determine whether Kingstonians thought of their town as a city. Although local editors often boasted of growth, delighted in discovering old newspapers which quaintly depicted "Rondout Fifty Years Ago,"[42] and boldly proclaimed that "Kingston village at no distant period will show all the territory in its corporate bounds covered by dwellings,"[43] they did not often use the word "city" to describe their new environment. But it must be remembered that "city" was a legal term and that Kingston had not yet received a city charter from the state of New York. By continuing to refer to Kingston and Rondout as villages, the editors were simply conforming to legal terminology, and we must be careful not to assume that they were either insensitive to growth or nostalgic for the pre-canal country village. Besides, they did occasionally use "city," and they most assuredly looked forward to the granting of a city charter in the immediate future.[44] Most important, the editors gloated over Kingston's importance as a commercial center for the mid–Hudson Valley, the Catskills, and the farms of Delaware County. In 1860, the *Republican* responded to the boasting of several downriver villages which had begun to grow as summer suburbs of New York:

> We can not certainly envy a kind of growth which is made up of country residences of city business men, who run out of New York to avoid taxation, and erect a country establishment as a branch of their city life. . . .
>
> Kingston is itself a centre. It prefers to dictate rather than adopt the customs and dress of such transient neighbors. . . . We think we speak the Kingston conceit when we rejoice that our growth is our own, depending upon the prosperity of a rich and thriving agricultural and manufacturing section of the country, of which it is the centre, and not merely the reflection of the business prosperity of New York.[45]

Finally, there is the question of whether the editors and local residents generally perceived a coalescence of the two villages into a single locality. This is still more difficult to answer, partly because the same individuals often gave contradictory opinions, and partly because these opinions (and, therefore, the contradictions) often arose in contexts that demanded one view or the other. In promoting the idea of a plank road, for example, the *Courier* wrote in 1849:

> The interests of the two villages are inseparable. . . . It is but a short sighted and bigoted envy which would put the one against the other . . . for it needs no great foresight to predict that in a very few years the twain will be one.[46]

Yet, eight years later, when the convergence of the two villages was far more of a reality than it had been in 1849, the *Courier* proclaimed that "Kingston and Rondout are so entirely distinct in every essential and trait, that it strikes every stranger of observing mind. They are a thousand miles asunder in character, interests and habits."[47] The context of this unneighborly statement was the promotion of the idea of a separate township for Rondout, which in turn sprang out of Rondout's failure to procure a second town polling place—the only existing town poll was in Kingston village. Moreover, the little editorial war that was fought over this issue had the distinct flavor of a domestic quarrel, with each paper accusing the other of "the desire to withdraw their fellowship."[48] Perhaps the most telling point is that the Kingston and Rondout papers were constantly responding to each other and to events and developments in the other village. In Kingston's paper we learn of cholera deaths in Rondout.[49] In Rondout's paper we learn of the "Isthmus," a neighborhood of brothels near Kingston village.[50] Interestingly, when the *Ulster Republican* carried a piece of fiction, written by an outsider, that described "the Dutch village of Kingston" as "a quaint, beautiful little place, that looks, with its grass grown streets and mossy houses, as if it were winking and nodding in a confirmed drowsiness,"[51] it was the Rondout *Courier* which responded with angered ridicule. Perhaps editor Hageman felt that only Rondouters were entitled to chide Kingston—that the sedate older sister and the growing younger brother (growing like a tree) were, after all, members of the same family.

7   The Development of
Local Institutions:
Government and Politics

The new physical entity at the terminus of the Delaware and Hudson Canal bred new social patterns, both by creating new institutions and by turning old ones to new uses. The transformation of existing institutions was particularly evident in the town's post-canal political development. Before the canal there were political parties in Kingston, and town and village governments. There were political newspapers, campaigns, elections, and a political community of candidates, party officials, campaign workers, and voters. In the decades following the construction of the canal, however, all these institutions and groups were transformed, some quite dramatically. By the time Abraham Lincoln assumed the presidency, this small portion of his constituency had acquired a far different set of political processes and a far different type of political consciousness than their fathers had possessed during the presidency of James Monroe.

In 1820, as we have seen, Kingston's political life was directed entirely toward campaigns, issues, policies, and personalities in the larger arenas of state and national government. Local government was functionally insignificant, and largely because of this, it was simply ignored by those whose responsibility it was to mobilize public support for one or another of New York's political factions. This was particularly so at the level of village government, where elections were not even reported in the local press and where the conduct of public affairs was informal, unimportant, and even infrequent. During the decades that followed, as the village grew and as the new village of Rondout appeared and outgrew its neighbor, local government acquired increasing significance, lost its informal character, and received increasing attention from the originally cosmopolitan political parties. At the same time, state and national issues, once quite remote from the affairs of the community, often became local issues as well, and sometimes were so transformed by local contestants that their origin in national or state politics was obscured or forgotten. By 1860, in short, there was a local dimension in Kingston's public affairs that had been nearly absent in 1820. Just how this came to pass, and the ways it influenced and reflected local conceptions of citizenship and community, are the subjects of this chapter.

The development of village government in Kingston and in Rondout is an interesting story made up of such uninteresting objects as sidewalks, cisterns, and grocery licenses, along with a few more dramatic elements such as cholera epidemics. Both the year-to-year, routine business and the occasional crises, however, contain the same message of development, and the former is probably the more telling. In the years immediately following the construction of the canal, routine village government was much the same as it had been in 1820. In 1829–30 there were only a dozen meetings of the Kingston board of directors, and half of these occurred during the first two months of the political year, April and May.[1] As in 1820, the directors' achievements consisted largely in setting up the village government for the year. Only thirty-four items came before the board, nineteen during the first two months, and thirteen of these were resignations, appointments, and other housecleaning operations. The remainder were mostly rather trivial chores that the directors accomplished themselves. In April, for example, director Joseph S. Smith was charged with calling upon a Mr. O'Neill about a missing ladder. In May, director Matthew Ten Eyck was paid $1 for having filled up a well in Wall Street. The purchase of two fire hooks and two ladders was a large enough project to require the appointment of two directors, Ten Eyck and Jacob Burhans, as a committee. Moreover, village government was as informal as it was inactive. There was still no village hall, and the directors met both at the courthouse and at Hannah Radcliff's tavern. Street repairs, like everything else, were performed under the supervision of specified directors, and their sites were generally designated as, for example, "between the old distillery and the bridge by Jonathan D. Hasbrouck's blacksmith's shop." Claims on the village treasury were presented directly to the board, which passed upon each one as it appeared. There were, perhaps, a few signs of change. In October the board divided into two committees, each with authority over the repair of streets in half of the village. In January there was a new fire ordinance and an application to the state legislature for a new village charter. The new charter, as published in the local press, is most notable for the creation of the office of street commissioner, an appointee of the board whose duty it was to enforce village ordinances concerning sidewalk obstruction, horse racing, and roving swine.[2] Beyond this, however, there seems to have been little that was not already within the board's power. The new charter, reflecting the limited activities of the village government, contained exactly thirty paragraphs and covered a small portion of a single page in the *Ulster Palladium*.

Minutes of the board's operations during 1830–53 are missing, so it is not possible to observe the precise evolution of local government in Kingston during this period. The newspapers are some help. Although they did not begin to take editorial notice of the village government until 1845, there are a few insertions written and paid for by the village itself, such as a call in 1838 for a special vote by the "taxable inhabitants" on a proposed tax of $1,000 for the liquidation of village debts, the widening of streets, and the construction of two enginehouses.[3] This one item tells us that the village government had begun to do things it would not have done ten years earlier. A treasurer's report indicates that disbursements during 1836–37 were $667.84, as compared with only $80.55 in 1821–22 and only $89.50 in 1829–30.[4] Two years later, disbursements of $1,396.38, of which $950 was financed by another special tax, are reported.[5] And yet another treasurer's report, published in 1841, indicates that the special tax was probably becoming an annual occasion. In that year disbursements by the village were $1,495.87 and the net "avails of village tax voted" were $924.53.[6]

Of particular value are the minutes of a half-dozen directors' meetings held in the spring of 1842 that, in a fit of extravagance (soon tempered), the directors decided to publish in the local press.[7] The spring directors' meetings had always been a great deal busier than those held during the remainder of the year, so the disappearance of the minutes from the newspapers after May 18 may well indicate that the traditional seasonal pattern of village government still obtained. But the spring meetings of 1842 were different from the spring meetings of 1829. There were the usual appointments to be made and resignations to be accepted, but there were at least three new elements that gave the board a significance it had previously lacked. First, many of the items concerned the opening of new village streets (Fair and Prospect), the creation of a village pound, and the management of other public properties such as cisterns, culverts, and the village cemetery. Second, there were several punitive items stemming from violations of village ordinances. Third, there was a special meeting devoted to the troublesome question of grocery and tavern licenses, which, we shall see a bit later, had become a local issue of great importance. The board (meeting at a temperance hotel) handled this problem by simply refusing to grant any grocery licenses (which were often "used as a cover for the purpose of selling liquor to be drank on their premises")[8] and by granting only five tavern licenses, that being the number "absolutely necessary for the accommodation of travellers in the village of Kingston."[9] The village board of 1842, in short, was both tougher and more active than it had been in earlier years, and its minutes reveal not only that it had more to do but that, in addition, the villagers themselves were beginning to pay close attention to its decisions and activities.

By 1854–55, the first full year after 1829–30 for which the village minutes are available, local government had been almost completely transformed.[10] Instead of the dozen meetings of 1829–30 there were now fifty-two, and instead of 34 items of business during the year there were now 184. Perhaps more important, the village government had become a truly year-round affair, conducting almost as much business during the summer and fall as during the spring. To some extent, this dramatic expansion reflected the fact that Kingston had just received another charter, this one running to fifty-nine paragraphs and occupying almost two full pages of the *Ulster Republican*.[11] The new charter greatly expanded the powers and duties of the board, increased their taxing authority, and, apparently, restructured and increased the number of village officers. The village government was now a fairly complex institution, with seven directors, one elected from each of seven village wards, three assessors, a treasurer, a collector, a clerk, a street commissioner, and no fewer than fourteen fire wardens, two from each ward. In addition to these elected officials, there were four fire engine companies and a hook-and-ladder company, whose members met annually to select the chief and assistant engineers of what was now known as the Kingston fire department. A "streets department" was created by an important provision in the new charter that turned the village into a separate road district and gave the village directors the taxing, assessing, collecting, planning, and executing powers of commissioners of highways—powers formerly in the domain of the town. In their new capacity, the directors were to draw up a list of inhabitants required to work on the village streets and were also empowered to transform this ancient corvée into a cash payment, at a rate not exceeding 50¢ per day. This the directors did (and apparently continued to do in subsequent years), collecting the "road tax" and placing the work itself under the supervision of the street commissioner.[12] Finally, the directors utilized another provision of the new charter to create yet another "department" in the form of three "public officers," or policemen, to be paid "for such time as they shall actually be on duty."[13] On March 5, 1855, this little police department was tripled in size, "to preserve order and suppress any riot in the Village of Kingston, on Tuesday, March 6, 1855."[14] Perhaps because of this impressive mobilization, no riot seems to have materialized.

Commensurate with the expanded functions of the village government was an expanded and compartmentalized treasury. In 1854–55 the village received into its general fund $2,692.43, most of it from the $2,000 tax now authorized by the charter (there was also a provision for an additional $1,000 tax if the voters approved), and the remainder from licenses and the village's share of the hayscales revenues. It spent $2,244.60, mostly on the fire department, and it is worth noting that expenditures for printing, office supplies, and other clerical items ($134.94) were considerably higher than the entire village budget had been twenty-five years earlier. There was also a separate road fund in 1854–55, in which expenditures of $1,627.56 were almost exactly matched by the "50¢ per day of labor" road tax. The total village budget was now over $3,800.

Village government was not quite professional in the 1850s (for example, directors still investigated nuisances personally), but it had certainly become more formalized. Indicative of this was the codification every few years of village ordinances, a trend subjected to a marvelous roasting by the *Ulster Republican* in 1855:

> Codification is a science now. It requires rare talents, and our Village codifiers have got 'em. . . .
> We intended going through the whole code perpendicularly, horizontally and diagonally, in order to be sure and hit all its beauties, but 4th of July comes but once a year, and as the code fixes it as the only day when we can fire "a pistol, squib, rocket,

cracker or fireworks of any explosive compound," or "make or create a bonfire or bonfires in said village except by permission of the Board of Directors," why we must ... be content to notice two or three remark-worthy provisions.[15]

The most "remark-worthy" of the ordinances concerned village brothels:

"That no person or persons shall, within the bounds of said village, set up, maintain or keep any disorderly house of assignation, brothel, bawdy house, or house of debauchery; nor shall any such person or persons within said village entertain lewd women for the purpose of prostitution, or procure or aid in procuring lewd women for that purpose, under the penalty of not less than twenty-five nor more than fifty dollars."

In deference to vulgar prejudice on such score, Sam [the lawyer who wrote the ordinances] don't bluntly say that for from twenty-five to fifty dollars we'll license these necessary evils, but under show of a penalty, does so in reality.—The fact is, Sam is progressive and keeps up with the age. If "Young America" and "fast America" are to be propitiated, why not do it on the sly, get up a nice license revenue in the operation, and not compel our hard up ardent youths to rush into Mormonism and all that sort of thing.[16]

The *Republican* was unable to reverse the trend toward the expansion and formalization of village government. In 1857 the treasurer reported expenditures of $5,572.23 and, for the first time, assigned the various expenditures to categories.[17] The 1860–61 directors' minutes contain 272 items, exactly eight times the number brought before the board in 1829–30 and a 48% increase since 1854–55.[18] At the first meeting of the year, the directors voted themselves a regular boardroom at the new Fireman's Hall, giving the village government a fixed place for the first time in its history. In general, the 1860–61 minutes reveal a greatly expanded village government, busily engaged in laying out new streets, erecting new streetlights, grading, curbing, and guttering old streets, operating and expanding the fire department (there were now seven companies and 191 active firemen), auditing and paying bills, disputing claims, hearing petitions, and enforcing village ordinances. Of greater significance, perhaps, was the attention now given to record keeping and to bureaucratic details. In May the directors published the latest edition of the village ordinances, now 93 paragraphs long.[19] In June they agreed to pay $75 for a bound copy of the federal census schedules pertaining to the village.[20] In July they began a sequential numbering of the bills presented to them for approval.[21] In October they authorized the president of the board to hire a clerk to put all of the village's documents into better order.[22] And at the end of the year, statistical summaries of the membership and activities of each of the fire companies were incorporated into the minutes.[23] Each of these actions directly reflects the new complexity of the village's public business. But there are two less obviously related items that tell the interrelated stories of urban growth and village modernization even more eloquently. On July 2 the directors ordered the usual 50¢ road tax but based it on every $500 of assessed property rather than on each day of required labor, thereby erasing the last remnant of the rural corvée.[24] And on April 23 they voted to sell the village hayscales to J. P. Osterhoudt and Co. for $50.[25]

The growth of the village government is reflected in the increasing attention paid to it by the local press and by the political parties. The first editorial comment on the operations of the village board was made in 1834, when the directors unsuccessfully petitioned the legislature for an amendment to the charter that would restrict the village electorate to taxpayers. This was apparently an anti-Irish maneuver and was denounced as such at a public meeting and in the editorial columns of the *Ulster Republican*.[26] But in the 1830s only an extraordinary item such as this could gain such publicity, and it was not until 1845 that a routine complaint (urging stricter enforcement of an ordinance prohibiting the storage of gunpowder in the village) would appear in a local newspaper.[27] "We seldom refer in our paper to village matters," wrote the *Republican* in 1847, as a preface to a long article complaining of a proposed village tax, and, unwittingly, as a preface to an era of increasing editorial comment on village affairs.[28] By the early 1850s the local press routinely commented on village fire-fighting facilities, sidewalks, and streets, and even reported an occasional news item, such as the election of fire department officials.[29] In 1860, under the bold heading, "Local News," the *Republican* began carrying the minutes of the directors' meetings, this time as *news* rather than as paid public notices.[30]

It is not surprising, in light of the political character of the local press, that the politicization of village affairs should have followed a similar, if somewhat faster, timetable. Originally, village elections and the conduct of village government lay entirely outside the domain of partisan politics. The first hint of partisan interest in the annual charter election was in 1832, when the local Anti-Masonic newspaper published the village election results as a news item, along with the returns of an explicitly partisan town election.[31] Two years later the *Republican* followed the same format, adding offhandedly, "Our village ticket is also elected throughout, by an average majority of about 40."[32] But the following years yield no mention of village elections, except in the traditional form of paid advertisements,[33] until 1839, when the *Republican* noted that the election "was contested on party grounds in relation to directors."[34] Even then the *Republican* claimed only three candidates and two winners, and those two ran on the Whig ticket as well. Furthermore, its commentary in the following year contradicts its earlier claim of village politicization:

> The annual Charter election of this village was held yesterday, and we had an animated brush on strict party grounds, the first that has occurred within our recollection. The opposition threw down the gauntlet and we were compelled to take it up, much as we regretted the introduction of party politics in our village affairs. Our nominations were not made out until a late hour on Monday night, and many of the candidates were not apprised of their nomination until the next day [the day of the election].[35]

The *Republican*, to be sure, was simply trying to explain away defeat, for its party elected only three officers in 1840. But the form of the explanation—the lofty moral position of reluctant partisanship—is significant.[36] There should be no doubt that the parties, including the *Republican's* own Democrats, had concerned themselves with village elections during the preceding decade. But it is fairly clear that they had not yet succeeded in transforming the annual charter election into a thoroughly partisan event. In all probability, they simply did not yet care enough about the village government (which still did little and dispensed practically no patronage) to mobilize party machinery for its capture.

The charter election of 1841 was again "held upon party grounds," and full returns were given for the first time. These reveal a close division of Democrats and Whigs, with enough ticket-splitting to elect six of one and five of the other. They also reveal that the turnout (about 350 votes, which later years' returns indicate was typical) was almost as high as the turnout for the county, state, and national elections held in the autumn.[37] The following year's election was the first in which an explicit issue can be discerned, with "the introduction of the temperance cause into the political arena, which exercised a controlling influence upon the election."[38] It was the board then elected, identified by the *Republican* as Whigs, who printed their early minutes in the local newspapers and took such a firm stand against the granting of grocery and tavern licenses. Their election, their actions, and perhaps even their publicly financed publicity, indicate that village politics could be based on more than the fact that there were offices to be filled.

However, despite the considerable enlargement of the scope of village powers and activities after 1842, there does not seem to have been a corresponding enlargement of village-oriented political activity. The town remained the smallest unit of party organization, and the town elections retained their monopoly on spring newspaper campaigning. Although most village elections were reported as political events, some were reported with no comment, and in a few instances partisanship was specifically downgraded. In 1843 and in 1848, the *Republican* actually played down the political significance of its own party's recapture of the village board; in 1855 it once again attempted to explain the Democrats' defeat by accusing the opposition (in this case the Know-Nothings) of unfairly introducing politics into the village election.[39] On the other hand, the pattern achieved by 1842 was retained. Party politics, although occasionally denied or downgraded by the local press, had become a permanent feature of village elections, which were occasionally enlivened further by important local issues. Thus, in 1846 another "no license" board was elected by a comfortable margin.[40] In 1855 the Native American or Know-Nothing party began a three-year reign over this thoroughly native village. When they were defeated in 1858 the delighted editor of the *Republican* recalled grimmer days, when "Daniel [Bradbury, Know-Nothing leader] could stride the streets of 'Old Sopus,' conscious that he was 'cock of the walk.' "[41]

The history of Rondout's government is in one sense the reverse of Kingston's, for in the newer village a large, dense population and a village-oriented local newspaper preceded the creation of a village government. Indeed, the *Courier* was actively encouraging the incorporation of the village as early as 1844 and gave a great deal of space to the successful drive toward incorporation in 1849.[42] After the charter had been obtained, the *Courier* actively promoted improvements in fire protection, streets and sidewalks, water supply, cleanliness, licensing, Sabbath observance, and police protection; it even went so far as to suggest the creation of a village hospital.[43] But in its formal and functional development, the Rondout village government was not much different from that of its older neighbor. Despite the obvious need for village services, particularly fire protection, the government of Rondout got off to an exceedingly shaky start.[44] The earliest meeting held on the issue of incorporation decided in the negative.[45] Later meetings (to judge from the tone of the *Courier*) may not have been much more enthusiastic.[46] When the first village election was held, only 288 votes were polled, and, interestingly, most of these were cast to *defeat* the ticket nominated at a citizens' meeting and printed in the *Courier*.[47] The two men elected to be the village's first treasurer and clerk declined the honor, and, despite the considerable task of building a government from the ground up, two of the first seven trustees' meetings were adjourned because a quorum was not present.[48]

For several years Rondouters treated their new government with considerable reserve, especially when it came to raising village taxes. Even when a tax proposal was intended for the settlement of existing claims against the village, the voters of Rondout were likely to vote it down, leaving the trustees with little choice but to resubmit the tax at a later date. For example, in 1852 the trustees took the bold step of acquiring a house and lot for $800 for use as a village hospital.[49] A year and a half later, when the trustees finally proposed a tax to pay for the property, the voters rejected it by a margin of 96 to 22. A second attempt also failed. Only on the third try did the trustees succeed, 76 to 60, and the new hospital was opened in time for a brief flurry of cholera in 1854.[50] But the fundamental problem remained. Rondout's charter was designed to provide maximum responsiveness to the will of the inhabitants of the village. This assumed, however, that the voters would regard the village government as basically legitimate and that votes on taxation would convey the popular will about various policy alternatives within the framework of a continuing institution. Apparently, this sort of commitment was not widespread in the young village, and the Rondout government was forced to function for several years under the very real threat that its own citizens would shut it down.

The trustees' minutes, too, reflect the marginal status of the Rondout village government during its first few years. As in earlier days in Kingston, the board met fairly often during the first month or two and then all but adjourned for the rest of the year. It is true that the trustees were quite active during the terrible cholera epidemic of 1849, but their activities were entirely restricted to the emergency and derived more from directives from Albany than from local initiative.[51] Once the epidemic had abated, moreover, the Rondout trustees reverted to comparative inactivity. During the following year they met only fourteen times and considered only two dozen items of business. They did not meet at all during the summer and conducted half of their business during the first two months of the political year.[52]

The Rondout government, however, gathered strength through the 1850s. A new charter expanded its powers in 1851, and in 1857 another made it almost identical to the government of the village of Kingston.[53] By 1860 the trustees of Rondout were meeting just as frequently as, and were accomplishing even more business than, the directors of the older village.[54] Politically, too, the Rondout government came of age, for even though there is little mention in the *Courier* of partisanship in village elections (there is an "American" ticket mentioned in 1858),[55] there was a substantial increase in voter turnout during the last few years of the decade—from 434 votes in 1856, and 492 in 1858, to 742 votes in 1860.[56] The 1860 election is particularly revealing of the development of village government in Rondout over the decade, for the incumbent board represented themselves as the "progress and improvement ticket" on the basis of a vigorous street-draining and grading policy followed during the previous year. They were reelected in a landslide and, crowed the *Courier*, "it would seem that the hearty popular endorsement stamps Rondout as a 'progress and improvement' place."[57]

Local government in Kingston and Rondout is not fully accounted for by the village corporations. If we wish to understand the evolution of public institutions on the urban threshold, we must give some attention to the township and the county, if only to understand better the villages themselves. The town, as we have noted earlier, was the smallest unit of government in rural areas lacking an incorporated village. Although a city replaced a town and automatically absorbed all its functions, a village such as

Kingston or Rondout existed within the framework of the pre-existing town (in this case, the town of Kingston) and absorbed only those functions specifically transferred to it by the village charter. Thus, Kingston and Rondout each became a separate highway district during the course of its development and acquired the road-building authority (including taxation) formerly invested in the town; the town was left authority over those roads outside the village boundaries. Other functions, such as the operation of the public schools and the care of the poor, were never transferred to the villages, even though school districts were created to coincide with village boundaries. Unlike the villages, however, the town did not really operate as an entity. Its officers performed their duties separately, and its chief officer, the town supervisor, presided over no organized body. Rather, he served as the town's representative on the county board of supervisors, which was in turn the legislative and administrative body of the county and, by extension, of all its towns. Between the incorporated village and the county, in other words, there was no single governmental unit that could be specified as the town, and the residents of unincorporated areas must have experienced no small amount of confusion when it came to sorting out the various responsibilities and rights that constituted their local government. That the town and county officers were themselves sometimes confused is evidenced by the publication of *The County and Town Officer* in 1816 by John Tappen, editor of the *Plebeian* and, for a time, clerk of Ulster County. Tappen states openly that his purpose in writing the book was to correct errors caused by ignorance:

> I have long been persuaded, as well from my own observation, as the information of others, that the errors and inaccuracies which have been frequently committed by county and town officers in the exercise of their several official duties, might in many instances have been avoided, through the aid of a Manual, such as this book presents to the public.[58]

This formlessness in rural local government underscores the basic theme of our discussion of village development—that as the village governments grew in size and significance, they provided a local dimension to public affairs that had previously been diffused and difficult to comprehend. The village not only greatly expanded the sphere of local government—organizing fire departments, erecting streetlamps, regulating traffic, and attempting to regulate morals through numerous ordinances on drinking, swearing, and prostitution—it also provided a more tangible and even more local organizational focus to functions previously performed by the town. Still, it would be a mistake to assume that the town itself was static during this period and that it could not contribute in its own way to the development of a significant local polity. Actually, as a governmental unit, the town changed very little. But as a unit of organization for local political parties, it changed dramatically, increasing in significance as parties developed their increasingly elaborate machinery of political mobilization.

In the 1820s, as we have seen, there was but one political season in Kingston, beginning during the summer and culminating with the fall election. The press paid almost no attention to the spring elections, except to note that "the following gentlemen" had been elected to the board of supervisors or to include an advertisement from the village clerk about the coming charter election.[59] The first hint of partisanship in town elections is found in the *Ulster Sentinel* of 1828, in a notice of a Saturday night meeting at the Ulster County House for the nomination of town officers.[60] Successful supervisor candidates are identified as "Adams men" and "Jackson men" (other town officers are ignored), but it is not clear to what extent their factional affiliations were provoked by the fact that it was a presidential election year.[61] It remained for the Anti-Masons, always a weak political force in Ulster County, to bring town politics out into the open:

> There is no duty which the Anti-Masons can perform with more advantage to themselves at this time, than by preparing for the approaching town meetings. . . . Towns form counties and counties form the state. Let the people once draw the line in towns, and the progress of antimasonry will be as rapid, and its success as certain as it has been in the western counties.
>
> Many of our friends . . . say that it is unnecessary to raise any opposition in the town elections, but leave that till the general fall election. . . . Remember that office gains influence, and that by obtaining official stations in the spring, your opponents can electioneer with greater effect for the fall.[62]

The focus here is not on the town or even on the county but on the state. In this sense, the emergence of town politics in the 1830s hardly indicates the development of a localized political conscious-

ness among the partisan. But the movement toward openly partisan town elections had just begun. In later years and among more
firmly established parties, the connection between town, county,
and state politics would not be articulated, largely because there
was no need to articulate what everyone already understood.
Nevertheless, the emergence of a second political season in each
and every year—of a completely separate political campaign for
town offices—must have produced an awareness of local politics
and government that could barely have existed before.

The spring political season developed a fairly regular pattern
during the 1830s. In 1834 the *Ulster Republican* reported "one of
the most important and desperately contested elections which has
ever been known in this town," but the contest had developed only
in the three or four days prior to the election, when a group of
"seceders" nominated a ticket.[63] The election of the following year,
although partisan, was quiet.[64] The Whigs were just beginning to
put together a party, the Republican factions were temporarily at
peace with one another, and the Anti-Masons were gone forever,
apparently absorbed into the emerging Whigs.[65] In 1836, although
still firmly in command of local politics, the Republican (or, by
now, Democratic) town committee printed the following notice in
the *Republican*:

> The democratic electors of the town of Kingston, friendly to the
> present state and general administrations, and *in favor of regular
> nominations*, are requested to meet at the Court-house . . . for the
> purpose of nominating candidates for the ensuing year.[66]

No campaigning appeared in the newspapers of that year or the
next. But in 1838, with the emergence of a more powerful Whig
party in the county, the spring season took a much clearer shape.
The call for nominations was followed by a weekly listing of the
party ticket at the head of the editorial column, just as in the fall
campaign. The editorials themselves were, for the first time,
devoted to the town election, and results were both listed and
discussed.[67] All that was lacking was the stridency of the fall
campaign, and this was supplied in the following year, when the
Democratic victory was greeted with the cry, "Ulster Redeemed!"[68]
Thereafter, the two political seasons, as manifested in the local
press, were indistinguishable in form. The fall campaign was longer
and the issues were usually different, but both the local mechanisms and the enthusiasm were the same.

The emergence of a separate, highly charged local campaign in the spring of each year is not in itself proof that party activists redirected or significantly extended their political frames of reference toward local affairs. The vehicles of involvement were, after all, the state and national parties, and the basic positions of these parties on state and national issues inevitably intruded into the contests for supervisor, county clerk, commissioner of highways, and the other local offices. The primary motive for the spring campaign, as we have seen, was to build an effective base for the conduct of state political warfare, and this is reflected in the emphasis given to the goal of achieving a majority on the patronage-dispensing board of supervisors. It may be significant in this connection that in 1860, despite a decisive defeat in the county, Kingston Democrats celebrated the triumph of their ticket in the town. "Our street was illuminated by burning tar barrels, and cheer after cheer, kept up till midnight, attested to the good feeling which it caused among the 'Boys.'"[69] Were the Kingston Democrats really so pleased, or was the *Ulster Republican* simply trying to distract attention from the countywide defeat? The state party leaders, surely, would not have appreciated a celebration in Kingston in the spring of 1860.

We cannot understand the influence of the development of local political structures, however, without looking at the political issues themselves. Perhaps intensified local campaigning was conducted entirely on behalf of Texas annexation, the abolition of slavery, or a fiscally responsible plan for improving the Erie Canal. Perhaps, on the other hand, the spring elections and conceivably even the fall elections were contests on local issues or between local interest groups or personalities, with little reference made to the larger issues or loyalties implied by party labels. Reality seems to lie somewhere in between. Political issues in post-canal Kingston were neither strictly local nor strictly nonlocal; nor, for that matter, were they simply a mixture of both. Rather, the growth of Kingston and the development of more fully articulated local political institutions transformed state and national issues into local issues by giving them a local relevance and a local medium of expression that had been lacking in the pre-canal country town. Nonlocal issues became local issues, in short, when Kingston began to experience those economic and social changes that altered the substance of government in the nation as a whole, and when

Kingston acquired the machinery to carry into politics the local manifestations of economic and social change.

It was by no means accidental, therefore, that in the 1830s Kingston had a bank war. We have already seen that the post-canal growth of Kingston's economy, and particularly of its economic prospects, resulted in the concentration of Ulster County's banking facilities in Kingston, despite the efforts of other towns, particularly Saugerties, to secure banks of their own. The bank memorial of 1834 presented Kingston as the inevitable economic nucleus of the county, as did editorials in the local Republican and Anti-Masonic press. But banks were more than economic institutions. The very fact that, until 1838, banks in New York were incorporated individually and quite selectively by the state legislature meant that they were valuable political commodities as well. A growing town's economic argument for a new bank, therefore, served only to raise the significant political question of *who* in that town should be awarded the valuable charter by having themselves or their friends put in control of the commission charged with distributing the new bank's stock. In some towns, perhaps, the decision was an easy one. In Kingston, where the old Clintonian and Bucktail factions had been combined into an uneasy Republican alliance, and where the newspapers of both the old factions survived, the application for a new bank caused a political eruption that dominated local politics for six years and focused political energies during that time almost exclusively on the parochial arenas of the town and the county.

The issue of a "second bank" in Kingston arose shortly after the doors of the first local bank were opened in 1832. For the first bank, though probably intended in part to knit together the local Republican party, had fallen into the hands of the old Clintonians. The latter had been leaderless since Clinton's death in 1828 but were still united by their antipathy to Martin Van Buren's Albany Regency.[70] It is not clear how the local Anti-Regency group managed to obtain control of the new bank, but their coup created a glaring imbalance of political reward and immediately renewed old animosities. By the following spring each faction was holding separate nominating conventions and running separate tickets in the town election. The basic issue separating the factions was now, of course, a strictly local one, and this seemed to require new factional labels. On March 2, the Anti-Regency group denounced the local Van Burenites as the "Kingston Junto" and in return became fixed in the popular mind as the "Anti-Junto."[71]

The Kingston Junto wasted little time in attempting to redress the political imbalance caused by the Anti-Junto's control of the Bank of Ulster County. In July of 1833, the *Ulster Republican*, voice of the Junto, began insisting on the need for a new bank in Kingston while accusing the Anti-Junto *Ulster Sentinel* of supporting the petition from Saugerties.[72] In August, the *Republican* carried a notice, signed by more than five hundred men, of a "bank convention" to be held that month in Rosendale (a little hamlet just up the canal from Kingston), and out of that convention grew the bank memorial we described earlier.[73] The Anti-Masonic *Palladium's* response to the convention is most instructive. Though enthusiastic in its support of a new Kingston bank, the *Palladium* suggested that "a sharp eye [be kept] on the most *clamorous* actors in this business" and that the commissioners in charge of the stock distribution be composed of the political *enemies* of the Kingston Junto, so that the bank "should be regarded separate from a mere party consideration."[74] A month later, recognizing the futility of such a suggestion, the *Palladium* withdrew its support of the bank petition.[75]

Through the four elections of 1833 and 1834, the Kingston bank war completely dominated local politics. The Anti-Junto organized sufficient strength in the county, particularly in the towns around Saugerties, to prevent hasty approval by the legislature of the bank petition.[76] By the end of 1834, however, the new Whig party had made its appearance in Ulster County, necessitating some kind of accommodation among the warring Democrats (as we should now call them). In February, 1835 a truce was effected, and was solidified further in April, when state senator John Sudam, leader of the Kingston Junto, died in Albany. The Junto now agreed to support Anti-Junto Ebenezer Lounsbery to serve the remainder of Sudam's term, and the Anti-Junto agreed to support a petition for a bank that both sides would control.[77] In the summer of 1835 the *Republican* coupled its arguments for a new bank with appeals for party unity.[78] Peace was seriously threatened at the autumn county convention, but the Democrats managed to stay together long enough to defeat the Whigs.[79]

The fruits of reunification were now at hand. In January, 1836, a bank meeting was held at Kingston. The two secretaries of the meeting were Alonzo L. Stewart of the *Ulster Republican* and William Culley of the *Ulster Sentinel*.[80] In February the banking committee of the state assembly reported favorably on the Kingston petition and unfavorably on the petition from Saugerties.[81] In April the town elections went by with barely a hint of intraparty conflict, and in May both houses of the state legislature granted Kingston its second bank charter.[82] The stock sale was set for the end of June. On the eve of the distribution Alonzo Stewart was in the best of moods, his long battle finally won:

> Our usually very quiet village has been a scene of general bustle and confusion for two days past, occasioned by the opening of the books of subscription to our new bank, and by the host of prospective Presidents, Cashiers, and Directors, fishing in the muddy waters of patronage.... May one half of the seekers for office be successful; and the Kingston Bank will resemble the army of the Prince of Little Schwarzingen, where fifteen generals command four trumpeters and a corporal.[83]

Stewart's high spirits would last only a few days, for he and the Kingston Junto had in fact been hoodwinked by their old adversaries. Anti-Junto leaders, including the officers and directors of the *first* bank, were given enough stock to control the new bank. Ebenezer Lounsbery, the Anti-Junto who had replaced John Sudam in the senate, was elected bank president—three years after Sudam himself had been accused by the Anti-Junto *Sentinel* of lusting after the office![84] Now the *Sentinel* defended the new bank against a scathing attack by its old promoter, the *Ulster Republican*, which called for a "people's convention" to condemn the stock distribution.[85] A year later the state banking committee heard Cornelius E. Wynkoop, one of the commissioners, testify "that the majority of the board intended making such a distribution as would give the control of the institution to that section of the party termed 'anti-Junto,' and to those who would go with them, in order to insure the election of the Hon. Ebenezer Lounsbery, president, and J. S. Smith, cashier of the bank."[86] The committee apparently accepted this testimony as truthful and accurate but did nothing to change the existing order.

After the betrayal of the Junto in 1836 nothing could hold the factions together. The *Republican* took to calling the Anti-Junto the "bank managers" and glumly reported their gradual absorption by the Whigs.[87] By the fall of 1838 only two tickets were in the field, with the Whigs triumphant.[88] In 1840, the *Ulster Sentinel* merged with the Whig *Political Reformer* to form the new local Whig paper, the Kingston *Democratic Journal*, and Kingston's political realignment was complete.

The details of the Kingston bank war should not obscure that conflict's relationship to the development of the town as a commercial center. Without the growth of Kingston there would have been no bank war, for the obvious reason that there would have been no question of a local bank. Nor is it likely that any equivalent political issue would have developed to focus the attention of Kingston's political leaders inward on the town rather than outward to the nation and state. Our concern here is not whether static rural townships could or could not have become convulsed in local issues, but whether these issues could have provided the substantive focus for the energies of those men who were already involved in more cosmopolitan political arenas. In other words, we are concerned with the political orientations of men whom we may call local political elites, and I suggest that the orientations of these elites became more localized as the local political arena expanded to a point where it could contain significant political issues. More accurately, I suggest that they *added* a significant local orientation to their previous cosmopolitanism, and that this new element of localism may have significantly altered their approach to the political system as a whole.

It is instructive to observe the course of Kingston's politics after the bank war and its attendant political realignments were over, for the above argument is not valid if there was a return to conditions prevailing in the pre-canal town. State and national issues could have reappeared on the local level, particularly with the reconstruction of a local two-party system corresponding with state and national alignments; but our argument is valid only if these issues did not *replace* local issues or reduce the local polity to its former insignificance. In fact, state and national issues did reappear in Kingston once the Democratic-Whig realignment had been effected. The fall campaigns of 1838 and later were fought over currency reform, internal improvements and the state debt (this was one issue), the extension of slavery, immigration and naturalization, and, perhaps most persistent of all, temperance. All these were state or national issues. In addition, the personalities of national (but not state) politics, and the new image-making campaign techniques of both parties, played an enormous role in local campaigns, at least during the years of presidential elections. Kingston Whigs erected a log cabin in 1840, where, according to the "Locofoco, agrarian leveller" *Ulster Republican,* one could see "our 7 per cent aristocracy, who doffed their robes of superiority so far as to enter the basement, where the crowd assembled, take a finger full of beans and pork, talk sentiment about '*us* poor people,' and then glide up stairs to partake of a sumptuous dinner."[89] Four years later the Democrats were raising hickory poles to the greater glory of "Young Hickory," and four years after that there were "Scott clubs" and "Pierce clubs" to supplement the rallies and torchlight parades. But the local polity was not crushed beneath the weight of log cabins and hickory poles. On the contrary, the politics of Kingston during the 1840s and 1850s continued the localizing trend begun in the 1830s. The spring elections for town and village officers retained their new importance, and the spring campaign was given no less attention than it had received during the local bank war. But more important, several of the great state and national issues were now local issues as well and were applied so intensively to the local scene that their existence at wider political levels was all but forgotten. With one exception, moreover, Kingstonians responded with enthusiasm only to those state and national issues that had obvious local relevance. The exception was slavery, and its career as a political issue in Kingston was restricted to the Free-Soil controversy of the late 1840s. During the 1850s slavery receded into the background of local political debate, while Kingston turned its attention increasingly to alcohol and immigration.

Although the temperance issue and the Irish arrived in Kingston at about the same time, the early 1830s, it is not likely that they were at that time considered by sober natives to be related. The Irish were few in number and lived off by themselves near the D & H docks. Native Americans were quite capable of getting drunk without any instruction or inspiration from the Irish, and it was a rare harvest which was not "gotten in" without a great deal of help from the whiskey barrel brought out to the fields by the farm owner. The drunkenness of native Protestants and the example of other Protestant places, therefore, were what inspired the formation in 1831 of the Ulster County Temperance Society, the Kingston Temperance Society, and the Temperance Society of the Kingston Academy.[90] But as long as the problem was a rural one and not especially associated with the villages or their diversifying populations, the temperance movement in Ulster County remained outside politics. In fact, the movement itself seems to have foundered until 1842, when it was revitalized and linked to the emerging local political system. The 1842 report of the Kingston chapter of the Ulster County Total Abstinence Society indicates that the chapter had been formed in 1837 with 42 members, that it had languished until 1842, and that it had been given a tremendous boost in that year by the lectures of John T. Romeyn, Esquire (a former Anti-Junto leader), who was responsible for 455 new members and the opening of a "temperance public house" in Kingston.[91] Romeyn's participation is itself a hint of a linkage between politics and the temperance cause, but there is also far more substantial evidence. The same year saw the election of the first temperance board of directors in Kingston village and the first official attempt to control the sale of intoxicating drink. Thereafter, local politicians could ignore the "cold water vote" only at considerable risk, for the temperance movement had fixed on a no-license policy to go along with their lectures, temperance dramas, separate July Fourth dinners (on several occasions their influence was sufficient to have the "official" celebration held on "temperance principles"), and their expanding structure of voluntary societies (which included the Delavan Temperance Union for blacks).[92] The movement peaked in the second half of the 1840s with an unsuccessful experiment in state-authorized local prohibition.[93] It revived again a few years later in the Maine law movement, which in 1855 actually produced separate temperance nominations for assemblyman and county judge.[94]

The temperance movement in Kingston was, of course, by no means isolated from the national crusade; even its local political goals were necessarily directed in part at the Albany legislature. But the goal of a strictly enforced no-license law focused much of the movement's energy inward on the community, where grocery and tavern licenses were actually distributed and where enforcement was supposed to reside. No-license advocates were active all over the county and were no doubt responsible for the invigoration of local politics in the smallest of places, but it is hardly surprising that they were most active in Kingston and Rondout, where thousands of native, Irish, and German men supported scores of licensed and unlicensed grogshops. That they were not more successful in their attempt to control the governments of these two villages, particularly Kingston, is attributable partly to the fact that the temperance issue became somewhat lost in the more fundamental, and by then closely related, national-local issue of immigrant citizenship.

While there may be some question about which movement, temperance or nativism, was more important to Kingston's politics in the 1840s, there can be no doubt about nativism's domination in the 1850s. Until the 1850s, both movements had followed similar patterns, becoming visible in the early 1830s and emerging as locally oriented political movements in the 1840s. The first explicitly nativist political effort in Kingston was in the town election of 1844; and when the Whigs won the election, the *Republican* attributed it to Democratic defections to the third ticket.[95] The *Republican* itself carried an "American Republican" town ticket as a paid advertisement during the following year's campaign. This time it was the Democrats who won, despite a Whig victory in most of the rest of the county, causing the *Republican* to reverse itself and speak of Whig defections. In Kingston itself, the "natives" had even beaten the Whigs.[96] The "natives" also offered a village ticket in 1845 and again ran second to the Democrats, so it probably was the Whigs who were fueling the new movement.[97] But temperance advocates may also have figured prominently in local political nativism, for no "American" tickets were run during the no-license controversies of the late 1840s.

Nativism reappeared in Kingston during the nationwide Know-Nothing movement, and this time carried all before it. In 1853 the *People's Press* was founded as a Whig newspaper in Kingston, but in less than a year the *Ulster Republican* had sniffed out its nativist connections.[98] Not that this realization was of much help to the Democrats. In the town and village elections of 1855 the Know-Nothings offered complete tickets and were elected in both from top to bottom.[99] The nativist victory was repeated in 1856, and by then the Know-Nothings were confident enough to run a ticket in immigrant-dominated Rondout—which, however, they were never able to carry.[100] The Know-Nothings completely dominated the government of Kingston village for three years and controlled the town offices until they were gradually absorbed into the new Republican party in the last years of the decade.[101]

What is most interesting about the Kingston Know-Nothings is that they focused their political energies on the town and the villages, while professing goals which could be achieved only in Albany and Washington. Obviously, neither the town nor the villages had any control over the criteria of citizenship or over public aid to parochial schools. They did have some control over office holding, and the first nativist campaigns in Kingston professed as their goal "the elevation of none but the American born to public office."[102] However, neither the Democrats nor the Whigs were at that time in the habit of nominating or appointing foreign-born men. Why, then, did the nativists even bother with the town and villages, particularly the latter, much less focus their efforts there? They could, of course, deny grocery or tavern licenses to immigrants, increase the size of the police department, and make sure that "none but the American born" were hired by the streets department. That is, they could use the expanded powers and facilities of local government to assure local natives that the Irish and Germans in their midst would not disrupt the community, and, perhaps more fundamentally, that the community still "belonged" to the native-born. This was probably the thrust of local nativism. Although the establishment of a twenty-one-year residency requirement for citizenship would have made the job of the community guardians that much easier to perform, this was a remote goal which could be achieved only by remote actors. Meanwhile, a far more tangible task existed within Kingston itself, and only Kingstonians could accomplish it. Once again, in short, the local manifestation of a national political issue turned at least a portion of Kingston's political community inward, and, in this case, transformed the issue into one of community membership rather than of American citizenship.

It should be reemphasized that Kingstonians did not ignore state and national issues that had no obvious local ramifications, and that Kingston's political leaders were not *parochialized* by the bank war, temperance, nativism, village "progress and improvement," or any other local or localized issue. Rather, the existence of these issues on the local level *added* both a local dimension to political action and a local orientation among the political community. Political elites, in particular, retained their Albany connections and kept up with the arguments on slavery at the same time that they planned for the coming village election. Still, it is apparent that political controversy in Kingston was most intense and endured for the longest time whenever fundamental local questions were involved. Sidewalks were not fundamental, but continued commercial development, community order, and the criteria of community membership were of the utmost importance. These were the issues brought about by growth, and it is for this reason (adding, perhaps, the simple expansion of local governmental machinery) that we may associate the growth of Kingston with the creation of both a local political system and an intensified consciousness of local citizenship.

8   The Development of
Local Institutions: Entertainment,
Refinement, and Reform

Far from absorbing functions and energies that had once belonged to organizations outside of politics, Kingston's parties and governing bodies represented only one phase of a general expansion of organized collective activity in the community. As the town grew, scores of organizations devoted both to public service and to personal pleasure were founded by local citizens, and existing ones expanded greatly the scope of their activities. Some of these organizations lasted just a year or two; others became permanent features of local society. Some were created by state law or were local branches of national or regional societies, but others were entirely local in structure and impetus. And all contributed, in varying degrees, to what appears to have been a dramatic alteration of the local social order, for pre-canal Kingston had contained but a handful of local organizations and had offered a modest calendar of recurring social and cultural events. Of course, we must determine the real significance of this organizational development. What importance should we attach to the greater eagerness of post-canal Kingstonians to associate in formally organized groups? How did these groups fit into the general life of the town? How did they reflect and affect the course of social change?

Unlike the political parties and village governments, Kingston's voluntary organizations did not develop steadily following the opening of the canal. For fifteen years or so there was very little change in the number of local associations or in the scope and intensity of their activities, despite a number of experiments. The early 1830s, for example, had given birth to a number of agencies of moral reform—the temperance societies we noted earlier, the Female Bible Society (whose officers and annual meeting speakers were all men), the Young Men's Branch Bible Society, and the Female Society for the Promotion of the Gospel—but none of these flourished.[1] A Kingston lyceum appeared briefly in 1833, as a magazine club did in 1839.[2] Indeed, Kingston's organized social life may well have declined in the 1830s, for the largest and most significant of the pre-canal organizations, the local Masonic lodge, was closed in 1833.[3] An interesting addition to the village calendar was the traveling circus, which began making annual visits to Kingston in the summer of 1833. But this had nothing to do with the organizational life of the village or the town and little to do with the modest growth that had occurred in Kingston after the opening of the canal.[4]

The early 1840s witnessed only a modest upswing in associational activity. A Kingston young men's lyceum was attempted once again in 1840, and was expanded two years later into a young men's association "for mutual improvement in useful knowledge."[5] For one season the association was quite active, sponsoring lectures and holding debates on a more or less regular schedule throughout the winter. By 1843, however, it had disappeared.[6] It was replaced the following year by an amateur histrionic association, formed by "a company of young gentlemen of the village," but this too lasted only one season.[7] Meanwhile, two new music societies had come and apparently gone.[8] Perhaps it is significant that these institutions apppeared at all, for they seem to have reflected a feeling by some of the younger men of the village that Kingston could attempt to do some of the things that were ordinarily associated with larger places. Still, it is more significant that, of the several institutions formed in the early 1840s, only the Kosciusko lodge of the I.O.O.F., which opened its doors in 1843, survived.[9] By 1845, the failure of the various lecture, debating, and music societies left Kingston with an organizational life not much different from what it had been a quarter-century earlier. There may have been those who thought that Kingston had become capable of supporting urban institutions of culture and refinement, but there was little in the village that year to prove it.

But Kingston in 1845 was on the brink of a radical transformation of its organized social life. During the next ten years a host of new organizations would be formed, a number of old ones would be expanded and altered in purpose and structure, and a new social calendar, complementing the rhythms of Kingston's new economic life, would be created. Let us look, for example, at Kingston's fire companies, for these show clearly the character of these developments. First, and least important, they grew in number, from two in the 1820s to seven in 1855 (in both villages) to twelve in 1860. Second, they changed in character, and in so doing added significantly to the calendar of social events in both villages. The fire companies had always served as social clubs for their members, but there is no evidence of organized social activity by the village firemen until 1839, when the three local companies combined for the first annual Kingston Fire Department Festival, held two days after Christmas at the Kingston Hotel. There may have been a parade, but all that is mentioned in the newspaper is a dinner, at which the usual toasts to the nation, the Constitution, the flag, "our free institutions" (and, for some reason, the navy) were supplemented by toasts to "the Citizens of Kingston" and the fire department itself.[10] The affair was repeated two years later, on Christmas eve, this time with a parade headed by the Kingston Brass Band.[11] There do not seem to have been any more such events until 1850 when in early November, a torchlight parade was followed by a dinner.[12] Thereafter, the festival was held annually, usually in the early spring, and by 1860 it had expanded to include some four hundred firemen, including visiting companies from Rhinebeck, Peekskill, and Newburgh.[13]

Meanwhile, a new and much more significant social function had grown up within and around the fire companies. In the winter of 1848 the Excelsior Engine Company No. 4 of Kingston village held its first annual ball, and although there had been many "first annual" but few "second annual" events in Kingston up to that time, this was one which immediately took hold. The Excelsior Company offered a formal ball every year through 1860, and the institution quickly spread to every other fire company and militia company in both villages as well as to several fraternal lodges. Simultaneously, a more or less standardized newspaper report—a polite congratulation—developed in the local press. For example:

A PLEASANT BALL.—On Thursday evening last, Mr. Clark, of the Eagle Hotel, did his good name and fame justice by the manner in which he got up the appliances for the ball of the Washington Fire Company, No. 3.—The Company also did justice to their reputation for spirit, by turning out in force, and getting up and keeping up one of the best balls of the season. There were 55 couples on the floor. The music, supper and all the arrangements and decorations were in the finest style, and every thing "went off" with celerity, except the company, which broke up at last with a general regret that "morning came too soon."[14]

This ritual newspaper article (morning always came too soon and each ball was the best of the season) may be somewhat misleading about the refinement of the affair. In 1851 Nathaniel Booth attended the fourth annual Excelsior Company ball:

> It was a miserable affair—a very small room—a very large company—a very rude set of men from the bar-room blocking the halls and passages—a very common supper—very ordinary women with few exceptions—very dusty floor—very foul atmosphere. . . . The co. had the bad taste or rather total want of taste to wear their red flannel shirts as at a fire or parade. . . . Red cheeks were therefore the order of the night among the women and red flannel and red noses among the men.[15]

Booth, who had once had a fling at polite society in Washington, was always rather crusty when it came to the subject of organized social affairs in Kingston. But he did attend many of them, and it is perhaps significant that he did expect them to meet certain standards of politeness. Occasionally he was satisfied, as on January 8, 1849, when he had attended an evening dancing school and found "the gentlemen particularly courteous" and "the ladies agreeable."[16] Dancing schools, incidentally, had found a new and eager market among the young people of Kingston, and their evening sessions were themselves social functions.

In short, by the early 1850s a thoroughly organized winter social season had emerged in Kingston. Each year, usually starting in early December, a dozen or more balls were given by local organizations, and an indeterminate number of "soirées" were offered by fire companies, militia companies, and dancing schools. In 1856, for example, the National Greys "hit upon one of the pleasantest modes of social enjoyment for our coming winter," a soirée which "will probably be repeated monthly during the gay season."[17] These were supplemented by the concerts of itinerant performers (the earliest apparently were a company of Swiss bell ringers who came to Kingston in January, 1847)[18] and of several newly formed local music societies. The local groups included the Kingston Amateur Musical Association, the Hudson River Musical Association (itself a collection of local societies), the Mendelssohn Union, the Rondout Brass and String Band, and the Kingston

Sacred Musical Association.[19] In addition, starting in the mid-1850s, there were regularly organized annual charity balls, managed by "respectable and active citizens."[20] And, to cap the "gay season," there was an increasingly elaborate celebration of the birthday of George Washington, an event that no one in Kingston had even thought of celebrating before the rise of the militia companies.[21]

There was also an intellectual side to the newly organized season. In November, 1851 a meeting was called in Kingston village to consider the possibilities of reviving the winter lecture and debating series.[22] At first, there was an attempt to form a single organization for both villages (which gave the *Courier* a fine opportunity to discourse on their inevitable unification) but the idea was clearly premature.[23] Rather, a separate lyceum was organized for each village, and each offered honorary membership to the members of the other. Schedules of lectures and debates were immediately drawn up.[24] Interestingly, the Rondout Lyceum was an instant success, with lively debates over such subjects as "the concession of an equal share of political, civil and social rights, by the male monopolists to their helpmeets,"[25] while the Kingston Lyceum was a decided failure.[26] The latter was replaced in 1854 by the Kingston Literary Association, which changed the focus to outside lecturers. With this format, it succeeded in maintaining a full winter lecture series (which often included such famous figures as Wendell Phillips, Theodore Parker, Henry Ward Beecher, and Horace Greeley) through the rest of the decade.[27]

The winter, when the canal was closed, the river frozen, and local businesses semidormant, was unquestionably the social and intellectual "season" of both villages. But winter did not monopolize all the organized social activity. After 1845, summer had its own regular events that, along with the traveling circuses and the celebration of the Fourth of July, gave at least some Kingstonians access to organized entertainment while the canal was open. One such event was the late-summer steamboat excursion, the first of which was held in September of 1846. The *Republican* of September 9, 1846 advertised the departure of the *New Jersey* on the 17th at 9:00 A.M. for Fort Independence in the Highlands, to return the same evening, fare $1.[28] In 1848 a more ambitious excursion carried passengers to the fishing banks off Sandy Hook, New Jersey. The *Highlander* left Rondout at 4:00 P.M. on an August

Tuesday for New York, passed through the Narrows early the next morning, and returned to Rondout that night.[29] By the early 1850s, river excursions (both by sunlight and by moonlight) and fishing excursions were regular late-summer events and often carried several hundred passengers. Excursions of a different sort also developed, as local fire and militia companies made frequent visits to other river towns where they were formally received and feted by their opposite numbers. For example, in September, 1853 all the fire companies of both villages, except one left behind for emergencies, went by steamboat to Hudson, where they paraded and were given a formal dinner by the Hudson fire department. They were officially greeted on their return that night and published a "card" of gratitude in a Kingston paper.[30] In 1859 there was a particularly large crop of excursions. The *Republican* of August 17 reported three: "The Great Rondout Excursion" of some 2,500 persons to Newburgh to benefit St. Mary's Church, a firemen's excursion to Newburgh, and an excursion of two Sabbath schools to "a beautiful spot about 15 miles down the river."[31] These were followed by another Sabbath school excursion, another journey of firemen to Newburgh, and an impressive voyage of the National Greys all the way to New Haven.[32]

Another form of organized summer activity appeared in 1858 with the formation of baseball clubs in the two villages. Intervillage competition was inevitable, and in April (of course) the village clubs met on a neutral field for what we can only call a "triple-header." Rondout won all three games, scoring an exhausting total of 104 runs to Kingston's 75.[33] A week later the *Courier* reported "a score" of new clubs since "the grand match," and a second intervillage match that was rained out.[34] The rematch was held on the following week, however, and Kingston obtained its revenge, winning three games (43 to 26, 42 to 35, and 26 to 22) while losing one (27 to 21).[35] A small editorial war broke out between the Rondout *Courier* and the Kingston *Democratic Journal* over the merits of the players of the two villages, with both papers maintaining a discreet silence on the subject of pitching. Of course, not all Kingstonians were willing to engage their ruder neighbors in either baseball games or debates about athletic prowess. In 1859 the Eclipse Cricket Club was organized in Kingston, with team captains bearing the venerable names of Masten and Schoonmaker.[36]

The warmer months of the 1850s also witnessed innumerable

parades by local and visiting fire and militia companies. Some were apparently unannounced:

> The Harrison Guards, Capt. Von Beck, of Rondout, dropped down among us on Friday evening last, to the inspiriting music of their excellent band. They mustered some fifty muskets, and in their neat and serviceable uniform looked like true soldiery. They called upon Gen. Smith, and, after a tour of the village, left us with a very flattering impression of the military spunk and energy of our sister village.[37]

Again, it seems necessary to record the dissenting opinion of Nathaniel Booth:

> A new fire-engine having been purchased by Kingston the fire companies turned out en masse and dragged their machines through the hot glare of the sun and dust for half a day while the immortal brass band of Kingston blew their brains out on their ill-tuned instruments.[38]

Finally, there were the continuing features of former summers— the traveling circuses and exhibits that first appeared in the 1830s, and, of course, the celebration of the Fourth of July. Though the latter had become quite ritualized even in pre-canal days, its form was by no means impervious to either temporary local influence or further formal development. For example, the local bank war produced separate Junto and Anti-Junto dinners in 1833 and 1834.[39] Temperance celebrations were held, sometimes as separate affairs and sometimes as the "official" celebration, in 1834, 1842, 1845 through 1848, and 1850.[40] Occasionally, local political tensions seem to have prevented the holding of any celebration. And in one or two places a hint of local politics breaks through the formal ritual, as in 1843, when John Van Buren's volunteer toast to "Ireland" was immediately followed by R. A. Chipp's toast to "the Dutch Colonists of Ulster."[41] The volunteer toasts in general reveal a parochializing trend of sorts, so that by the 1850s nearly half were offered to Kingston and its various institutions—quite a contrast to the virtual neglect of the town in the toasts of pre-canal celebrations.

More striking is the development of the form of the celebration itself. It had always been a fairly elaborate affair and had always drawn at least a few spectators from smaller towns in the county, but the full exploitation of the Fourth as a day of public celebration awaited the development of a large number of uniformed fire companies, militia companies, and bands, as well as the playing out of the rather stultifying influence of the temperance movement. Both were partly accomplished by 1852, when the parade to the church included the Kingston Brass Band and five fire companies, numbering 175 men, and the evening fireworks were witnessed by an estimated 7,000 persons. Interestingly, although it was customary for the spectators of the morning parade to fall in behind the organized companies and form the rear guard of the procession to the church, this time they simply watched and then dispersed, as though the event were professional rather than communal.[42] By 1857 the growth of the celebration required a number of changes that may be taken as symbolizing the whole course of social change in Kingston. The celebration of 1857 was a joint affair of the two villages, and the committee of arrangements was, by necessity, divided into eight subcommittees, each dealing with a different phase. The procession comprised all the militia and fire companies of both villages and, in an important break with tradition, led not to the First Dutch Reformed Church but to the Academy Green, where the Declaration of Independence was read and the oration delivered to a crowd that could not possibly have fitted into the church. After the ceremony, instead of the usual dinner attended by the gentlemen of the village, there were no fewer than four dinners, each hosted by a different fire company and serving two or three hundred patrons. Five thousand persons witnessed the evening fireworks display.[43] Clearly, this was no longer a village festival devoted to demonstrating the status of a few of its citizens. It was a large, complicated, carefully organized affair, closely tied to the new organizational life of both villages, reflecting the growing importance of Kingston and Rondout in the mid-Hudson Valley, and having little to do with the social pretenses of a small community elite. The distance Kingston had traveled in this respect is underscored by the 1859 celebration, to which 15,000 visitors "from the remote sections of Ulster and the river counties poured in by every train and steamboat, and from every road leading to the country,"[44] and by the 1860 celebration, which dispensed with the parade, the dinners, and the fireworks in favor of a balloon ascension by "Prof. Brooks of St. Louis."[45]

Kingston's new social calendar owed much to one type of local organization I have thus far slighted—the militia company. We have noted its role in the balls and soirées of "the gay season" and in the numerous parades of the warmer months, but we have not really conveyed the depth and extent of the militia fad of the 1850s. The local newspapers of that decade are filled with articles on musters, encampments, parades, presentations of colors, excursions, balls, and contests of marksmanship, with descriptions of new companies, and with titles—Col. Pratt, Capt. (and then Maj.) Von Beck, Gen. Sampson, Col. Hendricks, Capt. Van Buren. General S. S. Hommel, editor of the *Ulster Republican*, was particularly fond of referring to local militia officers by their impressive titles, regardless of whether the context was a brigade inspection or a dry goods sale, but other editors were only slightly less caught up in the military spirit. The increase in the number of local militia companies can be attributed to the growth of the town and to the tightening of state laws.[46] But the enthusiasm with which military obligations were embraced in some quarters during the 1850s is something of a puzzle. Surely, the social activities of the companies had something to do with it—the Jefferson Volunteers were organized in the summer of 1854 and held their first annual ball the following December[47]—as did the prestige of a military title and even of a military uniform. We may assume that at least two companies in Rondout functioned as ethnic clubs, for the Harrison Guards (Capt. Von Beck) consisted entirely or mostly of Germans, and the Jackson Rifles, whose uniforms were green, were "composed of adopted citizens of Irish birth."[48] The militia companies were certainly part of a larger trend toward organized social activity in Kingston and Rondout, and it is tempting to associate the enthusiasm they generated with local urban development. Such a view, however, may well be too narrow, for military fever seems to have been a statewide epidemic in the 1850s, and it is not clear whether it infected only urban places.

The social importance of the military in Kingston was supplemented, if not quite matched, by the militia's role in promoting the local economy. Military uniforms provided only a few merchants with extra business, but nearby military encampments benefited nearly everyone. The importance attached to them by local businessmen and perhaps by the town as a whole is illustrated by the encampment of the Second Division in August, 1855. The encampment itself was the crowning achievement of the local military, for it brought to Kingston an estimated ten to twelve thousand troops and visitors, constituting, in the frank anticipation of the *Repub-lican*, "a harvest for the village."[49] The harvest, however, was only partly gathered. During the exercises one day, a stray bullet fired by someone in the Seventh Regiment killed an infant feeding at his mother's breast. The tragedy caused the immediate cancellation of all further activities, including the military ball that had been anticipated to be the social event of the year—if not the decade. Mrs. Castle, the mother of the dead child, was made an honorary daughter of the Seventh Regiment and was promised $1,500 in cash and a pension from its treasury. This response was considered adequate in the local press; when, in the following spring, Mrs. Castle sued the Seventh Regiment for $5,000, the community was outraged. Two public meetings denounced the suit as extortion and ingratitude and reassured the regiment of the town's continued good will. The local press proposed the theory that Mrs. Castle had fallen into the hands of greedy lawyers and angrily pointed out that Kingston would obtain no more profitable encampments if her suit succeeded. Even when the *Courier* discovered that the Seventh Regiment had apparently backed down on its earlier cash offer, the other local papers continued to oppose the suit. The *Courier* alone was satisfied that justice had been done when the court awarded Mrs. Castle $1,500 in damages.[50]

I do not wish, however, to present an economic interpretation of Kingston's after-hours organizational development. It is true that military encampments and Fourth of July celebrations brought money into the villages, and that lodges and other fraternal organizations paid death benefits (the Masons, incidentally, were revived in Kingston in 1850 and opened a Rondout lodge in 1854).[51] But it would be foolish to explain the dramatic increase in formally organized social activity in Kingston in these terms. The Rondout *Courier* provided a different sort of explanation when it commented on the unusual "card" entered in its advertising columns by one John B. Smith, who thanked his personal friends for having attended his son's funeral and berated his brethren in the I.O.O.F. and the Sons of Temperance for having stayed at home. The *Courier* remarked:

These associations are necessary in crowded and busy popula-tions, to prevent the dominion and effects of the singular selfishness which seems to be an inseparable attribute of a high state of civilization. They endeavor to maintain, by organizing upon a common interest, a community of feeling akin to fraternal sympathy, that warmth of brotherhood which flourishes best and without effort in sparse and small communities, where perhaps these orders would be out of place because unnecessary.[52]

This is a familiar interpretation, to say the least. The *Courier* has simply anticipated a fairly standard sociological theory that associates urbanization with individualism, the compartmentalization of social life, the decline of intimate, "primary" interactions among the members of the community, and the use of formal structures as devices for recapturing some of the intimacy of the small town. As early as 1848, in other words, the Rondout *Courier* observed a fundamental difference between Kingston-Rondout and "sparse and small communities" and stated that difference in terms consistent with our own expectations about the course of urban development. Formal organizations and formally organized social activities developed in Kingston *because* the town itself grew past the point where "fraternal sympathy" flowed naturally among neighbors who knew each other well and interacted with each other in a wide variety of contexts. Even Marius Schoonmaker could no longer claim that he knew everyone in Kingston village, or even that he wished to. Paid newspaper notices relating to domestic quarrels or threatening public ridicule could now be scoffed at as totally without effect. The newspapers themselves could now claim a legitimate local news function, even though they still circulated only once a week, for the network of backyard gossip was no longer coextensive with the community. And so, in order to recover some sense of common feeling and in order to accomplish anything requiring common action, the members of this growing community subdivided into a large number of functionally specialized groups, fragmenting the community further in an effort to recover the feeling of unity.

The trouble with this interpretation is that it is just accurate enough to be seriously misleading. Kingston's lodges, fire companies, militia units, and literary societies did develop in response to the growth of the town, and they did function as social groups for men who undoubtedly felt that there were few other ways of establishing satisfactory fellowship.[53] But the *Courier*'s central assumption—that the organized and specialized social life of urban

Kingston *replaced* an earlier social process that had been more communal in both form and spirit—may be challenged on two grounds. First, it is by no means clear that informal social life, outside the formal organizations, was disrupted or significantly altered by the growth of the town. And second, it is even less clear that community identity was in fact well developed in pre-canal Kingston, either as "fraternal fellowship" or as a feeling among local residents of common origin, purpose, and destiny. With regard to the first of these points, it may be granted that Kingstonians of the 1850s no longer knew all of their fellow townsmen or villagers, and that an increasing proportion of their daily interactions did probably occur in compartmentalized and instrumental contexts. For example, Kingston merchants sold dry goods to some women whom they did not see at church, whose children did not play with their children, and who were married to men the merchants did not even know. But the loss of familiarity with the entire community need not imply a real contraction of anyone's circle of informal or intimate acquaintances, and the apparent increase in purely instrumental interactions outside that circle surely left a great deal of room for more satisfying (or agonizing) interactions within it. Nathaniel Booth's diary describes an informal social life in Kingston that in many ways was continuous with the rural, pre-canal town described by Henry Vanderlyn and Marius Schoonmaker. The "gay season" in the 1850s consisted not merely of formal balls and lectures but also of sleighing parties, New Year's Day visits, trotting races, ice-skating on the frozen river, evening songfests, and enough gossip to indicate that Kingstonians were not entirely strangers to one another. Somewhere between these informal activities and the organized winter social calendar were the donation visits held in early January by the members of most churches for the benefit of their ministers. The first donation visit was advertised in the local press in December, 1849, but later editorial discussion indicates that it was simply a revival of the "bees" that had been held in former times for the same purpose.[54]

In the warmer months, too, there is evidence of social activities much like those of the previous generation. Booth's diary turns mostly to matters of business in the spring and summer, but we must not suppose that the long hours of work entirely disrupted either the visits, songfests, and serenading tours of long summer evenings, or the picnics of summer Sundays. Nor should his relative silence on family affairs or neighborly relations mislead us. Booth was a widower during the years he maintained his diary in Wilbur, and his residence in that little hamlet physically removed him from his Kingston and Rondout friends. As for the role of family in his life, we may note the very last entry in his diary. Booth had remarried six months earlier and had brought the daughter of his first marriage back from his mother's house. He had reached the end of his second volume and questioned whether he would begin a third:

> At least it will rest a while—for life has now settled down into a calm, happy, contented state, that has not changed enough to furnish an item—it has but two phases—the office and its duties which are the same every day—home and its charms which cannot be greater and never be less—all the same happy faces greet me there morning noon and night.[55]

Perhaps it could be argued that this benediction (for Booth seems not to have begun a third volume) emphasizes the compartmentalization of social life in Kingston. Except for the reference to a daily return home at noon, this passage could have been written by any modern suburbanite possessed of a touch of sentimentality and a high tolerance for rush-hour traffic. It could be further argued that the sentimentality with which Booth regarded his family was itself a reflection of social compartmentalization ("functional differentiation" may be a better term), for the family as a local institution was now stripped of many of its old functions and given the more restricted task of providing emotional support for its members. On the other hand, it may be wiser to approach this passage in Booth's diary less boldly—simply to let it remind us that family life existed in Kingston long before and long after the construction of the D & H Canal, and that it provided a continuity to the structure of social life that may well have been understated in our examination of the evolution of the town's formal organizations.

There is, as I have indicated, a second objection to the *Courier's* discussion of the role of voluntary associations in the urbanizing setting of Kingston. The organizations described by the *Courier* as devices for recovering "fraternal fellowship" may have produced a sense of community that had never been there in the first place. The *Courier*, like so many subsequent theorists of urban life, assumed that "sparse and small communities" are closely knit organisms, characterized by communal action and a strong sense of local identity. We have already seen that the Dutch country village that was pre-canal Kingston may have possessed neither of these traits. Though the sources do not permit so close a view of village life as we would like to have, they do suggest a collectivity of individuated householders and money-makers rather than a cooperative, self-conscious community. Undoubtedly, relationships in the country village were familiar and often friendly. However, it is important to distinguish between the network and tone of interactions in a community, on the one hand, and the social cohesiveness of that community and the cultural orientation of its members, on the other. People can be friendly at the same time that they insist on privacy and eschew any form of collective action. They can become personally acquainted and even intimate with every coresident of their town, without ever fixing on the town as a source of citizenship or culture. And even though this may seem to be overly hypothetical, it appears to have been true of pre-canal Kingston. There is little, in surviving sources at least, to suggest otherwise.

The *Courier* was undoubtedly correct in asserting that Kingston's voluntary associations "endeavor[ed] to maintain, by organizing upon a common interest, a community of feeling." Now if these organizations succeeded in that goal, and if our assessment of pre-canal Kingston is correct, then we may assume that Kingstonians *expanded* both their group action and their collective awareness as the country town grew into a small city. There are, to be sure, possible objections to this assumption. First, the organizations of the community may not have produced or reflected any significant change in the sympathies and orientation of their members. Note, for example, that the funeral that set us on these reflections was attended by family friends but not by organizational "brethren." Second, most of the organizations were smaller than the community and even formed competitive units within it. Conceivably, this could have detracted from rather than contributed to an identification with the community as a whole. Third, most members of the community simply did not belong to any of the organizations we have reviewed in this chapter; and only a small minority attended the community's lectures, balls, and dinners.

The first objection is easily met—the competitive spirit and high camaraderie that permeate nearly every account of the activities of local organizations, particularly of the fire and militia companies, contradict it. We can be certain, moreover, that we are not being misled here by journalistic convention, for there is other evidence of group spirit besides the newspapers. For example, a fight between the chief engineer of the Kingston fire department and Gilbert Smith, a member of Excelsior Engine Company No. 4, led to the following testimony before the board of directors:

> Chief Engineer Sharp appeared and stated that he and the Assistant went to No. 4 house on the day of inspection and there saw Smith, told him that they had come to measure the cylinder of the engine. Smith replied that it should not be measured without taking his life etc. etc. When the engine was brought upon the ground... Smith used further abusive language to me [Sharp] and shook his fist in my face saying if I was chief engineer I was not of No. 4, called me a black son of a bitch and whorehouse lawyer.[56]

Of course, in removing the first objection in this way we only reemphasize the second and third. Granted that an active and often spirited group life was created in Kingston by the 1850s, didn't the competitiveness of the fire and militia companies, and perhaps even of the churches and reform societies, destroy any hope for the creation of a community-wide identity? To some extent it probably did. But the organizational structure of Kingston was not so fragmented as it may seem. The fire companies were, collectively, the Kingston fire department, and they presented themselves in that fashion on making excursions to other towns and when playing host to excursions themselves. The militia companies also served as emissaries and hosts for the town as a whole, even when only one company was involved in a particular excursion. The churches of Kingston often cooperated in Bible society and temperance society affairs, and the temperance movement was carried forward by numerous organizations whose memberships were interconnected. Several organizations did purport to represent at least their entire village—for example, the Kingston Literary Society, the Rondout Lyceum, and the Rondout Y.M.C.A. (the last was founded in 1858).[57] Lodges, music societies, reform societies, and churches sometimes drew members from all over the town. Finally, the sheer quantity of local organizations, many of which bore the names of the villages, the town, and the county, helped remind local residents, including those who did not belong to any of them, that Kingston was a unique and tangible entity.

This final point deserves elaboration. Just as its physical form became more imposing, its economic facilities became more complete, and its government acquired a day-to-day reality and significance that had been utterly lacking in 1820, Kingston developed a voluntary institutional structure that reinforced the *presence* of the town in the minds of its citizens. The activities of the voluntary organizations constantly reminded Kingstonians of the existence of the community and of their own membership in it and occasionally permitted them to be rather impressed by a town that could support a regular series of lectures, a full season of formal balls, a dozen fully equipped fire companies, an elaborate Fourth of July celebration attracting thousands each year, and all the other scheduled and impromptu activities of a growing and prospering place. To be sure, the other elements of Kingston's physical and institutional development—particularly its growth and its economic diversification—probably impressed them more. But my central point here is that the development of a townscape and of all the urban institutions we have surveyed in these chapters did not fragment a previously unified, self-conscious community. On the contrary, it appears to have provided Kingston with a group life and perhaps even a collective awareness and identity that seems to have been but weakly developed in the country town of the previous generation. It did not, of course, seriously affect the fundamental individualism that Kingstonians shared with their predecessors and with other Americans, any more than the development of a localized political consciousness interfered with the cosmopolitanism of Kingston's political elites. Local residents did not, we can be certain, begin to place the community above themselves and their families. But even if the changes we have surveyed here were culturally rather superficial, they are significant because of their direction. They speak of a town which moved toward community as it grew toward urbanism—not in spite of its growth, but because of it.

In the preceding discussion of institutional evolution and its communal implications in post-canal Kingston, we have generally treated the community as an undifferentiated whole. But we have also seen that the development of a more fully articulated and formally organized institutional structure was paralleled by the development of a far more heterogeneous local population. We cannot, therefore, realistically ignore the differences among Kingstonians when we describe the community and its institutions. "It is not enough," warns Robert K. Merton, "to refer to 'the institutions' as though they were all uniformly supported by all groups and strata in the society. Unless systematic consideration is given the *degree* of support of particular 'institutions' by *specific* groups, we shall overlook the important place of power in society."[1]

Local newspapers, village records, and Nathaniel Booth's diary have given us some idea of what local institutions did. In addition, they have provided occasional clues about, for example, the ethnic composition of local militia companies or the success of one political party based squarely on a platform of excluding foreign immigrants from citizenship. But such clues only begin to answer the basic question of how Kingston's new institutional structure was used and supported by the people who lived there. Did many Kingstonians or only a few actually participate in organized social life? Was this participation structured according to definable subgroups of the population? What are the implications of this structure for the critical questions of power and community membership?

One way of seeking answers to these questions is to attempt to locate the actual participants in the organizations described in previous chapters. Then, by locating these individuals on the manuscript census schedules, we may associate participation with the "groups and strata" of the local population. The procedure is a risky one, since it depends on the completeness and quality of surviving records, on the reliable "linkage" of participants to the census, and on the kinds of assumptions and decisions made in the evaluation of participation itself. Nevertheless, by carefully using the data that are available, we may describe and analyze the patterns of participation with a satisfying degree of accuracy and completeness.

The first step, of course, is the identification of participants. A review of virtually all the surviving records descriptive of life in Kingston during 1850–60 yielded the names of 1,256 men who participated in some fashion in the town's organized social life.[2] From the newspapers of all political parties in both villages, I obtained the names of nearly everyone who ran for village, town, county, state, or even national office in that decade, as well as the names of town, county, and district committeemen, convention delegates, campaign and club members, and those listed as having attended political rallies. The same sources contained the names of many other types of participants: directors of local banks, insurance companies, and plank road companies; directors, officers, and members of the Kingston Lyceum, the Kingston Literary Association, the Kingston Academy, the Ulster County Historical Society, the Rondout Y.M.C.A., the Ulster County Bible Society, the Rondout Library Association, and numerous other organizations devoted to refinement and useful leisure; the organizers of and official participants in the Fourth of July celebrations; the officers and listed attendants of a host of citizens' meetings called to mourn the death of Henry Clay, protest Mrs. Castle's suit against the Seventh Regiment, urge the relocation of the Rhinebeck ferry, and so on. Village records provided the names of the firemen and appointed officials of both villages, while a number of manuscript volumes in the possession of the New York State National Guard in Albany contained the names of the officers of Kingston's militia units (some enlisted men were mentioned in local newspapers). The local Masonic lodge provided a list of Masons active in the 1850s, and most of Kingston's churches have preserved records detailing their lay leadership. These two lists have been further extended by names included in Sylvester's history of Ulster County. Perhaps as many as five thousand instances of organized social participation have been ascribed to the 1,256 individuals identified.

To analyze this mass of information, I assigned each individual participant a "participation score" ranging from "1," representing minimal activity, to "5," representing the highest level of community leadership. At the same time, the details of his participation were preserved, so that it would be possible to analyze both the distribution of scores and the precise patterns of membership and activity. Of course, scores running from 1 to 5 are quite abstract, and the results that follow cannot be comprehended unless a few examples of what each score may mean in terms of actual participation are provided. The lowest score was assigned to men whose names appeared once, perhaps twice, in low-level, noncontinuing contexts. Augustus Huhne, for example, was a "4th Lieutenant" of the Rondout Wide Awake Club, which was an organ of the Republican presidential campaign of 1860. Leander Smith participated in Kingston's 1856 Fourth of July celebration. James Stanley offered himself as a candidate for fire warden in Rondout in 1852 and was defeated. Derrick Dubois attended a citizens' meeting in 1852, and Jacob Elting signed a temperance proposal that appeared in the *Republican* in 1853. None of these men appeared in any ongoing organizations or in any other activity. All were assigned a score of 1. Only 73 men, less than 6% of the total participation list, received this score.[3]

A slightly higher score was assigned to men whose participation in organized social life was not limited to one or two occasions but whose memberships were restricted to one or two organizations that did not confer much power or prestige. James Kenworthy was a member of Kingston's American Engine Co. No. 1. Thomas Murray served one term as a Rondout fire warden in 1850. Louis Gilsinger was a member, but not an officer, of the Jefferson Dragoons. Peter Gallagher was both a fireman and a member of the Ulster County Musical Association. There were many memberships and activities of this type in Kingston and Rondout, and it is not surprising that the score of 2 should account for just under 60% of the entire participation list.

The score of 3 is more of a dimensional hybrid than the others. It was given to two types of participants: those who did a number of things at a fairly low level; and those who served in one or two fairly high-level capacities. The largest number of the second group were high-level church leaders. Edward W. Styles, for example, was a trustee of the First Baptist Church for the entire decade, but his name did not appear in any other organization or activity.

Equivalent to the people categorized in this narrow but high-level participation were occasional political officeholders such as Jeremiah Smith, who was a director of Kingston village in 1858 and 1859, politicians such as Samuel McIntyre, who held important posts in the Democratic party but neither ran for office nor involved himself in any activity outside of politics, and a few men of narrow cultural or communal interests such as Anson Dubois, who served several terms as a trustee of Kingston Academy. More frequent, however, were men who combined several activities at a lower level. John Chipp, Jr., was a Mason, a sergeant in the National Greys, a Kingston fireman, and a participant in the Fourth of July celebration of 1860. Edgar Hudler was a Whig town committeeman, a one-time candidate for election inspector, and a class leader and steward of Trinity Methodist Church of Rondout. William Townsend ran for town clerk in 1854 and was a Mason and a one-term director of the Kingston Literary Association. In all, 281 men, about 22 % of the total number of participants, were given a score of 3 for either the level or the range of their organized activities.

The final two scores represent active, high-level community participation. Those who were scored 4 were invariably active in two or more organizations and demonstrated at least some leadership in community affairs. Solomon Brown, for example, was a fireman early in the decade, and became a Mason, a vice-president of the Ulster County Musical Association, and a participant in two Fourth of July celebrations; he was awarded a 4 because he combined these with a directorship of Kingston village. More characteristic of those in this category, however, were men whose leadership extended to more than one type of community institution, such as Henry Brodhead, Jr., who was a surrogate and then a county judge, a director of the State of New York Bank, and an active Whig and Republican leader throughout the decade. Abraham Crispell served as a trustee, assessor, or health officer of Rondout village during much of the 1850s and was a member of the board of the Union Plank Road Company, in addition to participating in the militia, the Republican campaign of 1860, and a meeting called to promote a railroad from Rondout to Ellenville. Cornelius H. Van Gaasbeck was the Kingston village treasurer in 1853, the Democratic candidate for county treasurer in 1854 (although he bolted his party to campaign for Frémont in 1856), a trustee of the Kingston Literary Association in 1855 and 1860, a member of the Ulster County Musical Association, and a multiple-term elder and perennial treasurer of the First Dutch Reformed Church. Each of these men was a community leader to some degree and was active in a variety of organizations. There are 128 of them in our participation list, accounting for just over 10% of the total number of recorded participants.

Finally, there were twenty-eight men whose activity stands out above even the Cornelius H. Van Gaasbecks and Abraham Crispells. They are, for the most part, exceedingly easy to identify, and it seems only proper to offer as a first illustration Marius Schoonmaker himself. Schoonmaker was active in all areas of the community's organized life. He was a congressman, a state senator, the New York State banking commissioner, a member of the Whig county central committee, and a delegate to four Whig and Republican conventions. In addition, he served two terms as deacon and two terms as elder of the Second Dutch Reformed Church and was a director of the Ulster County Bank. Schoonmaker spent only about half the decade residing in Kingston, but when he was there he seems to have moved easily and perhaps automatically into positions of local political, religious, and economic leadership. Johannes Bruyn was a special county judge, a deacon and elder of the First Dutch Reformed Church, a trustee of Kingston Academy and of the Kingston Literary Association, the secretary of the Hudson River Lecture Association, and a participant in two citizens' meetings. Unlike Schoonmaker's, Bruyn's leadership was almost entirely local, but the institutions he helped lead mark him as a Kingston aristocrat. Jacob B. Hardenbergh, who carried another ancient Ulster County surname, mixed trustee-ships and other offices of Kingston Academy, the Kingston Literary Association, the Masons, and the militia with all sorts of other activities, including the fire department, no fewer than four July Fourth celebrations, two citizens' meetings, and a rough-and-tumble political life that covered the entire spectrum of Kingston's political parties. Hardenbergh ran for district attorney as a Whig in 1850 (he was called "the Whig Warwick of Kingston" by the *Republican* in 1852), ran again for county judge and village treasurer as a Know-Nothing in 1855 and 1856, served as secretary of the "Fusion" (Republican–Know-Nothing) county convention in 1858, and wound up the decade by campaigning for the "Little Giant," Stephen Douglas!

Not all those who were scored 5 were members of old Kingston families, and the road to leadership did not always run through the directors' room of Kingston Academy. The most extreme exception is, unsurprisingly, George F. Von Beck, who was an immigrant, a self-made man, a resident of Rondout, and a leader of a different set of institutions than those led by such men as Johannes Bruyn. Yet Von Beck's leadership is just as impressive. He was a Rondout village trustee for four years, president of the first village board, and village assessor for one year. He was an active participant in Democratic campaigns and was rewarded with his party's nomination for town supervisor in 1859. He was the president of the board of trustees of the German Evangelical Lutheran Church and the president of the Laborers' Benevolent Society. He was a major in the militia, a founder of an Odd Fellows' lodge in Rondout, and, at the same time, a Mason. Rondout held very few July Fourth celebrations, so Von Beck was an official in only one; but he participated in each of Rondout's citizens' meetings. His leadership, although oriented almost entirely toward the new village, was nearly complete. No one in Rondout, not even the wealthy Thomas Cornell, could compare with Von Beck in the range and level of his leadership.

After scoring social participation, I searched for each participant in both the New York State census of 1855 and the United States census of 1860. In all, 54% of the participants were linked to the 1855 census and 59% were linked to the census of 1860. Considering the effects of death, out-migration, a policy of conservatism in linking participants to the census, occasional illegibility of manuscript records, and the phonetic spelling of one or two census marshals, these are gratifying results. Recall that the participation lists refer to the entire decade (actually eleven years, 1850 through 1860) and not merely to the census years. When we consider, for example, only those men whose participation extended into 1860, we find that exactly 80% were successfully linked to the 1860 census. And we must suspect that some portion of the remainder either died or moved out of Kingston before the midsummer census or in-migrated in the six months that followed.

Consideration of the numbers of men successfully linked to each census brings us back to substantive questions.[4] What proportion of the adult males included in each census is represented on the list of community participants? That is, how many of the men specified as residents of Kingston at a given moment were, according to our survey of social participation, active in some way in the organized life of the community? How many did not participate at all in the town's organizations and organized activities? These, surely, are the very first questions for any analysis of social participation, and it is both interesting and reassuring that the proportion of participants (to the number of males over fifteen years old) on the two censuses is almost precisely the same—15.7% in 1855 and 14.7% in 1860. These are conservative figures, depressed somewhat by gaps in the participation list and by missed links, but they are not far off the mark. We can say with some certainty, therefore, that at least one-sixth, and perhaps one-fifth, of the adult males of the town of Kingston participated in the organized life of the community in some way during the 1850s. And even the latter estimate begins to appear conservative when we consider that the summertime censuses include a significant (but unknown) number of seasonal inmigrants who perhaps should not be considered eligible for organized social participation.

A small majority of those identified as participants received scores of 1 or 2, so the proportion of men who were quite active in community affairs was probably not higher than 8%. Those men

Table 12   Participation Scores of the Adult Male Population, 1855 and 1860

	1855		1860	
	N	Percentage	N	Percentage
Score:				
0	3,665	84.3%	4,298	85.3%
1	28	0.6	37	0.7
2	353	8.1	393	7.8
3	180	4.1	184	3.7
4	101	2.3	103	2.0
5	21	0.5	23	0.5
Total	4,348	99.9%	5,038	100.0%

demonstrating community leadership (4 and 5) constituted perhaps 3% of the adult male population. In short, organized social participation in Kingston in the 1850s seems to have pyramided sharply upward from a fairly broad base. One of every five or six men joined some organization or participated in some activity beyond his family, job, neighborhood, or informal circle of friends and acquaintances. One man in twelve was more than minimally active in the community, either as a narrowly oriented leader or as a joiner of many things. One man in thirty or forty was a community leader; and one man in perhaps two hundred belonged to a select group whose leadership activities placed them above all others.

This aggregate pattern of participation and leadership is interesting in its own right, for it adds considerably to our ability to assess the effect of post-canal institutional development. Later, I will try to estimate whether the proportion of men who involved themselves in the expanded organizational life of urban Kingston was really greater than the proportion who participated in the more limited organized activities of the little country village and town of the 1820s. However, first we must answer more pressing questions about the pattern of participation we have discovered in the 1850s. Quite simply, we must ask, "Who did what?" How did the participants and leaders differ from those who did not join in Kingston's organized community life? How did participants receiving different scores, or simply participating in different organizations, differ from each other?

Each of the social variables available to us through the federal and state censuses confirms our expectation that organized social participation was far from randomly distributed among Kingston's adult males. More specifically, the variables associated with "class" (total reported property and occupational category) reveal strong relationships with both incidence and level of participation, while two others, place of birth and length of residence in the community, reveal associations at a somewhat lower level (see appendix B). Of course, each of these variables is also related in varying degrees to the others, so it will be necessary to consider all of them simultaneously—to ask how each contributes, *in combination with the others*, to our understanding of the pattern of participation in antebellum Kingston.[5] In table 13, therefore, the participation scores of Kingston's adult males are cross-tabulated with the three pertinent variables included on the 1855 census—occupation, place of birth (including county of birth for New York State natives), and years of residence in the community.[6] For ease of analysis, occupations are condensed into three ordinal categories. "High" occupations are those professions and proprietorships (including farming) which form the first three categories of earlier tables, "middle" occupations are the crafts and clerical jobs which comprise the fourth and fifth categories of those tables, and "low" occupations are those which we have earlier called semiskilled and unskilled.

The pattern of association table 13 shows between participation and the combination of these three social variables is complex but fairly clear. The most active community participants (those scoring 4 or 5) were nearly all high-occupation natives of Ulster County and high-occupation native in-migrants who had been resident in Kingston for at least six years.[7] Middle-level participants (those scoring 3) were somewhat more widely distributed but were most characteristic of high-occupation native Americans, middle-occupation native Americans with at least six years' local residence, and, most interesting of all, high-occupation foreign immigrants resident in Kingston for at least six years. The last were also well represented at lower levels of participation and reveal an overall

Table 13   Occupation, Place of Birth and Years of Local Residence by Participation Score; All Adult Males, 1855.

| | High Occupation | | | | | |
| | Ulster Co. | | Other U.S. | | Foreign | |
	6+ Years	0–5 Years	6+ Years	0–5 Years	6+ Years	0–5 Years
High Score (4, 5)	14.7%	17.1%	22.6%	7.8%	4.0%	0.0%
Middling Score (3)	14.7	9.8	21.7	13.0	10.5	1.5
Low Score (1, 2)	12.8	14.6	17.9	16.9	15.8	7.5
Nonparticipation (0)	57.8	58.5	37.7	62.3	69.7	91.0
Total	100.0%	100.0%	99.9%	100.0%	100.0%	100.0%
N	251	41	106	77	76	67

	Middle Occupation					
	Ulster Co.		Other U.S.		Foreign	
	6+ Years	0–5 Years	6+ Years	0–5 Years	6+ Years	0–5 Years
High Score (4, 5)	4.5%	0.0%	8.0%	0.5%	0.7%	0.0%
Middling Score (3)	10.3	4.7	10.2	2.2	2.7	0.6
Low Score (1, 2)	21.7	21.7	21.2	17.7	7.5	5.4
Nonparticipation (0)	63.5	73.6	60.6	79.6	89.0	94.0
Total	100.0%	100.0%	100.0%	100.0%	99.9%	100.0%
N	290	106	137	181	146	332

	Low Occupation					
	Ulster Co.		Other U.S.		Foreign	
	6+ Years	0–5 Years	6+ Years	0–5 Years	6+ Years	0–5 Years
High Score (4, 5)	1.1%	2.1%	0.0%	0.0%	0.0%	0.0%
Middling Score (3)	2.9	2:1	0.0	0.0	0.2	0.2
Low Score (1, 2)	8.2	2.1	8.6	1.6	4.7	1.6
Nonparticipation (0)	87.9	93.6	91.4	98.4	95.0	98.2
Total	100.1%	99.9%	100.0%	100.0%	99.9%	100.0%
N	208	47	70	61	422	812

profile quite similar to that of natives who were either more recent arrivals in the community or a step lower on the occupational scale. All other groups were significantly less active. Middle-occupation native Americans who were newcomers to Kingston were seldom identified as community leaders or activists but were often located as more minimal participants. Middle-occupation foreign immigrants and virtually all low-occupation workers, whether natives or immigrants, old-timers or newcomers, were seldom identified as participants at any level. Each of these points is emphasized by table 14, in which the cell frequencies of table 13 are recalculated into an index representing each socioeconomic subgroup's under– or over-representation within a particular participation score.

Several important points emerge from these two tables. First, it is evident that participation in Kingston's organized social life was an upper- and middle-class phenomenon, either closed to or simply ignored by all but a few of the town's many semiskilled and unskilled workers. Of the 1,743 workers identified on the 1855 state census schedules, only 71 are also identifiable as community participants. Of these, only 13 were more than minimally active in Kingston's institutions, and only 3 were active enough to receive a participation score of 4.[8] Obviously, there is little need to consider whether the participating workers were natives or immigrants, or whether they were long-term or short-term residents in the town. Very few of even the most deeply rooted workingmen were organized community participants in antebellum Kingston.

Second, the relationship between participation and ethnicity is somewhat weaker than the relationship between participation and occupational category, largely because those immigrants who were professionals, merchants, or manufacturers tended to become fairly active in community affairs after a few years of local residence. It is

Table 14   Participation Score Index for Occupation,
Place of Birth, and Length of Residence Sub-
categories, 1855.
Index = 1.00

| | High Occupation | | | | | |
| | Ulster Co. | | Other U.S. | | Foreign | |
	6+	0–5	6+	0–5	6+	0–5
High Score (4, 5)	4.78	5.50	7.29	2.59	1.23	.00
Middling Score (3)	3.33	2.17	4.87	3.00	2.45	.30
Low Score (1, 2)	1.37	1.58	1.87	1.86	1.68	.80
Nonparticipation (0)	.70	.67	.45	.77	.86	1.05

Middle Occupation

	Ulster Co.		Other U.S.		Foreign	
	6+	0–5	6+	0–5	6+	0–5
High Score (4, 5)	1.46	.00	2.60	.17	.21	.00
Middling Score (3)	2.32	1.06	2.30	.49	.60	.13
Low Score (1, 2)	2.31	2.32	2.25	1.89	.79	.58
Nonparticipation (0)	.76	.87	.72	.96	1.07	1.12

Low Occupation

	Ulster Co.		Other U.S.		Foreign	
	6+	0–5	6+	0–5	6+	0–5
High Score (4, 5)	.31	.64	.00	.00	.00	.00
Middling Score (3)	.66	.43	.00	.00	.05	.05
Low Score (1, 2)	.87	.21	.95	.15	.50	.17
Nonparticipation (0)	1.05	1.07	1.10	1.15	1.15	1.18

Index = Percentage of total in each score category divided by percentage of total in each occupational-birthplace-years of residence category.

true that, in comparison with native American participants, very few foreign-born participants were community leaders, that is, men who were assigned participation scores of 4 or 5. Indeed, there were only four, George F. Von Beck, Jacob and John Derenbacker, and Thomas Keyes, all at least moderately wealthy men who had lived in Kingston for twenty years or more in 1855. But at a slightly lower level of participation, among those men active enough to receive a score of 3, the more settled professional and entrepreneurial immigrants were quite well represented and were proportionately as numerous as similarly placed natives among the minimal participants, those scoring 1 and 2. Of course, we must remember that there were not very many foreign-born merchants and lawyers in Kingston, that foreign-born clerks and craftsmen were underrepresented on the roster of community participants, and that foreign-born dollar-a-day workers were no more active in community affairs than were the equivalent native workers. Nor should we underemphasize that Kingston's leadership consisted almost entirely of native Americans.[9] Still, the number of Irish and German immigrants who were active in community affairs is impressive. It points to a community where the criteria of membership and respectability were somewhat less closely tied to national origin than one might suppose from reading the pages of the Know-Nothing newspaper or from listening to the likes of Bob Baggs, leader of the Bumble Bees.

Both of these major points are highlighted in table 15, which substitutes the property entries of the 1860 census for the somewhat crude occupational categories of tables 13 and 14 as an indicator of "class." (Ulster County natives are not isolated here, and length of local residence is omitted as a variable, since this information is not included on the 1860 census. Also, the table applies only to heads of household; property entries do not exist for boarders, resident sons, and other nonheads.) For both natives and immigrants in this table there is a pronounced relationship between property and participation. Of every eight native-born men reporting more than $10,000 to the census marshal, five were community participants and three were community leaders. At the other end of the property scale, among those native householders reporting $1,000 and less, only 20% were participants in organized community affairs, and only 2% were community leaders. A similar but even more dramatic difference can be seen between wealthy and poor immigrants. Five of the seven wealthiest Irishmen and Germans were participants, while those reporting $1,000 or less were nearly all excluded from or unconcerned with community affairs. Not one of the 1,531 immigrant householders worth $5,000 or less in 1860 was a community leader. As this suggests, there are significant differences shown in table 15 between natives and immigrants, although, as in the earlier tables, these differences moderate among the higher categories of wealth. Irish and German householders worth $5,000 and more in 1860 were as well represented as the wealthier natives among community activists (those scoring 3) and were less numerous only among community leaders (those scoring 4 and 5). Again, these patterns are clearly revealed by recalculating the cell frequencies into a participation score index, as in table 16.

Table 15   Total Property and Place of Birth by Participation Score; Male Heads of Household, 1860.

			United States			
	$10,000+	$5,000– 10,000	$1,000– 5,000	$500– 1,000	$100– 500	$0– 100
High Score (4, 5)	37.8%	15.1%	7.6%	2.8%	0.8%	2.1%
Middling Score (3)	14.4	20.1	10.6	6.4	7.0	5.2
Low Score (1, 2)	10.8	14.4	16.1	9.9	12.4	10.3
Nonparti- cipation (0)	37.0	50.4	65.7	80.9	79.8	82.4
Total	100.0%	100.0%	100.0%	100.0%	100.0%	100.0%
N	111	139	341	141	242	497

			Foreign			
	$10,000+	$5,000– 10,000	$1,000– 5,000	$500– 1,000	$100– 500	$0– 100
High Score (4, 5)	(2)	6.5%	0.0%	0.0%	0.0%	0.0%
Middling Score (3)	(3)	22.6	1.1	1.3	0.4	0.4
Low Score (1, 2)	—	16.1	14.5	3.9	1.1	2.4
Nonparti- cipation (0)	(2)	54.8	84.4	94.8	98.5	97.2
Total	(7)	100.0%	100.0%	100.0%	100.0%	100.0%
N	7	31	186	155	274	916

Table 16   Participation Score Index for Place of Birth and
                Property Subcategories, 1860.
                Index = 1.00

	United States					
	$10,000 +	$5,000–10,000	$1,000–5,000	$500–1,000	$100–500	$0–100
High Score (4, 5)	10.55	4.20	2.13	.80	.23	.56
Middling Score (3)	2.88	3.98	2.10	1.28	1.39	1.04
Low Score (1, 2)	1.34	1.78	2.03	1.26	1.54	1.29
Nonparticipation (0)	.44	.61	.78	.98	.95	.99

	Foreign					
	$10,000 +	$5,000–10,000	$1,000–5,000	$500–1,000	$100–500	$0–100
High Score (4, 5)	7.83*	1.83	.00	.00	.00	.00
Middling Score (3)	8.70*	4.57	.21	.26	.07	.09
Low Score (1, 2)	.00*	2.06	1.82	.49	.13	.30
Nonparticipation (0)	.34*	.68	1.02	1.14	1.18	1.17

Index = Percentage of total in each score category divided by
percentage of total in each property-birthplace category.

*Based on seven cases.

Men of wealth and high occupational status, then, predominated
in Kingston's institutions. Moreover, they did so across nearly the

entire spectrum of community organizations and activities. Kingston's professionals, merchants, manufacturers, and farmers constituted only some 15 % of the adult male population in 1860. Yet they supplied more than half, and in some instances nearly all, of the participants in every type of local institution except the fire companies and perhaps the militia companies. Of Kingston's political party activists, 60 % held high occupations, as did over 70 % of the more important party officers. (Interestingly, there was only a modest difference in this respect between Democrats and Whig-Republicans—56 % of the former and 66 % of the latter held high-ranking occupations; 21 % of the Democrats and 23 % of the Whig-Republicans reported more than $10,000 in property in 1860.) Lawyers, merchants, and other professionals and white-collar entrepreneurs supplied 57 % of the village and town officers, 76 % of the county officers, 56 % of the lay leaders of local churches, and 58 % of the members of Kingston's Masonic and Odd Fellows' lodges. They also constituted 65 % of the official participants in local Fourth of July celebrations, 84 % of the officers of educational and cultural organizations, 68 % of the recorded members of Kingston's temperance societies, and 84 % of those who participated in the various ad hoc citizens' meetings. Of course, it must be recognized that many of these high-ranked entrepreneurs were actually owners of small stores and shops and did not necessarily earn more than a middling livelihood. The proportions of participants who could be considered wealthy are substantially lower—ranging from 5 % in the fire companies, to around 20 % or 25 % in most other organizations, to over 40 % of the officers of the educational and cultural societies and the recorded participants in citizens' meetings. These are very high proportions for a group making up only 4 % of the town's householders, but they fall short of a majority. Numerically, at least, Kingston's institutions were dominated by its middle-class entrepreneurs, and it seems, in final analysis, that membership in this broad group was the basic requirement for organized communal participation.[10]

We have seen that emigrants from Ireland and Germany could meet that criterion, and that the small numbers of immigrant entrepreneurs were in fact well represented among Kingston's social participants. But the participation scores do not in themselves reveal the degree to which natives and immigrants mingled within the same organization. If immigrant participants accumulated their participation scores entirely through such ethnic-based organizations as the green-clad Irish Jackson Rifles, the German Harrison Guards, or the German Laborers' Benevolent Society, we would recognize a deeper social division between natives and immigrants than would be implied by even a very dramatic difference in the amount of participation. A review of the specific patterns of association, however, reveals that such organizational segregation did not exist. Foreign-born men were scattered through a number of local organizations, and of these only the militia companies and one or two German *Vereine* seem to have been based on ethnicity. The most common type of immigrant social participation was fire company membership, and, perhaps surprisingly, the fire companies of both villages were ethnically integrated. It is true that each Kingston company contained only one or two immigrants, but it is also true that few immigrants lived in the old village. The Rondout companies provide a better test, and these were thoroughly integrated. Lackawanna Engine Company No. 1 did contain a majority of natives, and Ponckhockie Engine Company No. 3 was predominantly immigrant, but in both there were significant minorities of immigrants and natives; and Protector Engine Company No. 2 was a mixture of twelve natives, one Englishman, eight Irishmen, and four Germans in 1855. The same pattern is also visible in 1860. Foreign-born men also participated in local politics, which obviously placed them in the same organizations as those native-born men who did not flee to the Native American party. Interestingly, immigrant partisans involved themselves in both major parties, with only a hint of the expected pattern of allegiance. Eleven partisan Englishmen and Scotsmen were listed in the 1855 census; of these, six were Whigs or Republicans, four were Democrats, and one was a Know-Nothing. The same number of Irish activists divided into seven Democrats and four Whig-Republicans; while eight Germans were evenly split between the two major parties. The same pattern continued through 1860, despite the significant party realignments of the second half of the decade. Of course, these few men need not be considered typical of English, Irish, or German voters, nor do they seem to have been leaders or spokesmen for their respective ethnic groups. But that is precisely the point—despite the explicit response to ethnic heterogeneity by a portion of Kingston's native men (the Know-Nothings), local ethnic groups did not respond with any visible, concerted effort to acquire power for their "own kind."

Certainly the *Ulster Republican* did whatever it could to promote Democratic loyalty among the Irish, but it is difficult to discern from election returns whether the effort succeeded. The Whigs or Republicans were as likely to carry Rondout as any other place. Politics, in short, was ethnically exclusive in some senses but not in others. One movement was explicitly exclusive and proposed a fairly specific agenda of nativist measures. (We may recall that it succeeded in acquiring power but not in implementing substantive programs of immigrant exclusion or control.) No party, moreover, gave very many nominations or positions of party leadership to foreign-born men. On the other hand, those immigrants who participated in politics did so within the regular party structure, and there is no evidence that they were received specifically as spokesmen for organized and well-defined ethnic subcommunities.

The militia companies themselves present something of a puzzle. Why were they, unlike the fire companies, ethnically segregated? Both were the special province of young men. Both were social clubs, providing dinners, excursions, formal dances, and fellowship for their members, and both were based partly on the display of masculine skills. Was the difference in their primary function significant? Probably it was. Militia service evoked nationalism and, by a slight extension, the concept of national origin. Obviously, for those foreign-born men who wished to be assimilated into native society or simply to serve in the militia, the subject of national origin could be highly embarrassing. The situation seems to have called for a special response, one that would turn disadvantage to advantage by calling attention to national origins rather than trying to hide them. Thus, young Irishmen could proclaim their loyalty as "adopted Americans" by forming a distinctive Irish unit explicitly dedicated to the defense of American freedoms. Germans could do the same. Native Americans could be (and were) impressed by this evidence of good intent; at the same time, they could escape the uncomfortable feeling that native militia units were being undermined by men of uncertain loyalty. Seen in this light, the ethnically exclusive militia units appear not as an example of ethnic segregation but as a special form of assimilation, complementing rather than contradicting the integrated political parties and fire companies.

We should not, of course, lose sight of the fact that far fewer immigrants than natives actually participated in any of these organizations. Even when we control for the effects of occupational level and length of residence in the community, ethnicity remains visible as a correlate of social participation. Still, we have shown in these pages that this correlation is not as strong as we might have expected. It is consistently weaker than that between participation and class-related variables (occupational level and property) and no stronger than that between participation and residential tenure. Immigrants, we may suggest, were removed from organized community life primarily as workers and secondarily as newcomers and members of particular ethnic minorities. Those Irish and Germans who did not suffer the double disadvantage of class and recent arrival were almost as active as similarly placed natives and, as we have just seen, participated in the same organizations as the natives. On the other hand, the men we are attempting to describe did not concern themselves overly with multivariate analysis. Probably very few native men took the trouble to consider that most Irish and German immigrants were poor newcomers and that their poverty and their newness to Kingston could have had something to do with their behavior, their attitudes, and their interest in Kingston as a community. Fewer still must have systematically compared these immigrants to the significant number of American-born newcomers on the coal docks and in the quarries. Thus, it is not at all contradictory or especially surprising to find that native Kingstonians perceived the changes occurring around them primarily in ethnic terms, while the pattern of actual community participation indicates that ethnicity was of secondary importance. Native reaction and immigrant social participation are separate phenomena, to be viewed side by side rather than reconciled; and even in combination they fail to tell the whole story of the significance of ethnicity in antebellum Kingston. What of the opportunities open to the foreign-born to escape the dollar-a-day jobs that fixed them at the bottom of the community's social and economic hierarchies? Could not the native-born have achieved the semblance of an open community, incorporating into full community membership those immigrants who rose to a respectable economic level, while at the same time assuring themselves and each other that few immigrants would be permitted to leave the docks and quarries without leaving Kingston entirely?

In fact, only a small proportion—about one-sixth—of those foreign-born unskilled workers listed on the 1855 census remained in Kingston through the summer of 1860. Fewer than 10% of those who did remain (about 1.7% of those present in 1855) rose to skilled jobs or proprietorships in that five-year period.[11] Perhaps, then, the denial of economic opportunity was the hidden mechanism by which middle-class natives excluded immigrant minorities from full community membership. On the other hand, the local economic opportunities for native unskilled workers were apparently not that much greater. A large majority—about 72%—of those present in 1855 had left Kingston by 1860. A substantial minority—almost one-third—of those who did remain rose to skilled jobs and proprietorships, but these successes still represent only some 9% of those present in 1855.[12] Native workers were more often upwardly mobile than immigrant workers, but the rule for both groups was the most dramatic possible form of community nonparticipation—physical departure. We may conclude, then, that class was more critical than nativity in shaping the communal memberships and activities of antebellum Kingstonians.

This proposition may also apply to the opposite end of the participation spectrum, for foreign- and American-born working-men were not the only in-migrants to Kingston in the years of post-canal growth. The new opportunities in commerce also attracted men of greater means, mostly from elsewhere in the Hudson Valley and from New England. Many of these men prospered in Kingston, and in the process established themselves in the community as active participants in its new organizational life and often as community leaders. This is a third major pattern revealed in our analysis of participation scores—the seeming ease with which well-placed native in-migrants, particularly those from New England, acquired positions of leadership in this ancient town whose leading families could trace their contributions to the old corporation back to the seventeenth century. Slightly more than half the high-occupation, native in-migrants recorded on the 1855 census are identifiable as community participants. Moreover, among those residing in Kingston longer than five years, nearly half (44.3%) were evenly divided between active participants and community leaders (see table 13). All these proportions are somewhat *higher* than those pertaining to Ulster County natives of similar standing. Once again, however, we must raise the question of segregation. Perhaps the descendants of the farmers of Esopus maintained a firm grip on the old institutions, forcing the newcomers into newer institutions of their own making. Perhaps the seemingly heterogeneous elite was in reality two separate groups: one thoroughly local in origin, thoroughly Dutch in cultural background, and centered around such institutions as the Dutch church, Kingston Academy, and the Kingston village government; and the other consisting of New Englanders and other wealthy upstarts who centered their community life around newer churches, the newly created literary societies, and the government of Rondout.

As with the Irish and German workers, integration, not segregation, was in fact the rule among Kingston's leaders. With the exception of the First Dutch Reformed Church, whose lay leaders were almost all born in Ulster County to families that had been prominent in local affairs for generations, each of Kingston's institutions was led by a mixture of Esopus Dutch, Yorkers from other counties, New Englanders, and others. Indeed, in comparison with other native groups, Ulster-born men were somewhat underrepresented and New Englanders overrepresented on the boards of Kingston's banks, plank road companies, and cultural organizations, as well as in positions of leadership in local government, politics, lodges, temperance organizations, and the like. For example, though they constituted more than 60% of the population of American-born men, Ulster natives contributed fewer than 40% of the decade's village directors and trustees and about half the directors of the old village of Kingston. New Englanders, on the other hand, numbered fewer than 4% of the native adult male population but contributed about 8% of the leadership of the two villages and 10% of the leadership of Kingston. Of all the various forms of high-level community participation, only the planning and execution of the annual Fourth of July celebration was spread among the native groups in rough approximation to their proportions in the population.

Of course, the distribution of leadership positions does not automatically translate into the distribution of influence; and Kingston Academy may be a case in point. Trusteeships in the academy were, surprisingly, spread even more widely than usual: of fifteen trustees located on the 1855 census, seven were born in Ulster County, four were born elsewhere in New York, one was a New Englander, two were from other Middle Atlantic states, and one, William Kerr, was a well-to-do Irishman who had come to Kingston in 1830. Yet, in an extraordinarily candid editorial that must have shaken the community, Solomon Hommel of the *Ulster Republican* charged in 1857 that the academy was no more than "a curacy of the 1st Reformed Dutch Church." It was common knowledge, claimed Hommel, that the academy was "in its imbecility," and that the cause of its decline was the "purple and fine linen rule" of Kingston's original church and particularly of its pastor. Once, Hommel admitted, when the First Dutch Church was the only church in the village, its control of the academy was to be expected. But now that there were many churches, the control of the academy even by the oldest was plainly undemocratic and unjustifiable.[13] When the Kingston *Democratic Journal* responded that only a minority of the academy's trustees were members of the First Dutch Church, the *Republican* fired back that effective control did not depend on majorities and that elected "outsiders" were expected not to attend meetings.[14]

The dispute over the academy went no further, but it suffices to warn us of the possible differences between formal position and real influence. However, it is worth noting another article on the academy in Hommel's *Ulster Republican*, written two years after his attack on the First Dutch Church. In 1859, Hommel noted that the problems of the academy stemmed from the advanced ages of its trustees and from the fact that the principal, not the trustees, had directed its affairs over the years: "The control of the Trustees was, in truth, nominal."[15] There is not a word in this later editorial about the First Dutch Church, and Hommel's assessment of the impotence of the trustees plainly contradicts his earlier attack. Judging from other editorials attacking the church, the Classis of Ulster, and the Reverend Hoes, we may conclude that the original blast derived more from personal animosity than from the actual operations of the academy.

In any case, the pattern of organizational membership is clear— Yankees and Yorkers mingled in the same voluntary societies, in the same boardrooms, and on the same governmental bodies. Moreover, the sheer quantity of high-level participation by New Englanders and other outsiders suggests a considerable erosion of that continuity of community leadership that we earlier traced from the trusteeships of the seventeenth-century corporation to the town and village governments of 1820. The old families were not entirely replaced, but they could not dominate the growing little city as they could the country town. Note, for example, the directorships of the old village, where most of the old families and a much smaller proportion of the newcomers, lived. During the 1850s, there were 35 directors of Kingston village; of these, only eight carried the surnames that dominate the old corporation records. Another seven could trace their names back to at least one corporation trustee, but a majority of twenty men bore names that do not appear at all in Kingston's earlier leadership. Some of these men could no doubt point to an impressive maternal lineage, but the situation had greatly changed since 1820, when most village directors, and even most minor officers, were clearly descended from the same families that had led Kingston for generations.

The evolution of Kingston's leadership appears almost revolutionary when we consider the names of the twenty-eight men whose community participation in the 1850s placed them above all others. Sixteen of these men bore surnames that do not appear in the records of the old corporation; of the remaining twelve, only six were clearly descended from Kingston's leading colonial families. Even more striking is the fact that these six represent only three surnames— Schoonmaker, Hasbrouck, and Masten. Thus twenty-nine of the "top 32" corporation names are not included in our list of the twenty-eight leading community participants of the 1850s. We must be careful, however, not to overemphasize this apparently dramatic turnover. The most important *families* in Kingston were still the old ones, as is manifested by the recorded participation of fourteen Schoonmakers, twelve Van Gaasbecks, sixteen Van Burens, ten Houghtailings, seven Osterhoudts, fourteen Hasbroucks, ten Van Keurens, and similar numbers of men bearing equally venerable names. We should also reiterate the imperfect correlations between surname and family, on the one hand, and between organized social participation and either power or prestige, on the other. Nevertheless, I think it is fair to speak of a significant change in the pattern of local leadership in Kingston in the years following the opening of the canal—a change best described as an incorporation of new blood into a very old elite. Whether this incorporation constituted a significant alteration of the social order in Kingston is a question we will consider in the following chapter.

The subject of pre-canal Kingston brings me back to a question raised earlier in this chapter. Did organized social participation really increase as the country town gave way to the emerging city? Of course, we have no roster of social participants in pre-canal Kingston, but if we did it is very doubtful that it would include over

40% of the native-born adult white males of at least middling status and at least six years' local residence. Yet that is the proportion attributable to such men in the 1850s. For those who considered themselves the respectable core of the community, therefore, organized social participation almost certainly became more wide-spread as the town and its institutions developed. Moreover, participation in 1860 meant much more than it had in 1820. With the exception of the political parties and perhaps the churches, Kingston's organizations demanded far more time and energy from their members and in return gave them a far more regular and active group life. In both senses, organized social participation increased in Kingston during the years of its most rapid growth. We may be assured that the development of a fully articulated institutional structure did, in fact, bring more Kingstonians into more frequent contact with one another in group situations.

This increase in the amount of organized social participation makes it even more important that we understand which Kings-tonians we are discussing. For it is likely that, as local organizations proliferated and became more central to the life of the community, participation in them served increasingly to reflect and reinforce the social boundaries of the community itself. The problem of boun-daries was, as I suggested earlier, an urgent one by the 1850s—and an ironic product of the growth that made Kingston both more significant and more diverse. But we must not assume that it was a problem that went unresolved. If mere local residence could not suffice (as it did not, in the days of slavery), there were other criteria—class, ethnicity, length of residence—for establishing the social boundaries of the community; and an old mechanism—organized social participation—that could be put to the new use of making those boundaries explicit. Hence the pattern of social participation tells us something of the way in which old-stock Kingstonians reacted to the changes that were occurring around them, and something of the way in which Connecticut merchants, Irish quarrymen, German butchers, and Delaware County "canaw-lers" responded to their new home. It does not, of course, tell all. The real question remains: how did the expressed perceptions and reactions of Kingston's old and new citizens relate to the inferences made here? It is time, therefore, to let the Kingstonians speak for themselves.

Hurra for Business! Hurra for the grand activity of Steam, of Muscle, of Mind, that affords men, at the same time, occupation, amusement, instruction, development!—Hurra for the power that enables us to support our families, and to secure for them the comforts and luxuries, as well as the solid necessities of life! . . . Hurra for that mighty energy which imparts to civilization its whole spirit and impetus! Hurra for the conserving element which enables the great machine of society to work harmoniously . . . ![1]

With these words the Rondout *Courier* accepts our offer to listen to Kingstonians talk of their community. Or are we being a bit unfair? The quotation is taken from an article written in anticipation of the opening of the business season of 1856 and belies the somewhat more sober tone of J. P. Hageman's excellent journal. But, excessive enthusiasm aside, it does encapsulate the values that dominate the pages of the *Courier*, of the other Kingston newspapers, and of the diary of the young Wilbur merchant, Nathaniel Booth. In all probability, it represents the central beliefs of a large portion of the middling and prosperous residents of this busy commercial town. On the other hand, it is also likely that the average Irish dock worker or German teamster greeted the *Courier*'s remarks with a sneer and a well-aimed squirt of tobacco juice. We are dealing here with the unofficial ideology of middle-class, antebellum Kingston, not the "mind" of a culturally undifferentiated community.

The quotation, obviously, is above all a paean to business and commercial enterprise, but there are other elements as well. The benefits of business, first of all, are mentioned briefly but suggestively. Thus, business brings us not only bread but also "comforts and luxuries," and both can be accumulated without shame. Business enterprise not only occupies and amuses the businessman but educates and develops him as well. Indeed, business is the propelling force of modern civilization, providing "its whole spirit and impetus." But the most interesting portion of the *Courier*'s remarks comes at the end, where all the energy of what goes before is abruptly reined in by "the conserving element" that produces—not growth, not riches, not invention, but—*harmony*. The qualification is, I believe, of the utmost significance. Enterprise is embraced first as force, then as constraint; and the net result is orderly progress and a statement that, for all of its enthusiasm, is rather moderate after all. And perhaps most interesting, the counterpoint is made without a pause, without a change in mood, without grammatical qualification, and with as lusty a "hurra" as that which precedes the "mighty energy" itself. Enterprise and order, in short, are reinforcing parts of the "great machine of society" and function not in tension but in harmony.

It is, of course, hardly surprising to find that, in a growing commercial town, there should be a certain attachment to the idea that progress derives from the expansion of business in an orderly environment. There is much to be learned, however, from observing the specific ways this idea was actually implemented in the community. As a significant component of the prevailing system of values, it should have shaped responses to concrete situations of both ongoing and episodic characters, and, therefore, it can help us interpret the social patterns we have already described. As an ideology, it should have meshed in some way with other ideals, such as "liberty" and "democracy." And as a goal, it was necessarily more or less realized, informing us of the junctures and disjunctures between social thought and action.

Middle-class Kingstonians had nothing particularly subtle in mind when they urged themselves and each other on to lives of steady exertion. This is not to say, however, that "enterprise" was a simple concept with only one meaning and one application. On the contrary, the idea was intended to serve at least three critical and distinct communal functions, and, depending on the function and the group to which it was applied, assumed two rather different meanings. First, *imaginative* enterprise was the principal mechanism by which the upper levels of the community's stratification system were provided with specific personnel. Most, if not all, men worked toward economic success, but not all succeeded. Those who did were rewarded with comfort, security, and, in most cases, respectability.

Respectabilty, in turn, was often translated into tangible evidences of community leadership—directorships of the village, the academy, and the local banks; offices in the militia; church leadership; significant positions in political parties, citizens' meetings, and Fourth of July celebrations. To Kingston's middle class, this "filling out" of the economic and social stratification system with successful businessmen and professionals was extremely important, for it meant that society structurally embodied and rewarded their own aspirations. That economic and social inequality should exist was unquestioned; and that economic and social superiority should be based on demonstrated talent and achievement was, after all, what set America off from "feudal" Europe, perhaps even from an earlier age in America itself. Moreover, in a growing town like Kingston, the issue of organizational leadership was increasingly critical. Village directors built streets and sidewalks, enforced a growing list of ordinances, and controlled an increasing budget. Local bank directors helped shape the direction of local economic development. Even the committee of arrangements for the celebration of the Fourth of July had acquired responsibility for an event that was at once a great economic opportunity and a great danger to the peace of the village. Clearly, being a member of a leading family was no longer sufficient for assuming the leadership of organizations and meetings that now had serious business to accomplish. And finally, the belief had spread that fortune and respectability, and the community leadership that accompanied them, were no longer easily transferred from one generation to the next. "[A] few revolving years," wrote the editor of the *Ulster Palladium* without a trace of regret, "produce striking changes in society. Many, who, twenty years since occupied the first stations in their respective towns or cities, are now scarcely heard of, while those whose names were then unknown, are now uttered by every tongue."[2] How could local leaders be chosen except according to their demonstrated ability and commitment? And what better way was there of discovering the community's ablest men than by measuring their success in the world of business?

In truth, most of the Schoonmakers, Bruyns, and Van Keurens were capable of passing on to their children both an economic head start and the incentive to maintain it through hard work. As I earlier suggested and will note again a few pages hence, there was no war in Kingston between an embedded aristocracy and a rising class of entrepreneurs. All were entrepreneurs, and all were subject to the same criteria of diligence and achievement. Among the old leading families, to be sure, there was a tendency to confuse family name with individual worth, to "predict" that the community's natural leaders would be those who were bred in the "best" homes. But the criteria of assessment were the same. Note, for example, the juxtaposition of family and the individual on the opening page of Schoonmaker's *History of Kingston:* "Indeed, the history of a community is necessarily but little more than a compilation and combination of family histories. There are always in a stirring, active busy place some men of mark, who by their activity and energy give character to the place."[3] For Schoonmaker, this was more a boast than a contradiction. For us, it is an interesting example of how one Kingston "aristocrat" justified his position by pointing to individual "activity and energy."

Of course, the "activity and energy" that Schoonmaker applauded were converted to dollars and cents as well as to village director-ships. This permitted an error in judgment somewhat more dan-gerous than that provided by old families whose reputations exceeded their current usefulness. For too often a man was judged according to his wealth rather than his talent and character. Nathaniel Booth, who pursued his own "boyish dreams of pros-perity"[4] as diligently as anyone else, complained that "the Aris-tocracy ... of Kingston is more one of money than any village I have ever seen—man is wholly estimated by dollars—what he is worth determines his character and position at once—it governs the conduct of the ladies almost entirely."[5]

In May, 1851, Booth was invited to a party intended to display the new mansion of Judge James C. Forsyth:

> the Judge's new house is a splendid affair throwing all others in Kingston in the shade.—the delicately carved marbles—the rich carpets—mirrors—paintings and furniture would rather astonish the honest Dutch who built Old 'Sopus could they revisit old scenes—I wonder if they sleep guiltily in their graves while such changes are going on. The amusements of the evening were made up of music, champagne, and oysters, which immortal trio enabled the evening to pass agreeably.[6]

The "honest Dutch" may have passed a fretful night in the old Dutch churchyard, but if so they soon obtained satisfaction. Two years after his housewarming party, Judge Forsyth fled to England a step ahead of the discovery that his forgeries and illegal stock sales exceeded $200,000. The *Courier* commented:

> Mr. Forsyth was a spoiled child of fortune. . . . Placed unfortunately at once in a position where there was no need of the stern struggles which would have given direction and strength to mind and heart, and put his more ignoble tendencies in subordination, he gradually allowed his grosser inclinations to obtain the ascendancy.[7]

These sad remarks bring us back to enterprise. Though wealth nearly always translated into respectability (as it did for Judge Forsyth before his flight), wise men paid close attention to how it had been acquired. Men who steadily accumulated through years of application were those who could be trusted as men of character and wit, as men who would hold what they had achieved. Men who had inherited their fortunes or acquired them too quickly through some windfall—through gambling or through a fortunate speculation in stocks—were suspect.[8] What had they done to demonstrate their staying power? Perhaps a respected name or a splendid mansion was usually a good clue, but the Forsyth scandal demonstrated anew that "stern struggles" were a surer basis for continued fortune and respectability. On the other hand, it is worth reiterating that Kingston contained few "spoiled children of fortune," even among its most prosperous families. Unfortunately, there is no reliable guide to the sizes of individual fortunes in the pre-canal town, but it is likely that the children of even the wealthiest families applied themselves diligently to maintaining their initial advantage, and stood up well under the scrutiny of those who insisted that status-conferring wealth be retained in part through the hard work of the possessor.

A second communal function served by enterprise was its contribution to the growth and collective prosperity of the town itself. Kingston's spokesmen knew well enough that growth was neither impossible nor inevitable but depended in large measure on the aggressiveness of local businessmen. They and their fellow townsmen, especially those with investments in local businesses and real estate, also realized that their own prospects were bound with those of the town. Hence, the *Courier's* annual series of articles on Rondout's businessmen and the various preparations for the coming business season were far more than an exercise in local gossip or local color. Reportage of new stores, of enlargement, repairs, and new lines of goods, of increased shipping facilities, and of new attempts at local manufacturing expressed the most fundamental hopes and fears of those who maintained an economic stake in the community. "You will be delighted to learn," wrote the *Courier*, no doubt accurately, "that in spite of the failures of others in similar undertakings, the Rondout Machine Works have every assurance of becoming as solid and permanent as the great cement rock which overshadows them."[9]

The explicit basis for the *Courier*'s annual reassurance was the industry of local businessmen. In concluding his review of developments and prospects for 1852, editor Hageman wrote:

> There is one trait in the character of our business men that contrasts very favorably with many other places. All are busy. There is very little lounging about. . . . A young man wishing to establish a reputation, must be industrious, and forego all idle, vicious habits.[10]

But the enterprise demanded of Kingston's and Rondout's businessmen went beyond mere industriousness. If some men were to succeed and provide leadership for the community, and if the town itself were to prosper, hard work would have to be accompanied by a certain amount of ingenuity. In short, entrepreneurial enterprise required both industry and sagacity—and as steady an application of wits as of brawn. The more restricted concept of enterprise as simply putting one's nose to the grindstone was aimed specifically at the unskilled and semiskilled wage-earning portion of the work force, and at young men who were not yet expected to contribute ideas to the operations of their elders. Enterprise (as mere industriousness) had another major communal function—regulating the behavior, and particularly the public peacefulness, of these two groups.

Respectable Kingstonians undoubtedly realized that their own commercial energies (and those of the canal and cement companies) brought them more than prosperity and growth. Each new store, workshop, quarry, and dock opened several new job opportunities for skilled workers, clerks, and, most frequently of all, unskilled workers who were as willing to take a dollar a day in Kingston as in any other place. Most of the unskilled workers, and many of the artisans and clerks, were young men of native or foreign birth, whose presence in the town was correctly perceived as a potential threat to public order. Kingston and Rondout were not terribly violent or dangerous places, but there were sufficient minor disturbances and more than enough public drunkenness to worry the peaceful and sober (or discreet) folk and to earn the younger village, at least, a reputation for disorderliness. There were also the constant threats of major violence—particularly after the ethnic street fights of 1851 and 1853—a growing fear of crime, and the rather gleeful reminders in the Rondout *Courier* that the respectable old village of Kingston had acquired a neighborhood of houses of ill fame. All these evils were associated in the public mind with the young men, particularly the Irish, who had come to Kingston to provide muscle for its expanding economy and who were, therefore, indispensable. The problem was how to preserve the peace and perhaps even the purity of the community in the face of these troublesome but essential new residents.

It is interesting how seldom and ineffectively the dominant elements of Kingston and Rondout used overt methods of public control. Vigorous crusades were launched to limit or even prohibit the sale of alcoholic beverages and to control in less specific ways the new foreign element in the local population. But both crusades were unsuccessful. The failure of the second crusade was curious, for it controlled much of the machinery of local government for several years without seriously attempting to make even moderate changes in the public behavior of Irish and German troublemakers. Kingston's new ordinances for regulating brothels were justifiably lampooned in the Rondout press, and the village "police departments" remained the least developed of any of the areas of local government. Rather, the primary mechanism for establishing and maintaining order was "enterprise" itself, for the root of all disorder, Kingstonians believed, was neither youth nor Ireland but *idleness.* Hard work, whether or not it required much ingenuity, would absorb the time and energy of Kingston's young bucks, build their characters, and leave them little time, energy, or inclination to acquire vicious habits. A letter written to the *Courier* by a young clerk is instructive on this point. In it he complained of the long hours he was required to work each day and recommended a more reasonable general closing time of 7:00 P.M. or sunset during the summer, and 6:00 P.M. or 7:00 P.M. during the winter. It was true, admitted the overworked young clerk, that some would use their spare time to "contract vices," but most would use it for a profitable (and peaceful) pursuit of mental cultivation. Not trusting to this argument alone, however, he urged his fellow clerks, in the language of "enterprise," to "put their shoulders to the wheel and impel toward a reformation."[11]

Our dissatisfied clerk spoke directly to the fear of idleness among the young. The *Courier* itself was only slightly less direct when it boasted of the success of the Rondout Lyceum:

> The citizens of elder date have warmly entered into and furthered all plans for the improvement of the young men especially, and the healthy and full development of their intellectual powers. And they have been amply rewarded.... The great secret of this success is found in the fact of the industry of the young men hereabouts as a rule.—There are no loungers here as a class. Everybody is employed, and, for a great part of the year, *fully* employed to the extent of their powers. Hence they bring all their powers, thus trained by business, to bear upon the matter in hand, whether it be study or amusement.... Your dawdler (it *is* a good word, even if Fanny Kemble used it,) is equally in the way at a ball or a lecture.... Our Rondout youth understand the value of the maxim of being "a whole man to the object claiming the moment," and hence their vigorous improvement.[12]

"Enterprise" succeeded as a mechanism for preserving order, in short, wherever it carried over into the private lives of Kingston's and Rondout's young men. Having been "trained by business," they would apply themselves to constructive tasks off the job, improve themselves, and, not entirely by chance, save their elders a great deal of fear and worry in the process. Of course, the success of this cultural mechanism in preserving the peace and moral order of the two villages was a great deal less impressive than the *Courier's* statement suggests. Apparently, not all young clerks, and very few quarrymen, were impressed with the rewards of constant application and the evils of irresponsible idleness.

It should be mentioned that middle-class fears of social disorder, though often directed explicitly to the foreign-born, the poor, and the young, were not always quite so external; and neither was the notion that constant application was the best single inoculation against vicious habits. The scandal of James C. Forsyth was a painful reminder of the weakness of all men, however respectable they might appear to be at the moment. It is true that few expected wealthy merchants to riot in the streets (their sons in the Bumble Bees were another matter).[13] But there was no small amount of fear that respected citizens would fall from grace. Drunkenness was particularly feared.[14] However, if dishonesty and promiscuity were less frequently mentioned, they were brought to the attention of Kingstonians by two major scandals that occurred almost simultaneously, Forsyth's flight and the charge of adultery brought against one of Kingston's most respected ministers, Henry W. Smuller of the Second Dutch Reformed Church. Unlike Judge Forsyth, the Reverend Smuller survived his scandal, possibly because he was popular, and possibly because the judge's sin overshadowed the minister's. The Classis of Ulster did little to shape the community's reaction, for while they acquitted Smuller of the charge, they also expressed their "earnest disapprobation and reproof" for his having violated the "laws of decency and decorum."[15] Perhaps this curious adjudication did help, for it seemed unfair to declare "you're innocent, but don't do it again." When the classis attempted to ease him off to a new assignment in Philadelphia, a group of twenty-seven members of the Second Dutch Church (who had left the First Dutch Church only four years earlier) broke away to form Kingston's First Presbyterian Church, and declared Henry W. Smuller their pastor.[16]

The details of Forsyth's and Smuller's scandals are not so important as the fact that Kingstonians were forced by these events to recognize the precariousness of respectability. With little or no warning a respected judge could become a criminal refugee, and a respected minister could narrowly escape ruin, all within the space of several weeks. What, then, of one's own position in society? Once again, the villain was idleness, the unconstructive use of leisure time—to be feared as much as business misfortune, and in any case productive of the same result (Forsyth's downfall was caused by gambling debts and by the expenses of keeping up with New York and Newport society). When a "bowling saloon" was opened in Kingston in 1846, the *Republican* defended it in terms quite similar to those used by the overworked clerk: "Prejudices, we are aware, exist toward such establishments," but "It is conducted in the most orderly manner, and is frequented by our best citizens, who admire the manly and healthful exercise of bowling."[17]

By now it should be clear why the Rondout *Courier* could pass so quickly, in the quotation with which I began this chapter, from "enterprise" to "order." In several ways, the cultural value of imaginative or simply diligent application helped preserve the order and structure of local society, not only in the explicit sense of helping to maintain the peace and moral purity of the community but by performing more fundamental tasks as well—providing local institutions and local society with leaders, and promoting the economic well-being of the entire town. It is important that we recognize these conserving functions of enterprise, for we are otherwise likely to see it primarily if not exclusively as a radical and unsettling force, driving out previous systems of values and patterns of deference and unleashing the disturbing forces of industrial and urban growth, all in an increasingly vigorous pursuit of the dollar. Historians of this period of American history have justifiably emphasized the unsettling side of what is sometimes called "expectant capitalism."[18] In a few cases, they have traced its effects on the social structures of specific communities.[19] These historians have argued that a new business elite, comprising mainly self-made men, began replacing older elites whose important role in community life had been based on "family," that is, on fortunes earned by their grandfathers. But the drama of this transformation of the social order has probably been overstated. Most local elites of the "Federalist" variety were themselves businessmen or professionals, and the fortunes they inherited were based squarely and unashamedly on commerce and, as in Kingston, on commercial agriculture. And even where new elites did bring new values, their spirit of enterprise quickly acquired important elements of preservation. Growth must continue into a future of unlimited potential, to be sure, but it must occur within an orderly system which could confer maximum benefits on those who now stand in a position to receive them. Enterprise, in short, was both progressive and conservative, "a great machine of society" that retained its shape while it fulfilled the expectations of its creators.

Occasionally, the progressive spirit, which was never absent even when it meant only continued economic and urban growth, could inspire visions of a radically different society. Just two years after he had hailed the "conserving element," J. P. Hageman reflected on the day when "labor will be conducted in accordance with the laws of science" and mechanized production would replace back-breaking toil: "When that time has arrived, the iron sway of capitalists will be broken; the moneyed aristocracy will be a ruined institution; and liberty, equality and fraternity, have full sway over the human family." Distributive justice will accompany more satisfying labor, for "the laborers of a nation must be well recompensed for their services, before there can be a unity of feeling and interest among its various communities."[20] This is strong language from the man who wrote approvingly of the "conserving element" and, more to the point, who consistently took the side of the Delaware and Hudson Canal Company during the brief labor conflicts of the mid-1850s. But Hageman was no hypocrite. His sympathy for the working poor was genuine; it was simply exceeded by his faith in the "great machine of society." The strikers were underpaid, but this did not justify their upsetting the social order which, if allowed to run its natural course, would gradually and peacefully modify itself in the direction of "liberty, equality and fraternity." A peaceable Jacobin indeed! Elsewhere, Hageman saw New York State's suffrage extensions, abolition of slavery, and elimination of debtor imprisonment as "a fair return for the labor of thirty years," and conceded that socialism (he was probably thinking of Oneida communitarianism) had some good points. But he firmly declared that "we will adopt such ideas as are true in the course of time, and no more."[21] Meanwhile, the system of free enterprise was already bringing about a better world, a fact that strikers and abolitionists somehow failed to comprehend.

At least once during this period the twin ideals of enterprise and order stood in direct and irrefutable contradiction. No one who supported the entrepreneurial spirit, even when it resulted in large corporations, could see much good in the "feudal" land system that persisted in parts of eastern New York. Here was a system, though based on private property, that sapped rather than stimulated enterprise. The patroon was, according to popular belief, a country gentleman who lived in ease and comfort on his rents; the tenant farmer was a degraded serf who could not be expected to improve a farm he did not own.[22] Neither man conformed to the emerging figure of the industrious entrepreneur (indeed, these were the historical types that stood in the most direct contrast to it), and it was a standard element of local boosterism in Kingston to point out that the west shore of the Hudson was freer of this economically debilitating institution than the east shore.[23] Still, there was a certain amount of tenancy in Ulster County, mostly in the towns of Woodstock, Olive, and Shandaken, and when these nearby farmers joined in the anti-rent war of the mid-1840s, Kingstonians were forced to react. They did so unequivocally. In March, 1845, a large and eager sheriff's posse rode out of Kingston and easily subdued the tenants who had banded together to resist forcibly the collection of rents. The posse's success was hailed by the town and by the local press, and if there were any who were sympathetic to the defeated farmers there is no surviving evidence of it.[24] Later in the same year the murder of an undersheriff by anti-renters in Delaware County provoked a "law and order meeting" in Kingston, at which the anti-renters were thoroughly denounced and no concessions were made to the justice of their cause.[25] Over the course of the uprising, which troubled New York society and politics for several years, the Kingston press remained unswervingly opposed to the anti-renters, picturing them as violators of the public peace. The press utterly ignored the social and economic issues raised by their protest and the implications of its own position—the defense of order against enterprise.

With the exception of the anti-rent war, however, the tensions between enterprise and order were effectively, if not easily, reconciled. To most middle-class Kingstonians, no doubt, these were complementary rather than contradictory values that in combination went a long way toward defining the ideal community. Of lesser importance was the idea that at least some of the energies of the community should be applied to "intellectual and moral things," such as building churches and founding debating societies.[26] Even this, as we have seen, was generally cast in the language of both enterprise and order. Entirely missing from the writings—if not the minds—of antebellum Kingstonians was nostalgia for the smaller country town, for the simple ways of the old Dutch rural tradition, or for anything else that questioned the goodness of the growth of the town and its economy.[27] Also missing from the surviving documents is any significant challenge to the existing order by those who may have felt that it was moving too slowly toward "liberty, equality and fraternity," or by any who may have felt that it was moving in the opposite direction. J. P. Hageman wrote occasionally of "capital's duties to labor," but these generally turned out to consist of such things as the provision of better housing for workers and were, in any case, duties that Hageman fully expected would be met.[28] Ironically, the most direct written challenge to the local order appeared in the more conservative, less visionary, and thoroughly partisan Ulster Republican. In 1838 and 1839 editor Rodney A. Chipp had printed a series of attacks on the

Delaware and Hudson Canal Company, primarily to close Democratic ranks after the terribly destructive local bank war, to belittle
Whig currency and internal improvements legislation, and, most
important of all, to draw Kingston's new Irish population to the
Democratic party.[29] Probably with the last objective in mind,
Chipp's successor, S. S. Hommel, sided with the workers during
the strike against the D & H in 1855.[30] But as these remarks suggest,
the *Republican*'s commitment to the workers and its resistance to
corporate monopoly were sporadic and highly suspect. There is
barely a word on behalf of the one or in defiance of the other in the
years between 1839 and 1855. Moreover, the language of its attack
on the company in 1855 is squarely within the tradition of
"enterprise":

> What kind of a nation will this be when it is composed of
> luxurious and indolent capitalists and their griping agents on
> the one hand, and struggling and starving beggary on the
> other![31]

In sum, these two values, "enterprise" and "order," constitute
both the core and the bulk of community-oriented writing by men
who considered themselves spokesmen for Kingston's middle
classes. Indeed, the intersection of these two values—the convic-
tion that enterprise shapes and strengthens the social order—lies at
the very center of what was written about Kingston by men who
lived there in the decades preceding the Civil War. Of course, I am
not suggesting that the social thought of antebellum Kingstonians
was entirely contained within these simple categories. As private
individuals, as husbands, mothers, and daughters-in-law, as friends,
and lovers, as employers, and customers, they grappled with a
Victorian morality that was at once consistent with and distinct
from the idea of an orderly community of industrious workmen
and imaginative entrepreneurs. As citizens of the state and nation,
they professed allegiance to the political philosophy of republican
democracy and the inalienable rights of man and sought to
translate these ideas into support for or opposition to the Democratic party, state-sponsored internal improvements, John C. Frémont, and the Fugitive Slave Law. As Americans and as Yorkers,
they worried over and wondered at the power of the railroad
companies, crime in New York City, "complex marriage," California, and bloomers, and did their best to square these phenomena

with their own notions of equality, progress, freedom, and tradition. If they thought of their community in fairly simple terms, it is partly because Kingston was not the world and did not evoke the full range of ideas and ideals that its citizens were capable of expressing. Democracy, for example, though equally relevant to all levels of political organization, was somehow most appropriately discussed with reference to the nation rather than to the community. "Enterprise" and "order," on the other hand, were freely applied to all levels of social organization, including the community, where, after all, individual fortunes were made and lost, and where the threat of disorder was a threat to one's own family and property. Of course, these values are no less interesting for having represented the more tangible concerns of day-to-day social life rather than the results of abstract speculation on the course of civilization and the fate of man. And as for abstract speculation in antebellum Kingston:

> the denizens of our village ... have no time or disposition to yield to the ghostly reflections of a melancholy hour. What has reflection to do with the accumulation of wealth, or the over-reaching of our neighbors? What has intellect to do with man, except in helping him to cast compound interest and loss and gain? The main thing is utility; we are too impatient of the present, and build all our imaginings on the future; and ... the future must of necessity evolve plans of better worth and more practical utility. Until that time arrives we go for anything and everything which, while it increases our intelligence, must of necessity add to our actual wealth and power.[32]

Perhaps the most interesting aspect of social thought is its intersection with the social processes to which it refers. We have noted in these pages, for example, the congruence of the idea of enterprise and the actual community leadership of successful entrepreneurs who were as likely to have been relative newcomers from Albany or Connecticut as the descendants of the schepens of Wiltwyck. We have also noted the insistence on social and moral order in a community that did, in fact, contain organized gangs, brothels, innumerable grogshops, and a floating population of young men and aliens for much of the year, and that did see a great deal of drunkenness, a fair amount of minor violence, and an occasional major street fight between the "boys" and the "lads." And we have watched the community, or at least a portion of it, respond to scandals involving prominent citizens and to the challenges of strikers and anti-renters. These were the social realities that were most visibly and most directly related to the values of enterprise and order and that gave these abstractions much of their substance. But for this very reason, the picture I have drawn here is incomplete and perhaps seriously misleading. Social life in Kingston was not simply a refined process of adjustment between values and perfectly visible behavior. What of those events and conditions that were not perceived, or were not grasped, or were ignored, but that bore significantly on dominant community values? What of the *incongruities* between values and behavior, particularly those that remained uncorrected?

An excellent example of these incongruities is revealed to us in the pages of Nathaniel Booth's diary, where enterprise as a common practice appears somewhat at variance from enterprise as an ideal. There can be no question of Booth's industriousness or of his absorption in business affairs. But the young merchant's descriptions of business practices suggest that business was not the breeding ground of character that one finds portrayed in the Rondout *Courier*:

> Mixing and diluting is brought to the most scientific perfection— and drugs especially . . . are cheated first by the producer—then the importer, lastly by the retailer and the poor consumer ig- norantly swallows beans and peas for coffee . . . chalk and marble dust for sugar—etc. etc. . . . The retailer must suffer indeed if he takes for granted the weight in measure he pays for it—pork—fish and beef in barrels "warranted" 200 pounds will weigh about 180. . . . This mode is so well understood by *business* men that it is looked for as a matter of course and met with counter-knavery.[33]

The counter-knavery is illustrated by a sale of bluestone in which the buyer measured and the seller counted the slabs, each knowing that the other would count to his own advantage, and each satisfied that fairness would result from their combined dishonesty.[34] Other entries describe the hamlet of Wilbur as a competitive jungle, and its merchants as bitter enemies capable of using competitive devices ranging from dock monopolies down to personal slander.[35] We need not concern ourselves with the accuracy of Booth's specific complaints or with the implied honesty of the complainant himself, for the ignoble side of competitive enterprise in the age of patent medicines is well known. Booth's comments merely remind us that the seemingly smooth conjunction of enterprise and order did have its flaws. Would the "stern struggles" of business competition, as described by Nathaniel Booth, really have strengthened the character of James C. Forsyth? This can certainly be doubted. Did the mixing of marble dust with sugar really impart a sense of community responsibility to Kingston's young men? This, too, can be doubted. On the other hand, we should not be surprised to find dishonest businessmen serving the community in a variety of ways, acquiring the respect of their townsmen, and providing apparent confirmation of the idea that enterprise preserved the social and moral order of the community partly through the character, including the honesty, of local entrepreneurs.

Another perspective on the system of values we have described here is gained from the successes and failures of the men who tried to make their livings in Kingston. The concept of enterprise, as we well know, was closely bound with the concept of economic success, and the conjunction of the two was of great significance to both the individual and the community. Indeed, enterprise could hardly have functioned as a social value if there were not at least some visible confirmation of the endlessly repeated prediction that the industrious would prosper while the lazy would fail. How well, then, did this prediction hold up in Kingston? Traditional methods for the study of mobility do not, of course, provide us with an answer to this question, for they cannot tell us which men were industrious and which were not. What they do provide, perhaps, is some sense of the possibilities open to the men who worked in antebellum Kingston. For example, we observed in the previous chapter that a small percentage of native-born unskilled workers and a virtually negligible proportion of foreign-born unskilled workers visibly improved their occupational positions between 1855 and 1860, while a large majority of both groups moved away from Kingston to pursue their luck in other towns. On the basis of this combination of low vertical and high geographic mobility, we suggested that the chances for economic success for unskilled workers, particularly those born outside America, were not very great in Kingston during these sometimes troublesome years. Many workers, no doubt, worked diligently toward the goal of economic advancement, but few who remained in Kingston had much to show for their efforts by 1860. We may suspect, along with others who have speculated on the matter, that those who left fared no better and probably fared worse than those who remained.[36] For this large portion of the work force, therefore, "enterprise" was seldom buttressed by tangible evidence of economic success, and those among Kingston's dollar-a-day workers who continued to believe in the goodness (as opposed to the mere necessity) of hard work had to find other justifications for their belief. Undoubtedly, most agreed with the young boys who sang out to the boatmen who "locked through" at Eddyville:

> Canaler, Canaler, you'll never get rich
> You'll spend all your money and die in a ditch;
> You son of a bitch.[37]

The mobility of the middle classes and the rich is more difficult to assess through traditional means than the mobility of the poor. The word "laborer," so vague about function or activity, is not at all vague about status or income. "Grocer," "carpenter," and "foundryman," on the other hand, may each describe a variety of conditions superior to those of the laborer but forming no clear and reliable hierarchy with respect to one another. It is true that most attorneys may be placed above most tailors in the order of things, and that the tailors may be safely considered as at roughly the same economic level as most shoemakers, but even these fairly clear distinctions and equivalences do not justify our inferring economic success or failure from the simple study of occupational transitions. Most transitions are extremely difficult to interpret, while many fortunes were made and lost without any change of title.[38] We may note, perhaps, that there were a fair number of occupational changes between 1855 and 1860 that *appear*, especially at first glance, to have been significant. Thus, of seventy-five men who appeared as craftsmen or clerical workers on the 1855 census, ten, or 13%, were listed in what seem to have been more profitable occupations on the 1860 census, while four, or 5%, seem to have slipped to the working class. About 10% (five of fifty-one) who had been professionals, merchants, or farmers in 1855 were listed as craftsmen, clerks, or less skilled workers in 1860. This is a fairly impressive amount of change for a five-year period. On the other hand, a closer look at these transitions raises doubts about the significance of about half of them. Had the tailor who became a "clothier" changed his operations or just his title? Was the carpenter who had become a teacher making more or less money in

1860? Was the farmer who had been reduced to farm laborer by 1860 really an independent farmer in 1855, or had he been a farm laborer all along?

Fortunately, there is another means for gaining at least some insight into the realities of success and failure among Kingston's entrepreneurs. As far back as the 1850s, and perhaps slightly earlier, the Mercantile Agency, predecessor to Dun & Bradstreet, maintained and constantly updated records of their investigations into the economic affairs, financial standing, prospects, and reliability of men and firms all over the country. These early records, organized by state and by county, are available to the historian. Even though they vary considerably in detail from one entry to the next, they go far beyond such sources as city directories and census schedules in providing a real picture of the changing fortunes of local businessmen, sometimes over their entire careers. The entries, moreover, appear to cover the whole spectrum of business and businessmen, from wealthy merchants of seemingly unquestionable standing to the smallest and most marginal of tradesmen. And perhaps most interesting of all, a number of the entries combine the hard facts of success and failure with commentary on the diligence, ability, and character—the "enterprise"—of the entrepreneur himself!

A sample of twenty entries, descriptive of the careers of local businessmen active in 1860, conveys both the variety and the dominating themes of economic life in Kingston before and after the Civil War.[39] Perhaps the most significant and certainly the most striking of the patterns these little histories reveal was the vulnerability of all but the wealthiest men to sudden business failure. The accumulation of wealth was invariably a lengthy process in Kingston, but defeat could, and often did, come in a single stroke, particularly during times of general depression. Jacob S. Joy, for example, was doing a fine business in dry goods and tobacco in 1860, but a steam sawmill that he owned with his brother James ruined him a year later. James, who was a baker, had reported $15,000 in property to the census marshal in 1860, but apparently he went down with his brother. William Golden was an Irishman who had come to Kingston in 1853, had entered the grocery business, and after almost twenty years of "steadily accumulating," fell on hard times in 1872, barely holding onto his business until his final failure in 1881. James Pine was a baker of good habits and steady industry who had built $3,000 into $15,000 between 1856 and 1862 and continued to prosper until 1876, when he was ruined by stock market speculation. Each of these men (and others) had experienced some success before his failure. Others simply never got going. Parr Harlow had been a major force as a young man in Kingston's politics during the nativist controversies of the 1850s, but his Know-Nothing newspaper never brought him more than a small income. He continued to publish it as a Republican paper for some years after the war, but 1875 found him in a "subordinate capacity" on the Brooklyn *Daily Union*. Abram Flaton made no money repairing jewelry in Kingston until 1880; and apparently he would have failed years earlier if it had not been for a millinery store maintained by his wife. In all, eleven of the twenty men either failed, approached failure, or moved out of Kingston in apparent poverty. A twelfth, a successful German grocer named Lawrence Kigner, began to feel the effects of the depression in 1873, but the entry about him concludes without revealing whether he survived or failed. Of the six men whose entries carry into the depression years only one, the wealthy Cornelius Burhans, came through financially intact.

Of the eight entries that terminate without any indication of failure, four end inconclusively. Jonathan Schoonmaker is described only once (the entry claims he was a "front" for his son-in-law, whose business had failed and who had transferred title to Schoonmaker to escape his creditors). John S. Langworthy is described as fairly successful from 1857 to 1864. Two other entries end ominously just before the 1873 depression. Only four men, therefore, were unquestionably successful until the very end. Interestingly, three were quite wealthy and may have inherited a good portion of their wealth. Cornelius Burhans, the son of bank president Jacob S. Burhans, certainly did; the other two, James W. Baldwin and Charles W. Schaffer, were prosperous for at least most of their lives. The only clear example of permanent success from humble beginnings is that of Volney Shades, a carriage maker who stumbled along for some years with little profit, but who managed to leave a net estate of $6,000 and a going business to his sons at his death in 1871, two years before the depression. This is success of a modest order, and there is no telling what would have happened if Shades had survived for a few more years.

This rather dramatic vulnerability of Kingston's entrepreneurs should not obscure the fact that many were at least temporarily successful. At least six of the twenty in our sample improved their economic conditions for at least a portion of their lives, while only five, at most, had no success at all. In short, the records of the Mercantile Agency confirm the notion that Kingston's entrepreneurs experienced considerable changes in fortune over the course of their careers. What is perhaps surprising about the picture that emerges here is that it does not divide men neatly into the successful and the unsuccessful; rather, Kingston's merchants and tradesmen rose and fell, partly in rhythm with the national business cycle and partly in reflection of their own unique circumstances, efforts, and luck. The latter idiosyncratic pattern of success and failure no doubt underscored the need for an explanation by the "expectant capitalists" themselves of why certain men prospered while others did not; and this, of course, once again suggests "enterprise." Do the Mercantile Agency records reveal any association between industry, sagacity, and actual success?

There *is* a fairly close correspondence between the "good habits" and the fortunes of those men whose entries permit comparison. Of course, we must recognize that the function of the Mercantile Agency investigation was to facilitate or impede the granting of life-giving credit, so that the hypothesis we are making here is to some extent self-fulfilling. James Henry, for example, was a tailor of modest means and "questionable habits" who failed in 1863, partly, one supposes, because of his personal characteristics, and partly because this very judgment kept him from getting the credit he needed to survive. Still, there must be some meaning to the fact that those men who failed or simply did not prosper in times of business growth were, with one or two exceptions, the very men who are noted as lacking the personal qualities conforming to the ideology of enterprise. Eugene Best, whose business habits were "bad" and who is identified as a member of the Bumble Bees (the census identifies him as the brother-in-law of Bob Baggs), lasted in the hat business only three years despite good times. Parr Harlow and Abram Flaton, two men who made little money in the best of years, were simply bad businessmen. At the same time, those men whose industriousness and ability were noted in the entries invariably succeeded during years of general business prosperity, even though several were ultimately brought low by the depression. Lawrence Kigner, Samuel Frame, James Pine, Nicholas Matthews, William Golden, and Joseph Tubby were all men of "good habits" who improved at least temporarily on modest means, and wealthy Cornelius Burhans, who was personally and financially "good as wheat" (a compelling recommendation in the Esopus Valley), survived the 1870s without any difficulty at all.

Perhaps the most effective illustration I can provide of the correspondence between enterprise and success among the entrepreneurs of Kingston is the career of Nathaniel Booth. Booth does not appear in the sample, but he has left us a complete record of his thoughts and activities during a critical seven years of his life. As we have seen, he was a talented young man who applied himself assiduously to the business of getting rich and began to see the fruits of his labor by the time he brought his diary to a close in 1854. In 1847, a few months short of his twenty-eighth birthday, he purchased a small grocery store in Wilbur. For several years he supplemented its uncertain income with bookkeeping services for larger firms, and increasing participation in the bluestone trade, and occasional ventures in gunpowder and tanning bark. By 1852 Booth had become cheerful about his prospects and for the first time reported them in detail to his diary: grocery and other retail sales of $12,000, bluestone sales of $50,000 (his operations would involve twenty to twenty-five daily wagonloads and the full services of two sloops), limestone sales of $6,000, and the construction of a new store and two new docks.[40] His projections for 1852 were almost completely correct, and Booth, who had now brought his two brothers into business with him, was launched toward the prosperity he had begun to think would elude him entirely.[41] His diary ends in 1854, but the Mercantile Agency picks up where Nathaniel leaves off. As we would expect, Booth and his brothers are given the highest praise for their industriousness and talent, and the entries about them tell a story of continuing success, right through the difficult times of 1857 and 1858, the Civil War, the postwar period, and the early 1870s. By then Nathaniel Booth was a wealthy man, with a solid reputation based on twenty years of unbroken success, prompt payment of debts, and personal reliability and character. Then, under the date of July 22, 1872, appears the following jolting entry for the firm of Booth & Bros.: "Hard up & our banks hold a large amt of their discounted paper &

it is all going to protest. If our former estimates are nearly
correct ... they will come out OK."[42] Apparently, Nathaniel
himself did survive this crisis, although there are no further entries
for the firm. In April, 1875 he was reported to be worth over
$50,000, and received the usual compliments to his character. But
in 1876 Booth's good fortune came to an end. As a young man
Booth had complained bitterly about indebtedness and longed for a
time when he would be free of notes and mortgages. The older
Booth had forgotten the fears and vows of the younger man,
however, and overextended himself in mortgaged real estate. Late
in 1876 he found himself unable to meet his debts; by the following
July he was bankrupt, the fortune accumulated over a lifetime lost
in one stroke. There is no indication of what Nathaniel Booth did
with himself during the next year, but by June of 1878 he had found
someone to back a new business. It did not succeed. The final entry
under the name of our old friend sweeps him quickly, impatiently,
and poignantly off the stage: "March 8/81 Out of bus."[43]

11   Conclusion:
The Urban Threshold

By the 1850s, the town of Kingston was no longer rural. The people, the streets, the docks, the stores, and even the "rural cemeteries" of its lower portion had transformed both the village and the countryside of the pre-canal town into something that was visibly quite unlike anything that had previously existed in the mid–Hudson Valley. Two villages, both considerably larger and more densely settled than the pre-canal village of Kingston or any other early nineteenth-century settlement between New York and Albany, now pressed together on the north side of Rondout Creek. A modern canal, etched into the southern border of the town, reached more than a hundred miles into the coalfields of Pennsylvania, and a branching plank road climbed into the Catskills to the west and north. Even the seemingly unaltered fields and woods now supported almost as many quarrymen as farmers.

On the other hand, Kingston was as different from the large and medium-sized cities of antebellum America as it was from old Esopus, that "granary of the whole New Netherlands."[1] David Delamater, who smoked his pipe by the door of his farmhouse in Kingston at the turn of the century, would have been astonished at the Kingston of 1860, particularly if he had stirred himself to walk down to the old Van Gaasbeck and Hasbrouck farms at Kingston Landing. But he would not have been completely lost. Kingston village would have appeared much more imposing, but many of its streets and buildings would have reassured him that this was in fact the place in which he had quietly passed his years. More important, at 3 North Front Street he would have found the cabinetmaking shop of Peter Delamater, and at St. James near Kingston Avenue, the home of Tjierck Delamater, blacksmith.

The fact that Kingston in 1860 stood only on the threshold of urban life does not detract from its usefulness for our understanding of the process of urban growth. On the contrary, its experience as a small, emerging city serves to bring into sharper focus questions we may have concerning that process. Is the transition from rural to urban really as cataclysmic as some have made it sound? Does it necessarily involve the fragmentation of a closely knit community, the loss of intimate relationships, and the erosion of the autonomy and self-sufficiency of the community as a whole? Is there any general meaning to the term "urban threshold"? Does it invoke a set of processes, heretofore largely ignored, through which growing rural towns are *generally* transformed into cities? Does it help us understand, for Kenosha as well as for Kingston, the first steps away from rural social organization? Of course, there are limits to the general statements that can be drawn from a single community and from the experiences of a single era. In many respects, Kingston's experiences were probably typical of most emerging cities in nineteenth-century America. In other respects, they may have been atypical, if not unique. Before attempting to place these experiences in the larger context of an urbanizing society, however, we must first consolidate our narrative of antebellum Kingston. How did this town, as a social and cultural system, as a more or less complete human environment, change during the years we have thus far reviewed only in piecemeal fashion? In what ways did it remain the same?

The most dramatic changes experienced by this ancient New York town in the years following the construction of the D & H Canal were in the most tangible elements of local life. Most basically, Kingston grew and in the process began to take on the appearance, the sounds, and even the smells of a small city. The central portions of both villages were now clearly devoted to commerce and finance and were just as clearly set off from the residential neighborhoods that surrounded them. Within these village cores, where land was becoming increasingly precious, barnyards and trees were giving way to new business structures. Few of these were imposing in size or style, but each contributed to the overall impression of congestion and commercial specialization. The streets themselves had also changed, with broad bluestone sidewalks, curbs, and crosswalks, regularly spaced cisterns, streetlamps lighted with gas, and more than enough traffic to justify all these improvements. In Rondout, the port of the new little city, the scene, the noise, and the smells were probably as hectic and noxious as any comparably sized dockside portion of New York City.

But the visible changes in post-canal Kingston were not restricted to townscape and traffic. The population had visibly changed in association with even more tangible changes in the economy. At the turn of the century, the working class of the village and town consisted of slaves, hired hands, and journeymen, nearly all of whom lived in the households of their masters. By midcentury the canal company, the quarries, the cement companies, and the general increase in trade changed this structure dramatically. As the freedmen disappeared they were more than replaced by men who were physically almost as distinguishable from the white middle class. These new men lived in their own households and in their own neighborhoods, and they generally worked in large gangs for companies not even owned by local citizens. Most of them, moreover, were Catholics and foreigners who spoke English in strange accents when they spoke it at all, and who seemed to outdo the natives in both drinking and fighting. For the first time, in short, Kingston contained a large proletariat that threatened the peace and the moral order of the community, and that worked and lived beyond the reach of old vehicles for social control.[2] Whether the actual behavior of these new proletarians (and of others in the community who responded to their presence) was visibly different from the behavior of those who had lived and worked in the pre-canal town is another question. We do not really know, after all, how much drunkenness and violence there were in Kingston before the Irish came to work the coal docks and the quarries. We can only restate the common prejudice that Kingston became more disorderly as its population grew and changed in composition— and perhaps wonder if there are not a few missing links between the Committees of Safety and the Bumble Bees.

David Delamater would have required only one round trip on Joseph F. Davis's omnibus to see most of these changes. A somewhat longer stay would have revealed the dramatic development of Kingston's institutions. The board of directors of the village of Kingston and the board of trustees of the new village of Rondout now met on a weekly basis throughout the year and dealt with a great many things besides the disposition of the village hayscales. Local political parties, which once paid no attention whatsoever to village affairs, now mobilized their complicated machinery in an annual spring campaign for local offices. Voluntary and semivoluntary organizations devoted to public service, refinement, and leisure now flourished where before they had languished. More than a dozen fire companies fought fires, paraded through the village, sponsored formal balls, organized excursions to other towns, and played host, on behalf of the village, to the companies of other villages from all over the Hudson Valley. Militia fever had spread through Kingston, creating at least seven militia companies that seemingly never rested from dinners, balls, soirées, excursions, parades, musters, target practice, and receptions of colors. Both villages (how strange that phrase would have sounded to David Delamater) could boast of active literary societies, debating societies, libraries, brass bands, and even baseball clubs. Temperance and Bible societies still flourished, and there were several Masonic and Odd Fellows' lodges. Rondout contained a Y.M.C.A., and there were music societies without number. There were other local organizations, too, and on top of them we must pile a succession of citizens' meetings called to protest, celebrate, mourn, or promote just about anything. The one casualty of Kingston's urban development, the Kingston and Hurley Horse Thief Association, which by 1859 seems to have lost its purpose, may be safely considered the exception that proves the rule.

One effect of this greatly expanded organizational structure (we should add here certain commercial operations, such as traveling circuses, concerts, and steamboat excursions) was the creation of a new village calendar. Local life now had an organized dimension that maintained itself throughout the year. There were still seasons, of course, and the economic life of Kingston was as firmly controlled by the ice in the river as the farmer's life was controlled by the snow on his land. Organized social life, however, merely altered in form to fit the season. The winter brought an endless succession of balls, dinners, and lesser parties, and an equally relentless schedule of lectures, concerts, and debates. The opening of the canal in March or April signaled the end of the "gay season" and a return to longer, harder days at work, but it did not close off organized social life. The spring political campaign absorbed various amounts of energy from various groups, the fire and militia companies simply changed gear in preparation for an endless succession of parades and excursions, and various other groups and activities came to life. Balls and lectures gave way to picnics, steamboat excursions, traveling circuses, and the annual celebration of the Fourth of July. When we add all these activities together, no season stands out as the "social season" in antebellum Kingston.

More accurately, all do, for any month of the calendar year now brought more Kingstonians together in group activity than had the entire year in pre-canal days.

These were at once the most visible and the most dramatic changes that had accompanied urban growth. There were others, of course, that happen to have been both harder to perceive and of a lower order of magnitude. For example, it would have been difficult to discern and to analyze, even after a fairly long visit to the community, the various relationships that Kingston and Kingstonians maintained with the outside world. The resurrected David Delamater would have been quite struck with the telegraph, we may suppose, and with the fact that one could now travel to New York City in a few hours on almost any day of the week, in any season.[3] But what would he have made of such names as the Delaware and Hudson Canal Company or the Newark Lime and Cement Company? Would he have judged the relationships of the local Whig and Democratic parties to Albany and Washington to be different from the state and national connections of the Federalist and Republican factions of his own day? Would he have seen Kingston, as a whole, as having more or less control over its "own" affairs? Obviously, this would have required some study on his part—more, no doubt, than this quiet, pipe-smoking old Dutchman would have actually undertaken. Moreover, he would have had little patience with an answer that would have gone both ways at once; for, in fact, Kingston was both more and less autonomous and self-contained than it had been at the turn of the nineteenth century.

Kingston's growth and most of the changes that attended it were stimulated, if not caused, by the decision of the board of directors of the newly formed Delaware and Hudson Canal Company to run their canal into Rondout Creek and to locate their coal dock on the old Van Gaasbeck farm at Kingston Landing. No Kingstonians took part in that decision or, unless surviving commentary deceives us, had any influence at all on it. In this sense, the history we have traced in this book is one of community impotence in the face of the combined will of a regional corporation and two state legislatures. Kingstonians could not have prevented the construction of the canal, nor could they have influenced its route; they could therefore not have prevented the growth of Rondout, the settlement there of large numbers of Irish and German immigrants, or any of the other phenomena that can be attributed, directly or indirectly, to the D & H. Kingstonians had little or no influence over the operation of the canal company—the dates of the annual opening and closing of the canal, freight charges and policy, dock construction, or the potentially dangerous question of whether dock workers would receive 87½¢ or $1 per day. Even the question of *whether* the canal would open in the spring was outside local hands, and though the suggestion that the company might abandon or even reduce operations on its valuable canal would have been ridiculed in antebellum Kingston, there was nothing ridiculous about this threat after the war, when the D & H turned increasingly to railroads.[4] But it would be entirely mistaken to see Kingston as a company town (or, considering the Newark Lime and Cement Company, a two-company town), and it would be quite misleading if we focused only on the ways in which the presence of the company reduced local autonomy. Perhaps surprisingly, the company was not a manifest political presence in Kingston. Despite the nearly continual, extremely vigorous, and increasingly localized contest between local parties, the D & H only once became the target of political attack, and even then it was by a contrivance that had little to do with the company itself. Had the company actually tried to participate in local politics, we may be certain that it would have received far more credit in the newspapers of its opponents. Of course, it is important to recognize that the Delaware and Hudson Canal Company had no particular interest in the affairs of Kingston and Rondout and, therefore, made little or no effort to control their politics, economy, or social development. All it required from the town was a hands-off policy (of which there was no question) and enough space for an office and a dock. Its labor force was imported rather than recruited locally, and, unlike many corporations of the twentieth century, it felt no need to "serve" the community by having its executives take over the local school board. Nor was Kingston a market of any significance to the D & H. In short, the company threatened the autonomy of the community only in the sense that it was a significant dimension of Kingston's incorporation into the emerging national transportation network.

It is quite easy, moreover, to overstate the degree to which the canal, the steamboats, and the plank roads brought Kingston closer to the rest of the world. Kingston was never an isolated community, and in several important senses it was far from autonomous before it was conscripted into the transportation revolution.

Almost from its inception it derived its living from commercial agriculture and the shipment of forest products. Its undeveloped retailing sector meant not merely that most things were made in the home but also that many local residents traveled regularly (but not necessarily frequently) to New York City to shop. Politically, Kingston was anything but self-enclosed. Its earliest local governments were, in the Dutch colonial tradition, mere local agencies of the provincial governor, and later ones established by the State of New York were as inactive as they were theoretically self-sufficient.[5] Parties, meanwhile, focused political energies on the government at Albany, and their newspapers brought Esopus news of a much wider world. Some Kingstonians left town to attend college, where they established relationships with young gentlemen from other towns. Many of these relationships would endure and would constitute what I have called a "regional elite community." The town's earliest church had followed a varying course, but during most of its history it had been integrated into the synodical structure of the Dutch Reformed Church, while other, more specialized groups—the county medical society, the agricultural society, the militia—reached upward in similar fashion to larger, external organizations. Many of these links to the outside world were strengthened in the decades following the construction of the canal, and some may have reduced the autonomy of the town and the parochialism of its citizens. But the transportation revolution did not initiate contact between Kingston and an unfamiliar world and did not bring about the disintegration of a previously self-sufficient community. Indeed, the growth that followed the construction of the canal, and the institutional development that accompanied that growth, served to strengthen the community where it had been weakest and helped turn the attention of cosmopolitan minds inward on the town. To the latter, in particular, I will return in a few moments.

Perhaps as difficult to discern by the casual visitor to antebellum Kingston were certain changes in the structure of family life. In the early years of the nineteenth century, Kingstonians lived in fairly large households, more than a third of which contained from one to ten slaves.[6] For every woman in the town of childbearing age (16–44) there were 1.5 children below the age of ten.[7] And in most households, even in the village, domestic life was combined with both commerce and the daily chores of the barn and barnyard. By the 1850s, domestic arrangements had come to resemble those more commonly associated with the present century. The slaves, of course, had disappeared from households headed by whites, although in some cases they were partly "replaced" by one or two domestic servants, usually young Irish girls. Where before there had been 1.5 children below the age of ten for every woman of childbearing age, there was now only one. And, seemingly commensurate with the shrinkage and simplification of the typical household, commerce was more frequently removed from the home; the barns of the pre-canal village began to disappear from residential neighborhoods as well as from the commercial core. It is true that husbands walked but a few blocks to work each day, and that the "modernization" of the household was as characteristic of commercial farms as it was of compact villages in the maturing Hudson Valley. However, this does not alter the fact that domestic arrangements in Kingston had changed, quietly but significantly, and constituted one dimension of both the town's and the valley's economic and social development.[8]

The least volatile elements of community life appear to have been precisely those that are most difficult to document—the informal interactions of family members, neighbors, storekeepers, and customers, and the basic values which constituted their local culture. We should not be surprised at this, not only because these phenomena are generally more resistant to change than such things as village charters and merchandising practices, but also because local observers shared the historian's inclination to comment on those things that changed and to disregard those that did not. On the other hand, the values and face-to-face relationships of antebellum Kingston are not entirely beyond our view, and we probably have seen enough of them in preceding chapters to be relatively assured of their essential continuity between the early nineteenth century and the Civil War. The diary of Nathaniel Booth is not terribly different in these respects from the diary of Henry Vanderlyn, which describes people and events of a half-century earlier, and there is a similar continuity between the *Ulster Sentinel* of the 1820s and the Rondout *Courier* of the 1850s. The *Sentinel* does contain hints of an older, less aggressive culture of Dutch bottomland farmers, and it is possible that we would be more impressed with cultural change in Kingston if we could push our inquiry back a generation or two. Other clues, however,

suggest the opposite—that Kingston was an individualistic, entrepreneurial community from its inception, and that however much
it may have changed in other respects, these elements of its system
of values were present in significant degree throughout its history.
In short, if Kingston was, as one correspondent at the turn of the
century had claimed, "a parcel of old Dutchmen, here before only
remarcable [sic] for doing nothing,"[9] it was not for lack of trying.

Whatever the truth of the matter may have been for Wiltwyck
and colonial Kingston, the early nineteenth-century town appears
to have been quite similar, culturally, to the little city that was
emerging in the 1850s. Indeed, the most significant apparent
difference between the two consisted of the greater sense of
community identity and common purpose, and the greater importance attached to the abstract ideal of "community," not in the
country town but in the emerging city, at least among its middle
classes. The growth of Kingston undoubtedly reduced the proportion of townsmen each resident could personally know. The
development of numerous different churches, fire companies, and
other local organizations separated people who *might* have come
together in a single church or company or lodge if the town had
remained small. But it is by no means certain that townwide
acquaintance will be automatically translated into "community,"
or that local residents *will* come together in one lodge or one church
or one town meeting simply because there are no other organizations. With the possible exception of attending church, the alterna-
tive of simply staying home does seem to have been rather widely
exercised in pre-canal Kingston. More important, the fact that most
Kingstonians knew most other Kingstonians does not seem to have
impressed them with a sense that the town was an important
organization to which they all belonged.

The growth of the town, I have argued in several places,
increased this feeling of belonging among significant numbers of
Kingstonians. Far more of them joined in organized activities of the
sort that emphasized and reinforced their membership in the town
itself. Larger numbers participated financially and emotionally in
Kingston's economic battles with Newburgh, Saugerties, and Catskill. And virtually everyone found himself surrounded by evidence of Kingston's success—a phenomenon of no small significance in a society that placed achievement, particularly practical,
tangible achievement, in the front rank of social values. Kingston,

in short, was now large enough, important enough, and supportive enough of collective action to confer a sense of local citizenship on its residents, and it does appear that many began to regard the town more consciously, more seriously, and more often. And if there were newcomers in the local population with whom older residents could feel no sense of community, this served only to increase, by "negative reference," the solidarity of the native-born, Protestant middle class. The point, of course, should not be overstated. Kingstonians signed no sacred covenants of collective responsibility and sacrificed few, if any, personal prerogatives or opportunities on behalf of the town. That is, the growing sense of "community," and of membership in *this* community, did not mitigate the basic individualism of local citizens. The significance of its development derives more from its direction than from its depth, for a heightened awareness of community membership is perhaps the very opposite of what we might have expected to find in this growing, urbanizing town, particularly if common assumptions about the nature of urbanization had been our guide.

Was Kingston, then, an aberration, a place where urban growth produced effects quite unlike and even opposite to those produced in other emerging cities? Most of the specific elements of change in urbanizing Kingston were typical—increasing ethnic diversity and economic inequality, declining fertility, new transportation facilities, banks and other economic institutions, mass-based political parties and popular movements such as temperance and nativism, new social institutions and activities, patent medicines, daguerrotypes, and dry goods sold for cash. These were occurring and appearing all over nineteenth-century America, particularly in the Northeast and the urbanizing Midwest, and most particularly in the nation's cities. In the details of urban growth and social change, therefore, Kingston's history was certainly well within the American mainstream. It is more difficult to determine, however, whether the overall effect of these changes on the community was the same in other places as it was in Kingston. Indeed, the individualism of Dutch-American culture, and the confinement of this culture to New Jersey and eastern New York, suggests the possibility that one of our central observations—that Kingston grew toward "community"—may be of the least general significance. But individualism was hardly peculiar to the New York and New Jersey Dutch. It was, of course, a central value in most regions of early nineteenth-century America and was expressed, from New York to Kentucky, in part by the relative autonomy of the individual household.[10] Thus, the creation of a nationally integrated economy and society (via railroads, corporations, the telegraph, *Harper's*, and all the other institutions and agencies of nonlocal social organization) did not *simply* create a national consciousness among Americans. By vitalizing secondary urban centers, it also created a countercurrent of parochial, community-based action and identity. Perhaps on Yankee soil, as Michael H. Frisch has recently suggested, this simply altered a strong, preexisting sense of local community.[11] But on Yorker soil, and no doubt in other regions outside communal New England, the effect seems to have been more creative: urban growth and regional integration strengthened communal sentiments and processes that earlier had been only weakly developed. Perhaps this was true only where towns stood at the urban threshold in space and time. It remains to be proved that in larger cities, and in a later era, continued growth and more highly developed nonlocal communications and trade truly destroyed the sense and reality of local community in America.

Appendix A

Rank Order of American Cities and Towns
Containing 10,000 or More Inhabitants, 1860

Rank	City	Population
1	New York, N.Y.	805,658
2	Philadelphia, Pa.	565,529
3	Brooklyn, N.Y.	266,661
4	Baltimore, Md.	212,418
5	Boston, Mass.	177,840
6	New Orleans, La.	168,675
7	Cincinnati, Ohio	161,044
8	St. Louis, Mo.	160,773
9	Chicago, Ill.	109,260
10	Buffalo, N.Y.	81,129
11	Newark, N.J.	71,941
12	Louisville, Ky.	68,033
13	Albany, N.Y.	62,367
14	Washington, D.C.	61,122
15	San Francisco, Calif.	56,802
16	Providence, R.I.	50,666
17	Pittsburgh, Pa.	49,217
18	Rochester, N.Y.	48,204
19	Detroit, Mich.	45,619
20	Milwaukee, Wisc.	45,246
21	Cleveland, Ohio	43,417
22	Charleston, S.C.	40,522
23	New Haven, Conn.	39,267
24	Troy, N.Y.	39,235

Rank	City	Population
25	Richmond, Va.	37,910
26	Lowell, Mass.	36,827
27	Mobile, Ala.	29,258
28	Jersey City, N.J.	29,226
29	Hartford, Conn.	29,152
30	Allegheny, Pa.	28,702
31	Syracuse, N.Y.	28,119
32	Portland, Maine	26,341
33	Cambridge, Mass.	26,060
34	Roxbury, Mass.	25,137
35	Charlestown, Mass.	25,065
36	Worcester, Mass.	24,960
37	Reading, Pa.	23,162
38	Memphis, Tenn.	22,623
39	Utica, N.Y.	22,529
40	New Bedford, Mass.	22,300
41	Savannah, Ga.	22,292
42	Salem, Mass.	22,252
43	Wilmington, Del.	21,258
44	Manchester, N.H.	20,107
45	Dayton, Ohio	20,081
46	Paterson, N.J.	19,586
47	Lynn, Mass.	19,083
48	Indianapolis, Ind.	18,611
49	Columbus, Ohio	18,554
50	Petersburg, Va.	18,266
51	Lawrence, Mass.	17,639
52	Lancaster, Pa.	17,603
53	Trenton, N.J.	17,228
54	Nashville, Tenn.	16,988
55	Oswego, N.Y.	16,816
56	*Kingston, N.Y.*	16,640
57	Covington, Ky.	16,471
58	Bangor, Maine	16,407
59	Taunton, Mass.	15,376
60	Springfield, Mass.	15,199

Rank	City	Population
61	Newburgh, N.Y.	15,196
62	Poughkeepsie, N.Y.	14,726
63	Norfolk, Va.	14,620
64	Camden, N.J.	14,358
65	Norwich, Conn.	14,048
66	Peoria, Ill.	14,045
67	Fall River, Mass.	14,026
68	Mill Creek, Ohio	13,844
69	Sacramento, Calif.	13,785
70	Toledo, Ohio	13,768
71	Newtown, N.Y.	13,725
72	Quincy, Ill.	13,718
73	Lockport, N.Y.	13,523
74	Harrisburg, Pa.	13,405
75	Newburyport, Mass.	13,401
76	Chelsea, Mass.	13,395
77	Bridgeport, Conn.	13,299
78	Smithfield, R.I.	13,283
79	Dubuque, Iowa	13,000
80	Alexandria, Va.	12,654
81	New Albany, Ind.	12,647
82	Augusta, Ga.	12,493
83	Hempstead, N.Y.	12,376
84	Yonkers, N.Y.	11,848
85	North Providence, R.I.	11,818
86	Elizabeth, N.J.	11,567
87.5	Evansville, Ind.	11,484
87.5	Donaldsonville, La.	11,484
89	Davenport, Iowa	11,267
90	New Brunswick, N.J.	11,256
91	Auburn, N.Y.	10,986
92	Gloucester, Mass.	10,904
93	Concord, N.H.	10,896
94	Newport, R.I.	10,508
95	St. Paul, Minn.	10,401
96	Wayne, Ind.	10,388

Rank	City	Population
97	St. Landry, La.	10,346
98	Flushing, N.Y.	10,188
99	New London, Conn.	10,115
100	Cortland, N.Y.	10,074
101	Nashua, N.H.	10,065
102	Newport, Ky.	10,046
103	Waterbury, Conn.	10,004

SOURCE: *Population of the United States in 1860; Compiled from the Original Returns of the Eighth Census* ... (Washington, 1864). [Table No. 3, "Population of Cities, Towns, and Other Subdivisions"]

Appendix B

Patterns of Participation: Data and Methods

The tabulations and discussion contained in chapter 9, "Patterns of Participation," comprise the end product of a relatively complex research exercise, much of which was excluded from the chapter in order to simplify the presentation. Although the general reader may have little interest in a more extended methodological discussion, the specialist in social research may consider certain important questions unanswered. What are the two-way relationships between each of the independent variables—occupational level, personal wealth, place of birth, and length of local residence—and the dependent variable, organized social participation? How effectively are the patterns of these two-way cross-tabulations expressed by the categories of the multidimensional tables of chapter 9? What statistical procedures guided the analysis of these latter tables, and how do their quantitative results relate to the verbal descriptions that are the culmination of the chapter? This appendix will answer these questions.

Tables B.1 through B.5 present the cross-tabulations of participation scores with five different variables, including one (age) that was not incorporated into the multidimensional tables of chapter 9. Table B.1 reveals a sharp distinction between the participation scores of the "high," "middle," and "low" occupational groups. Only about 4% of those men working in semiskilled and unskilled jobs in 1855 were located as community participants during the decade, and almost all of these received scores of 1 and 2. Clerks and craftsmen exhibit a higher level of participation (about 22%) and a heavier weighting of active participants. Low-level participants are still numerically dominant, but over 7% of this middle category were active participants and leaders, twenty-seven of whom received participation scores of 4 and 5. Finally, no less than 40% of Kingston's professionals, merchants, manufacturers, and

Table B.1 Occupational Level by Participation Score, 1855

Occupational Level	Participation Score						Total	N
	0	1	2	3	4	5		
High	60.4%	1.4	12.2	13.2	10.2	2.5	99.9%	637
Middle	78.4	0.7	13.5	5.2	1.8	0.3	99.9	1,255
Low	95.8	0.3	3.2	0.6	0.2	—	100.1	1,743
Others	88.4	0.6	7.0	2.5	1.4	0.1	100.0	713
Total	84.4%	0.6	8.1	4.1	2.3	0.5	100.0%	
N	3,668	28	353	177	101	21		4,348

farmers were located as participants, and most of these (over 25% of the total category) were quite active in the community. The overall participation rate of these men was about ten times higher than that of the unskilled and semiskilled workers and was almost double that of the clerks and craftsmen. More importantly, they dominated the highest levels of participation by supplying about 65% of the men scoring 4 and 76% (16 of 21) of the men scoring 5, despite the fact that they constituted less than 15% of the total adult male population.

An even more dramatic indication of the relationship between socioeconomic status and social participation is obtained by substituting the property listings of the 1860 census for the broad occupational categories of table B.1. As table B.2 indicates, the wealthiest men of Kingston participated as a rule, rather than as an exception, in local organizational life and were found more often in positions of leadership than in more casual types of participation. Only one-third of the men reporting more than $25,000 in total property failed to participate in local organizations, while some 43% were scored as community leaders. At the other extreme, 92% of those reporting $100 or less did not participate, and most of the remainder participated at low levels. There were ten community leaders (all 4's) among this poorest group, but these may well reflect a weakness in the census data (occasional omissions of property entries) rather than real conditions. Between the two extremes there is a regular and dramatic progression, with the members of each property category participating more frequently and at higher levels as the value of the category increases. Men reporting between $1,000 and $3,000, for example, advance significantly, at each level of participation, over men reporting between $500 and $1,000. Those reporting between $3,000 and $5,000 add a noticeable degree of leadership to an increase in participation at lower scores. Men worth between $5,000 and $10,000, an impressive level of wealth, were almost evenly divided between participants and nonparticipants, and the former were significantly more active than were participants at lower levels of wealth. Above the level of $10,000 community leadership was characteristic rather than exceptional. Given this regular progression, it is apparent that any simplification of the property variable for multivariate analysis should approximate as closely as possible the continuum that table B.2 reveals. It is for this reason that the tables in chapter 9 employ six categories of personal wealth.

Table B.2   Total Property by Participation Score: Heads of Household, 1860

Total Property	Participation Score						Total	N
	0	1	2	3	4	5		
$25,001 and over	33.3%	—	4.8	19.0	33.3	9.5	99.9%	42
$10,001–25,000	38.2	1.3	11.8	14.5	26.3	7.9	100.0	76
$5,001–10,000	51.5	1.8	11.7	21.6	9.4	4.1	100.1	171
$3,001–5,000	58.0	1.5	21.7	7.2	10.1	1.5	100.0	138
$1,001–3,000	77.3	1.0	11.8	7.2	2.3	0.3	99.9	389
$501–1,000	83.3	0.3	6.4	3.7	1.3	—	100.0	297
$101–500	89.7	1.0	5.4	3.5	0.2	0.2	100.0	516
$0–100	91.9	0.4	4.9	2.1	0.7	—	100.0	1,414
Total	83.4%	0.7	7.3	5.0	2.9	0.7	100.0%	3,043
N	2,537	21	223	153	88	21		

In contrast, table B.3 reveals only one sharp break—between native Americans and English (including Scottish) immigrants, on the one hand, and Irish, German, other European, and Canadian immigrants, on the other. Consequently, it seems most reasonable to transform "place of birth" into a dichotomous variable, with one category representing native Americans, Englishmen, and Scots and another representing all other immigrants.

The cross-tabulation of participation with years of local residence, in table B.4, reveals no significant differences in participation among residents of fewer than five years but a rising progression of participation frequencies and levels among groups of increasing tenure. No doubt, local tenure could have been represented in chapter 9 with a large number of categories. However, since the differences among these categories would not be as pronounced as those among other variables, and since the critical distinction here seems to be between an initial period of virtual nonparticipation and a subsequent period of gradually increasing participation, the decision was made to dichotomize this variable. In chapter 9 one category represents the initial period of five years, and the other represents six years or more of local residence.

Finally, there is one variable on the state and federal censuses that does not bear significantly on social participation. This variable is "age," as defined in terms of traditional ten-year cohorts. Perhaps surprisingly, as table B.5 shows, the proportions of overall participation increase only slightly as we move from younger to older cohorts. Leadership and frequent activity do seem somewhat more characteristic of middle-aged and older men, and lower-level participation does seem more characteristic of younger men, but the differences are not nearly as dramatic as those in previous tables. It may be safely concluded that the incorporation of age differences would have added little or nothing to the multivariate analysis of social participation in chapter 9.

And what of the statistical measures that underlie this multivariate analysis? Locating an appropriate statistic is less easy than it might seem, since the most common measures of the relationships between cross-classified variables—chi square and its derivative measures of association—are not readily applicable to multidimensional tables such as those in chapter 9. Nor are such specifically multivariate measures as multiple regression and partial correlation, for these require that all of the variables be interval in scale, a

Table B.3 Place of Birth by Participation Score

Place of birth	Participation Score						Total	N
	0	1	2	3	4	5		
Ulster County	73.5%	0.9	12.8	7.7	4.2	0.8	99.9%	1,308
Other New York	72.2	1.2	12.4	7.3	5.8	1.1	100.0	564
Other U.S.	67.2	1.5	15.3	9.5	4.4	2.2	100.1	137
England, Scotland	76.3	2.1	15.5	3.1	3.1	—	100.1	97
Ireland	96.1	0.3	2.7	0.7	0.1	—	99.9	1,483
Germany	93.4	—	5.3	1.0	0.3	—	100.0	694
Other	94.2	—	1.9	1.9	—	1.9	99.9	52
Total	84.3%	0.6	8.1	4.1	2.3	0.5	99.9%	4,335
N	3,656	28	352	177	101	21		

Table B.4   Years of Residence in Kingston in 1855 by Participation Score

Years of residence	Participation Score							
	0	1	2	3	4	5	Total	N
Less than 1	94.2%	—	4.6	0.4	0.8	—	100.0%	260
1	93.0	0.3	5.2	1.0	0.5	—	100.0	383
2	87.9	0.3	8.4	1.7	1.4	0.3	100.0	356
3	93.3	0.5	5.2	1.0	—	—	100.0	420
4	92.2	0.6	4.1	2.2	0.6	0.3	100.0	319
5	90.1	0.3	5.8	3.2	0.6	—	100.0	313
6–10	84.3	0.4	7.9	4.1	2.6	0.8	100.1	775
11–20	75.8	1.1	14.7	4.9	2.6	0.8	99.9	611
21 +	71.2	1.4	10.2	10.1	6.0	1.1	100.0	761
Total	84.3%	0.7	8.2	4.0	2.3	0.5	100.0%	
N	3,540	28	344	170	95	21		4,198

Table B.5   Age at 1855 by Participation Score

| | | | | Participation Score | | | | | |
Age	0	1	2	3	4	5	Total	N
16–19	86.6%	0.6	12.3	0.6	—	—	100.1%	506
20–29	86.5	0.5	9.2	2.5	1.1	0.1	99.9	1,480
30–39	84.4	0.3	7.2	4.2	3.0	0.9	100.0	1,196
40–49	79.6	1.0	6.6	7.3	4.7	0.8	100.0	661
50–59	82.4	1.0	4.8	8.0	3.2	0.6	100.0	312
60–69	81.7	0.8	4.0	7.1	5.6	0.8	100.0	126
70 +	81.5	3.1	7.7	7.7	—	—	100.0	65
Total	84.4%	0.6	8.1	4.1	2.3	0.5	100.0%	4,346
N	3,666	28	353	177	101	21		

condition that is not met by most of our variables. Even the multi-way analysis of variance, which does permit ordinal and nominal scales within the independent variables, requires an interval-scale dependent variable; and our participation scores, though expressed as equal-interval numbers, in reality form only an ordinal scale. Thus, there exists a real problem as to the selection of appropriate statistical procedures for the analysis of the present data.

In recent years, a small number of statisticians have turned their attention to this problem, and one result of their labors is log-linear modeling, an imposing term referring to an even more imposing set of mathematics. There is no need (nor have I the ability) to discuss log-linear modeling and its underlying mathematics in any detail. For an extremely thorough discussion the reader may wish to turn to Yvonne M. M. Bishop, Stephen E. Fienberg, and Paul W. Holland, *Discrete Multivariate Analysis: Theory and Practice* (Cambridge, Mass., 1975) and to various articles by Leo A. Goodman, most notably "The Multivariate Analysis of Qualitative Data: Interactions among Multiple Classifications," *Journal of the American Statistical Association* 65 (1970): 226–56. Here we need indicate only the more important properties of the measure. Log-linear models (in the present instance at least) are various hypotheses of the independence of variables, sensitive to the n-factor interactions present in n-dimensional tables (that is, to the fact that the relationship between two variables may be different at different levels of a third, controlling, variable). These hypotheses of independence are expressed as log-likelihood ratios (G^2), which in turn are based on maximum-likelihood estimates for the various cells. Each independence hypothesis, or model, is evaluated in terms of "goodness of fit" by comparing G^2 to the appropriate degrees of freedom (which are greater in more complex tables). A good fit is obtained when G^2 is about the same as the degrees of freedom, or slightly lower; when this occurs, the hypothesis of the independence of variables is not rejected.

Table B.6 presents log-likelihood ratios for a number of models, each expressing the independence of variables in a different way. Each model, moreover, is applied to three somewhat different versions of the data file in which participants are linked to the state census of 1855: (1) nonparticipants and participants, with scores ranging from 0 through 5; (2) a dichotomized version of the above,

Table B.6 Log-linear Models Relating to Participation File as Linked to the New York State Census of 1855

Description of Models:	All Participation Scores (0 through 5)		Incidence of Participation (0; 1–5)		Level of Participation (1 through 5)	
	Degrees of Freedom	Log-likelihood Ratio (G^2)	Degrees of Freedom	Log-likelihood Ratio (G^2)	Degrees of Freedom	Log-likelihood Ratio (G^2)
Independence of all variables	133	2,877	63	2,685	98	387
Independence of participation:						
From occupation, birthplace and years of residence	105	902	35	710	70	192
From occupation and birthplace, controlling for years of residence	96	665	32	507	64	158
From occupation and years of residence, controlling for birthplace	99	472	33	313	66	159
From birthplace and years of residence, controlling for occupation	99	368	33	263	66	105
From occupation, controlling for birthplace and years of residence	78	340	30	230	48	110
From birthplace, controlling for occupation and years of residence	72	203	24	146	48	58
From years of residence, controlling for occupation and birthplace	81	165	29	90	58	75

dividing the entire data file into nonparticipants and undifferentiated participants; and (3) the participants only, with scores ranging from 1 through 5. Consider first the log-linear models as applied to the first variation of the data file, found in the first two columns of table B.6. The first model hypothesizes the complete independence of all variables, that is, the absence of any statistically significant relationships among any of the dependent or independent variables. The G^2 of 2,877, compared to the degrees of freedom, 133, is obviously a very poor fit. There are indeed relationships among at least some, and probably all, of the variables.

The remainder of the models hypothesize the independence of one variable—participation—from all, each, and various combinations of the other variables. The second model hypothesizes the independence of participation from the separate and combined effects of all three of the other variables. It, too, is a very poor fit, although G^2 is quite a bit lower because of the narrower focus of the model. Obviously, participation is associated in some way with the independent variables. The remaining six models reveal this association more precisely. The next three hypothesize the independence of participation from each combination of two independent variables, controlling for the third. As these are equivalent models, we may order them in terms of relative goodness of fit. The poorest fit occurs when occupation is combined with birthplace (in terms of their combined independence from participation); the second poorest occurs when occupation is combined with years of residence; and the best (but still poor) fit is obtained when years of residence is combined with birthplace. This suggests that the three independent variables—occupation, birthplace, and years of residence—are associated with participation in descending order of significance. This is corroborated by the final three models, which hypothesize the independence of participation from each of the independent variables while controlling for the other two. Occupation provides the poorest fit by a wide margin. Birthplace follows, but is not dramatically different from years of residence, which in turn is still far from providing a good fit with the independence hypothesis. All three of the variables are significant in their relationships with participation, and I have tried to reflect the above *pattern* of these relationships in my discussion of the tables presented in chapter 9.

The final columns of table B.6 show the results of applying the same models to the other variations of the data file. This was done to test the idea that the above relationships might vary when we refer, on the one hand, to the incidence or nonincidence of participation, and, on the other hand, to the levels of participation among participants alone. The results are, in fact, much the same as those in the first pair of columns, with the exception that in the "level of participation" file the final two models (hypothesizing the independence of levels of participation from birthplace and years of residence, respectively) come fairly close to a good fit. Even here, though, the fit is not good enough to confirm the independence hypothesis; and in the model which hypothesizes the independence of participation from the separate and combined effects of birthplace and residence the fit is not good at all. We may conclude that in all three variations of the data file the pattern of association between participation and the three independent variables is much the same.

One of the difficulties presented to the nonstatistician by log-linear modeling is the interpretation of its results in terms of the traditional concept of strength of association, usually expressed as a coefficient of correlation ranging between 0 and ± 1. The log-linear models express only the relative goodness of fit of various hypotheses. But if this method lacks the comforting simplicity of a coefficient of correlation, it also provides an insight into the complex relationships present in a multidimensional table. In the present instance, it has served as an excellent guide to the extended verbal analysis of the complex tables in chapter 9.

Notes

Chapter 1

1. During each of these four decades the increase in the urban population exceeded 60%, and in 1840–50 reached 93%. The only subsequent decades to approach antebellum levels were 1860–70 and 1880–90. See *The Statistical History of the United States from the Colonial Times to the Present* (Stamford, Conn., 1965), p. 14; George Rogers Taylor, "American Urban Growth Preceding the Railway Age," *Journal of Economic History* 27 (1967): 309–39.

2. Blake McKelvey, *American Urbanization: A Comparative History* (Glenview, Ill., and Brighton, England, 1973), p. 37.

3. *Statistical History*, p. 14.

4. Ibid.; U.S. Census Office, *Population of the United States in 1860; Compiled from the Original Returns of the Eighth Census* . . . (Washington, D.C., 1864), table 3, "Population of Cities, Towns, and Other Subdivisions." There is a significant disparity between these two sources. The *Statistical History* indicates only fifty-eight towns in the 10,000–25,000 range, while an actual count of the towns listed on the *Eighth Census* yields sixty-eight. See appendix A, below, for a list of American towns larger than 10,000 in 1860.

5. Marius Schoonmaker, *The History of Kingston, New York* . . . (New York, 1888). This is by far the best history of Kingston, even though it carries its story only to 1820. Other local histories are Nathaniel Bartlett Sylvester, *History of Ulster County, New York* . . . , 2 vols. (Philadelphia, 1880); Alphonso T. Clearwater, *The History of Ulster County, New York* (Kingston, N.Y., 1907); William C. DeWitt, *People's History of Kingston, Rondout and Vicinity* (New Haven, Conn., 1943); Andrew S. Hickey, *The Story of Kingston* (New York, 1952).

6. George Rogers Taylor, *The Transportation Revolution: 1815–1860* (New York, 1951).

7. A classic discussion of American political party development in this period is M. Ostrogorski, *Democracy and the Party System in the United States: A Study in Extra-Constitutional Government* (New York, 1910), esp. pp. 16–35. A more recent and thorough discussion is Richard P. McCormick, *The Second American Party System: Party Formation in the Jacksonian Era* (Chapel Hill, N.C., 1966).

8. William G. McLoughlin, Jr., *Modern Revivalism: Charles Grandison Finney to Billy Graham* (New York, 1959). See also Bernard A. Weisberger, *They Gathered at the River: The Story of the Great Revivalists and Their Impact upon Religion in America* (Boston, 1958); and Whitney R. Cross, *The Burned-over District: The Social and Intellectual History of Enthusiastic Religion in Western New York, 1800–1850* (Ithaca, N.Y., 1950).

9. See Cross, *Burned-over District;* Alice Felt Tyler, *Freedom's Ferment: Phases of American Social History from the Colonial Period to the Outbreak of the Civil War* (Minneapolis, 1944); and a host of works focusing on specific reform movements. A recent and superb study placing several related reforms within the broader context of social change is David J. Rothman, *The Discovery of the Asylum: Social Order and Disorder in the New Republic* (Boston and Toronto, 1971).

10. Russel Blaine Nye, *The Cultural Life of the New Nation: 1776–1830* (New York, 1960), p. 251; Harvey Wish, *Society and Thought in Early America: A Social and Intellectual History of the American People through 1865* (New York, 1950), p. 303.

11. Frank Luther Mott, *American Journalism: A History of Newspapers in the United States through 250 Years, 1690 to 1940* (New York, 1941), p. 216; Carl Bode, *Ante Bellum Culture* (Carbondale, Ill., 1970), p. 251.

12. Frank Luther Mott, *A History of American Magazines* 1 (1741–1850 [New York and London, 1930]): 120, 199; 2 (1850–65 [Cambridge, Mass., 1938]): 4–5, 10–11.

13. The classic discussion of the wage earner in the age of "merchant capitalism" is John R. Commons et. al., *History of Labour in the United States* 1 (New York, 1921): 88–107.

14. *Statistical History,* p. 57; Marcus Lee Hansen, *The Atlantic*

Migration: 1607–1860 (Cambridge, Mass., 1940), pp. 199–306; Oscar Handlin, *Boston's Immigrants: A Study in Acculturation* (Cambridge, Mass., 1941), pp. 25–53.

15. See Edward Pessen, "The Egalitarian Myth and the American Social Reality: Wealth, Mobility, and Equality in the 'Era of the Common Man,'" *American Historical Review* 76 (1971): 989–1,034; and Pessen, *Riches, Class, and Power Before the Civil War* (Lexington, Mass., 1973).

16. On American consumption before the Civil War, see Edgar W. Martin, *The Standard of Living in 1860: American Consumption Levels on the Eve of the Civil War* (Chicago, 1942). On the difficulties of the urban master craftsman in this period see Commons, *History of Labour*, pp. 88–107, and Commons, "American Shoemakers, 1648–1895," *Quarterly Journal of Economics* 24 (1909): 39–84.

17. See Page Smith, *As a City upon a Hill: The Town in American History* (New York, 1966); and Lewis Atherton, *Main Street on the Middle Border* (Bloomington, Ind., 1954).

18. See Darrett B. Rutman, *Winthrop's Boston: A Portrait of a Puritan Town, 1630–1649* (Chapel Hill, N.C., 1965); Frederick B. Tolles, *Meeting House and Counting House: The Quaker Merchants of Colonial Philadelphia, 1682–1763* (Chapel Hill, N.C., 1948); and Carl Bridenbaugh, *Cities in the Wilderness: Urban Life in America 1625–1742* (New York, 1938).

19. See Richard C. Wade, *The Urban Frontier: The Rise of Western Cities, 1790–1830* (Cambridge, Mass., 1959); Blake McKelvey, *Rochester*, vols. 1–3 (Cambridge, Mass., 1945–56), vol. 4 (Rochester, 1961); Bessie L. Pierce, *A History of Chicago*, vols. 1–3 (New York, 1937–57); A. Theodore Brown, *Frontier Community: A History of Kansas City to 1870* (Columbia, Mo., 1964).

20. A recent exception is Michael H. Frisch, *Town into City: Springfield, Massachusetts, and the Meaning of Community, 1840–1880* (Cambridge, Mass., 1972). Frisch's study, the first to examine systematically the consequences of mid-nineteenth-century urbanization for a preexisting, rural American community, will provide useful comparisons with my present study in the final chapter. But it must be noted that Springfield was itself founded as a trading center and never did establish a firm

agricultural base to its economy. Moreover, Frisch begins his close analysis of the town after it had already acquired 11,000 inhabitants.

21. Although cultural subregions have not yet received a great deal of attention from American social historians, the broader regions or sections provide one of the major themes of American historical writing. And even among those who would argue over whether the West was a wholly new and unique section or mainly an extension of seaboard sections, the specific delineations of America's major regions provoke little or no dispute. See Frederick Jackson Turner, *The Rise of the New West, 1819-1829* (New York, 1906); Howard W. Odum and Harry E. Moore, *American Regionalism: A Cultural-Historical Approach to National Integration* (New York, 1938); Merrill Jensen, ed., *Regionalism in America* (Madison and Milwaukee, 1951), particularly the essay by Fulmer Mood, "The Origin, Evolution, and Application of the Sectional Concept, 1750-1900," pp. 5-98.

22. In the early editions of Jedidiah Morse's *American Universal Geography*, the West was seen as an extension of the Middle Atlantic states, and not as a separate section. See Morse, *The American Universal Geography*, 5th ed., vol. 1 (Boston, 1805); Mood, "Sectional Concept," pp. 38-46.

23. See John Allen Krout and Dixon Ryan Fox, *The Completion of Independence, 1790-1830* (New York, 1944), pp. 107-11; Percy W. Bidwell, "The Agricultural Revolution in New England," *American Historical Review* 26 (1921): 686.

24. U.S. Census Office, *Population of the United States in 1860*, table 3.

25. Conrad M. Arensberg, "The Community as Object and as Sample," in Arensberg and Solon T. Kimball, *Culture and Community* (New York, 1965), pp. 7-27.

26. Kenneth A. Lockridge, *A New England Town: The First Hundred Years* (New York, 1970).

27. Frisch, *Town into City*, p. 257.

28. My understanding of "community" has been shaped largely by Roland L. Warren, *The Community in America* (Chicago, 1963); Irwin T. Sanders, *The Community: An Introduction to a Social System* (New York, 1958); Rene König, *The Community*, trans. Edward Fitzgerald (New York, 1968); Robert Redfield,

The Little Community (Chicago, 1955); E. T. Hiller, "The Community as a Social Group," *American Sociological Review* 6 (1941): 189–202; Albert J. Reiss, Jr., "The Sociological Study of Communities," *Rural Sociology* 24 (1959): 118–30; Willis A. Sutton, Jr., and Jiri Kolaja, "The Concept of Community," *Rural Sociology* 25 (1960): 197–203; Harold F. Kaufman, "Toward an Interactional Conception of Community," *Social Forces* 38 (1959): 8–17; Gordon W. Blackwell, "A Theoretical Framework for Sociological Research in Community Organization," *Social Forces* 33 (1954): 57–64; and by a number of excellent empirical studies of particular communities.

29. Louis Wirth, "Urbanism as a Way of Life," *American Journal of Sociology* 44 (1938): 1–24.

30. Ibid.; see Herbert J. Gans, "Urbanism and Suburbanism as Ways of Life: A Re-evaluation of Definitions," in Arnold Rose, ed., *Human Behavior and Social Processes* (Boston, 1962), pp. 625–48.

31. Legally, there is no question—Kingston was *not* a city until 1872, when the New York legislature granted it a city charter. But it hardly needs stating that Wirth's (and my own) conception of a city has little to do with the particular acts of state legislatures and involves many phenomena other than political institutions.

32. Perhaps the most explicit statement of this point is W. W. Rostow, *The Stages of Economic Growth: A Non-Communist Manifesto* (Cambridge, 1960). For other statements to the effect that this was a period of rapid and fundamental change in America, see Arthur M. Schlesinger, *New Viewpoints in American History* (New York, 1922), p. 200; Carl Russell Fish, *The Rise of the Common Man* (New York, 1927), p. 325; Frederick Jackson Turner, *The United States, 1830–1850* (New York, 1935), p. 578; Richard Hofstadter, *The American Political Tradition, and the Men Who Made It* (New York, 1948), p. 56; Arthur M. Schlesinger, Jr., *The Age of Jackson* (Boston, 1945), p. 8; Robert E. Riegel, *Young America: 1830–1840* (Norman, Okla., 1949), p. 131; Bray Hammond, *Banks and Politics in America* (Princeton, N.J., 1957), p. 327; Marvin Meyers, *The Jacksonian Persuasion: Politics and Belief* (Stanford, Calif., 1957), p. 87; John William Ward, *Andrew Jackson: Symbol for an Age* (New York, 1955), p. 169; Lee Benson, *The Concept of*

Jacksonian Democracy: New York as a Test Case (Princeton, N.J., 1961), pp. 12–13.

Chapter 2

1. $6 to Albany. I have been unable to determine the fare to Kingston. See the *Craftsman*, May 10, 1820.
2. Ibid., May 21, 1821.
3. Frances Trollope, *Domestic Manners of the Americans* (1832; New York, 1949), pp. 366–68.
4. Marius Schoonmaker, *The History of Kingston, New York* . . . (New York, 1888), p. 470.
5. Ibid., p. 469.
6. William Darby, *A Tour from the City of New York to Detroit* . . . (1819; Chicago, 1962), pp. 24–26.
7. John Allen Krout and Dixon Ryan Fox, *The Completion of Independence* (New York, 1944), p. 111.
8. Schoonmaker, *History of Kingston*, p. 426.
9. *Craftsman*, March 29, 1820.
10. Ibid., July 29, 1820.
11. See, for example, ibid., October 28, 1820.
12. Ibid., May 10, September 2, 1820.
13. Schoonmaker, *History of Kingston*, p. 426.
14. Ibid., pp. 426–27.
15. Ibid., p. 423.
16. *Craftsman*, October 28, May 10, 1820.
17. The village map, including the description of each building, is drawn from Schoonmaker, *History of Kingston*, pp. 435–71. Schoonmaker's descriptions are extremely useful and as complete as we can possibly expect them to be. He seems to have missed no more than a half-dozen businesses and about twenty-five or thirty dwellings. Schoonmaker himself lived in the middle of the stockade area in 1820, near the corner of Wall and John streets.
18. An excellent discussion of the significance of this continued unity of residence and work is included in John Demos, *A Little Commonwealth: Family Life in Plymouth Colony* (New York, 1970). In early Plymouth, the family performed most of the major social functions: it was business, school, vocational in-

stitute, church, house of correction, welfare institution, and old people's home (p. 184). Gradually, however, the family surrendered most of these functions to other institutions, and as it did it became increasingly significant as an emotional bulwark against what was now the "outside" world (pp. 186–87). "The biggest single factor" producing this highly significant change, writes Demos, "seems to have been the separation of work from the individual household, in connection with the growth of an urban, industrial system" (p. 187). I will return to this question in chapter 6.

19. Letter by the Reverend Laurentius Van Gaasbeck, printed in the *Ulster Republican*, August 30, 1843.

20. Schoonmaker, *History of Kingston*, p. 426; *Craftsman*, October 28, 1820; *Ulster Sentinel*, March 18, 1827. See also Robert Greenhalgh Albion, *The Rise of New York Port: 1815–1860* (New York, 1939), p. 80, where Kingston in the period immediately preceding the construction of the Erie Canal is described as "a particularly rich wheat region."

21. Albion, *Rise of New York Port*, pp. 128, 397.

22. Schoonmaker, *History of Kingston*, p. 413.

23. See various issues of the *Craftsman*, 1820–21.

24. Mortgage Register, 1818–20, Office of the Clerk of Ulster County, Kingston, N.Y.

25. Short-term operating capital was, of course, in part provided by credit extended to farmers by Kingston's merchants.

26. Schoonmaker, *History of Kingston*, p. 373; *Craftsman*, July 15, 1820.

27. Schoonmaker, *History of Kingston*, pp. 405–6.

28. Ibid., p. 405.

29. Marius Schoonmaker, manuscript fragment intended for a second volume of his history of Kingston, Senate House Museum, Kingston, N.Y. Cited hereafter as Schoonmaker MS.

30. Schoonmaker, *History of Kingston*, p. 406.

31. Ibid., pp. 408–10.

32. Wiltwyck appears to have resulted from the initiative of a single local resident, a young man named Roeloff Swartwout, who journeyed to Amsterdam and persuaded the directors of the West India Company to create a government at Esopus and to

appoint him as its chief officer. Stuyvesant at first refused to honor Swartwout's commission and did honor it only after being rebuked by the directors. Swartwout appears to have been a local maverick. When a local militia unit was formed to fight the Indians, he was at first given a minor office and was then dropped entirely. Ibid., pp. 23–47.

33. Ibid., pp. 58–61.

34. Ibid., p. 82.

35. It is not entirely clear what the status of the corporation was after the new state divided the counties into towns. Sylvester claims that a new town was superimposed over the corporation, and gradually eroded its powers; see Sylvester, *History of Ulster County, New York* ..., 2 vols. (Philadelphia, 1880), 1:198. Schoonmaker makes no mention of this. It is possible that the local governors themselves were unsure of how many governments they had.

36. Patricia U. Bonomi, "Local Government in Colonial New York: A Base for Republicanism," in Jacob Judd and Irwin H. Polishook, *Aspects of Early New York Society and Politics* (Tarrytown, N.Y., 1974), pp. 29–50.

37. Schoonmaker, *History of Kingston*, pp. 379–82.

38. Though the word "township" has no legal meaning in New York, I have occasionally used it here in place of "town," which is the legal term for the smallest unincorporated subdivision of the county. I have also occasionally used "town" in the more common sense of a medium-sized human settlement. I hope that I have been able to avoid ambiguous use of these terms. See chapter 7, below, for a more complete discussion of the legal meanings of "village" and "town" in New York. And see Robert Stephen Litt, "Urbanization and Social Control: An Analysis of Kingston, New York, 1820–1872" (unpublished senior honors thesis, Harvard University, 1971), pp. 38–53, for a fine discussion of local government in Kingston in 1820.

39. [New York State] Division of Archives and History, *Historical Account and Inventory of Records of the City of Kingston* (Albany, 1918), p. 19.

40. Schoonmaker, *History of Kingston*, p. 384.

41. Ibid.

42. Minutes of the Board of Directors of the Village of Kingston, 1820–21, City Hall, Kingston, N.Y. Cited hereafter as Kingston Village Minutes.

43. *Craftsman*, March 20, April 10, 1822.

44. *Ulster Sentinel*, August 23, 1826.

45. Alvin Kass, *Politics in New York State, 1800–1830* (Syracuse, N.Y., 1965), pp. 65, 67, 173. The idea of the primacy of state politics is basic to Lee Benson, *The Concept of Jacksonian Democracy: New York as a Test Case* (Princeton, N.J., 1961).

46. *Ulster Sentinel*, November 14, 1827, April 9, 1828.

47. Schoonmaker, *History of Kingston*, p. 400.

48. Kass, *Politics in New York State*, p. 137.

49. *Ulster Sentinel*, December 6, 1826.

50. Schoonmaker, *History of Kingston*, p. 212.

51. Ibid.

52. Ibid., pp. 349–50.

53. Ibid., p. 363.

54. Ibid., p. 353.

55. Ibid., p. 424.

56. *Ulster Sentinel*, July 25, 1827.

57. Sylvester, *History of Ulster County*, 1:227, 230.

58. Schoonmaker, *History of Kingston*, p. 422.

59. Ibid., p. 420.

60. *Ulster Sentinel*, October 4, 1826.

61. Ibid., August 23, 1826.

62. Ibid., October 11, November 22, 1826.

63. Schoonmaker, *History of Kingston*, p. 226.

64. Ibid., pp. 214–21.

65. Ibid., p. 226; *The Acts and Proceedings of the General Synod of the Reformed Dutch Church, in North America, at Kingston, October, 1817* (Albany, 1817).

66. Record of the Proceedings of the Eldership and the Consistory of the Reformed Dutch Church of Kingston, 1841–78, First Dutch Reformed Church, Kingston, N.Y. See especially the entry for April 11, 1842.

67. Schoonmaker reports fifty-three students in 1803: thirty-one

from Ulster County, twenty from other New York counties, one from Pennsylvania, and one from Maryland. The Corporation of Kingston (which included the post-1811 towns of Kingston, Esopus, and Saugerties) contained approximately 1,100 white boys and girls of school age in 1800. The village itself probably contained between 250 and 300. Schoonmaker, *History of Kingston*, p. 359; *Return of the Whole Number of Persons Within the Several Districts of the United States* . . . (Washington, D.C., 1802), n.p.

68. Schoonmaker, *History of Kingston*, pp. 352–53.

69. Ibid., p. 353.

70. Ibid., p. 430; *Ulster Sentinel*, June 28, 1826.

71. Kingston Village Minutes, April 13, 1829.

72. Schoonmaker, *History of Kingston*, pp. 430–33; *Ulster Sentinel*, December 27, 1826, March 14, July 25, 1827.

73. *Ulster Sentinel*, July 19, 1826.

74. *Craftsman*, February 28, 1821, October 7, 1820.

75. Ibid., April 12, September 23, 1820, January 10, 1821; Sylvester, *History of Ulster County*, 1:122.

76. *Ulster Sentinel*, April 16, 1828.

77. *Craftsman*, June 14, 1820.

78. *Ulster Sentinel*, June 28, 1826.

79. Ibid., July 12, 1826.

80. *Craftsman*, July 11, 1821.

81. The communalism of the "covenanted" communities of early New England is a subject that has received a great deal of attention from historians. Somewhat less fully examined was the apparent moderation of this communalism during the eighteenth century. See Kenneth A. Lockridge, *A New England Town: The First Hundred Years* (New York, 1970); Sumner Chilton Powell, *Puritan Village: The Formation of a New England Town* (Middletown, Conn., 1963); Conrad M. Arensberg, "American Communities," in Arensberg and Solon T. Kimball, *Culture and Community* (New York, 1965), pp. 103–6; Richard L. Bushman, *From Puritan to Yankee: Character and the Social Order in Connecticut, 1690–1765* (Cambridge, Mass., 1967); Charles A. Grant, *Democracy in the Connecticut Frontier Town of Kent* (New York, 1961).

Chapter 3

1. *Census for 1820* ... (Washington, D.C., 1821).
2. *Ulster Sentinel*, September 27, 1826.
3. Ibid., November 21, 1827.
4. This proportion is based upon a total enumeration of the manuscript schedules of the federal census of 1860 pertaining to
   Kingston.
5. Marius Schoonmaker, *The History of Kingston, New York* ...
   (New York, 1888), p. 203.
6. Ibid., pp. 423–24.
7. Schoonmaker's genealogical notes on fifty-four Kingston family
   names indicate that John and Henry were first cousins; ibid.,
   p. 491. But Henry's diary refers to John as his uncle. Manuscript
   diary of Henry Vanderlyn, at New York Historical Society, New
   York, May 6, September 25, 1827. Cited hereafter as Vanderlyn
   diary.
8. Vanderlyn diary, April 29, 1827.
9. Ibid.
10. Ibid.
11. Ibid.
12. Edward L. Merritt, "Kingston Academy," *Proceedings of the
    Ulster County Historical Society* (1937–38), p. 42.
13. Vanderlyn diary, May 16, 1830.
14. Ibid., May 13, 1827.
15. Ibid., May 20, 1827.
16. Schoonmaker, *History of Kingston*, pp. 531–36.
17. Department of Commerce and Labor, Bureau of the Census,
    Heads of Families at the First Census ... *1790: New York*
    (Washington, D.C., 1908), pp. 171–73.
18. Patricia U. Bonomi, "Local Government in Colonial New
    York: A Base for Republicanism," in Jacob Judd and Irwin H.
    Polishook, *Aspects of Early New York Society and Politics*
    (Tarrytown, N.Y., 1974), p. 35.
19. Mack Walker, *German Home Towns: Community, State, and
    General Estate, 1648–1871* (Ithaca, N.Y., 1971), p. 56.
20. Bonomi, "Local Government," p. 34.

21. Schoonmaker, *History of Kingston*, p. 203.
22. Ibid.
23. Ibid., p. 421.
24. Ibid., p. 198.
25. Ibid., pp. 422–23.
26. Vanderlyn diary, May 13, 1827.
27. *Craftsman*, August 26, 1820.
28. *Ulster Sentinel*, October 24, 1827.
29. Sir Arthur Conan Doyle, *The Complete Sherlock Holmes* (Garden City, N.Y., n.d.), 1:347.
30. Roland L. Warren, *The Community in America* (Chicago, 1963), p. 161.
31. *Ulster Sentinel*, October 11, 1826.
32. Ibid.
33. Minutes of the Board of Directors of the Village of Kingston, City Hall, Kingston, October 24, 1820. Cited hereafter as Kingston Village Minutes.
34. The idea that elites may derive their status from sources beyond the community is best understood in the context of European society. See, for example, Peter Laslett, *The World We Have Lost* (London, 1965), pp. 22–52.
35. Oscar Lewis uses the term "rural cosmopolitanism" to describe certain phases of life (particularly a very striking degree of exogamy) in a village in northern India. It is an excellent term, for it forces us to surrender the assumption that the lives of simple, rural people *must* be enclosed within their immediate locality. See Oscar Lewis, "Peasant Culture in India and Mexico: A Comparative Analysis," in McKim Marriott, ed., *Village India: Studies in the Little Community* (Chicago and London, 1955), pp. 145–70.
36. Warren, *Community in America*, pp. 161–62; italics added.
37. Ibid., p. 53; italics added.
38. Ibid., pp. 9–11.
39. Albert E. McKinley, "The English and Dutch Towns of New Netherland," *American Historical Review* 6 (1900): 5.
40. Dixon Ryan Fox, *Yankees and Yorkers* (New York, 1940), especially pp. 66–71.

41. Lee Benson, *The Concept of Jacksonian Democracy: New York as a Test Case* (Princeton, N.J., 1961), pp. 298–304. Benson's book is essentially a revision of Fox's *The Decline of Aristocracy in the Politics of New York* (New York, 1919). But Benson (p. 5n) is explicit in his admiration of *Yankees and Yorkers*.

42. Vanderlyn diary, April 29, 1827.

Chapter 4

1. *Ulster Sentinel*, November 29, 1826.

2. Ibid.

3. Marius Schoonmaker, manuscript fragment intended for a second volume of his history of Kingston, Senate House Museum, Kingston. Cited hereafter as Schoonmaker MS.

4. The first shipment of anthracite down the D & H Canal was completed on December 5, 1828 and consisted of about 1,100 tons. The first full year of operations was 1829. See *A Century of Progress: History of the Delaware and Hudson Company, 1823–1923* (Albany, 1925). This is the "official" company history. Other discussions of the D & H may be found in Dorothy Hurlbut Sanderson, *The Delaware and Hudson Canalway: Carrying Coals to Rondout* (Ellenville, N.Y., 1965); Noble E. Whitford, *History of the Canal System of the State of New York . . .* (Albany, 1906), pp. 728–51; and Alvin Harlow, *Old Towpaths: The Story of the American Canal Era* (New York and London, 1926), pp. 185–94. Annual tonnage figures are included in the *Annual Report of the Board of Managers of the Delaware and Hudson Canal Co. to the Stockholders . . .* (New York, 1832–61).

5. According to Schoonmaker, most local stockholders sold out in panic in 1832, when an early spring freshet severely damaged the Eddyville lock. The canal opened in early May, the damage repaired, and coal shipments advanced nearly 60% over the previous year. See Schoonmaker MS.

6. *Ulster Republican*, September 11, 1833.

7. Ibid., January 22, 1834.

8. Manuscript diary of Nathaniel Booth, Senate House Museum, Kingston, December 13, 1850. Cited hereafter as Booth diary.

9. *Ulster Palladium*, March 9, May 18, 1831. The Middletown

referred to here was in Delaware County and should not be confused with the present town of that name in nearby Orange County.

10. Ibid., January 4, 1832.

11. *Ulster Republican*, December 5, 1838.

12. Ibid., March 2, 1842, November 29, 1843.

13. Ibid., January 23, July 24, 1850. Kingston did fail, despite numerous attempts, to obtain a rail connection before the Civil War. But this failure was probably a great deal less important than local capitalists believed it to be, for, unlike the Lackawanna anthracite carried to Kingston by canalboat, the western grain carried in freight cars required no reloading when it reached the Hudson Valley. Regional trade carried over branch lines could cause a way station to prosper, but Kingston had already secured a large portion of this trade by means of her canal, plank roads, and port. For a small sample of Kingston's many railroad schemes, see: *Ulster Palladium*, January 4, 1832; *Ulster Republican*, December 23, 1835, September 30, 1836, March 19, 1845, March 22, 1854, April 18, 1860; Rondout *Courier*, September 24, 1852.

14. Rondout *Courier*, January 21, 1848.

15. Ibid., December 7, 1849; Nathaniel Bartlett Sylvester, *History of Ulster County, New York* ..., 2 vols. (Philadelphia, 1880), 1:277.

16. Rondout *Courier*, December 7, 1849.

17. See Alphonso T. Clearwater, *The History of Ulster County, New York* (Kingston, N.Y., 1907), pp. 541–44, for a technical discussion of bluestone.

18. Ibid., p. 414.

19. Rondout *Courier*, April 26, 1850.

20. *Ulster Republican*, January 26, 1853. Note, on table 1, that the amount of stone shipped through the canal was comparatively small. Most of the quarries were in and around the town of Kingston, below the terminus of the canal.

21. *Kingston and Rondout Directory* ... (New York, 1858), pp. 99, 103–4.

22. *Ulster Palladium*, May 16, 1832.

23. *Ulster Republican*, January 22, 1834.

24. Ibid., February 24, 1836.

25. Ibid., July 5, 1848, June 25, 1851, April 13, June 22, 1853.

26. Ibid., December 30, 1835, March 16, May 28, June 8, October 21, 1836, March 12, 1851.

27. Every fifth entry was sampled. In 1818–20, no entry listed the Middle District Bank as mortgagee, although the Dutch Reformed Church of Kingston is listed twice. The church is not listed in the mortgage records of 1858–60.

28. If surnames are any indication, family ties do not seem to account for a significant number of mortgage contracts. Only thirteen of 137 mortgages involved parties with the same surname.

29. Harvey H. Segal, "Canals and Economic Development," in Carter Goodrich, ed., *Canals and American Economic Development* (Port Washington, N.Y., and London, 1972), pp. 216–48.

30. That Kingston's stores were typical of country stores all over the state is indicated in Ulysses Prentiss Hedrick, *A History of Agriculture in the State of New York* (New York, 1966), p. 200. That they were characteristic of the nation as a whole is indicated in John Allen Krout and Dixon Ryan Fox, *The Completion of Independence, 1790–1830* (New York, 1944), pp. 241–42.

31. *Ulster Palladium*, January 19, 1831.

32. Ibid., August 24, 1831.

33. *Ulster Republican*, December 2, 1840.

34. Ibid., January 1, 1840.

35. Ibid.

36. There were more than eighty local advertisers, but the sheer volume of newspaper advertising made sampling necessary after 1820. All the advertisements from every fourth newspaper were recorded for 1831 and 1840, so few—if any—local firms were missed. By 1850 and 1860, however, every advertisement was recorded from only four papers (one in each season of the year), so some businesses were probably missed.

37. *Ulster Republican*, January 4, 1860.

38. *Kingston and Rondout Directory*, pp. 91–114.

39. Rondout *Courier*, August 28, 1857.

40. Ibid., May 8, 1860.

41. *Ulster Republican,* February 10, 1836. Domestic manufacturing was, of course, declining all over the more developed parts of America and was disappearing from the homes of New York State farmers as rapidly as from those in Kingston. See Rolla Milton Tryon, *Household Manufactures in the United States, 1640–1860* (Chicago, 1917), esp. pp. 304–5; and Jared Van Wagenen, Jr., *The Golden Age of Homespun* (New York, 1963).

42. *Ulster Republican,* April 2, 1845.

43. Ibid., July 4, 1860.

44. If I am marrying here the terminology of regional geography and community sociology, it is a marriage at which I am pleased to carry the shotgun. For an excellent application of "central place" theory to an American region, see James T. Lemon, *The Best Poor Man's Country: A Geographical Study of Early Southeastern Pennsylvania* (Baltimore, 1972), pp. 118–49. "Locality-relevant functions" are described in Roland L. Warren, *The Community in America* (Chicago, 1963), pp. 9–11.

45. Unfortunately, there are no reliable accounts of manufacturing in Kingston before the 1850s. The "McLane Report" (House Executive Document 308, 22d Congress, 1st Session, 1831–32, published as *Documents Relative to the Manufactures in the United States* ..., 2 vols. [Washington, D.C., 1833]) mentions only one firm in Kingston, an iron furnace employing six men (2:115). But this survey is quite incomplete for New York State as a whole and is certainly incomplete for Kingston. The 1840 census lists a handful of firms, mostly small rural shops and mills, but omits the new bluestone and limestone quarries, Baldwin's foundry, and a number of small shops and boatyards mentioned (but not described) in state gazetteers. See U.S. Census Office, *Aggregate Value and Produce, and Number of Persons Employed in Mines, Agriculture, Commerce, Manufactures, Etc....* (Washington, D.C., 1841), pp. 128–31; J. Disturnell, *A Gazetteer of the State of New York* ... (Albany, N.Y., 1842), pp. 347–48.

46. Rondout *Courier,* June 13, 1856.

47. *Ulster Republican,* March 7, 1860.

48. Rondout *Courier,* April 17, 1857, July 27, 1860.

49. *Ulster Republican,* August 12, 1836.

50. Ibid.

51. The most thorough discussion of this is still John R. Commons, et. al., *History of Labour in the United States* 1 (New York, 1921): 88–107.

52. *Ulster Republican*, August 4, 1841.

53. Rondout *Courier*, March 29, 1850.

54. Ibid., April 14, 1854; *Ulster Republican*, April 19, 1854.

55. Rondout *Courier*, April 14, 1854.

56. Ibid., April 21, 1854.

57. *Ulster Republican*, April 26, 1854.

58. Ibid., June 27, 1855.

59. Rondout *Courier*, May 9, 1856.

60. Booth diary, July 18, 1854.

61. Ibid., January 3, 1853.

62. Ibid., January 10, 1853.

63. *Ulster Republican*, February 11, 1852.

64. Rondout *Courier*, May 20, 1859.

65. The numbers employed are difficult to tabulate, as teamsters, laborers, and other types of workers besides quarrymen worked in the bluestone trade. The *Ulster Republican* estimated three hundred workers in 1854, but this may be high. Ibid., January 18, 1854.

66. The figure is based on total enumerations of the population schedules of the two censuses. These enumerations will be analyzed in greater detail in the next chapter.

67. Rondout *Courier*, April 14, 1854.

68. Ibid., April 9, 1852.

69. Ibid., November 30, 1849.

70. Ibid., January 21, 1859.

Chapter 5

1. Kingston's growth slowed considerably during and after the Civil War. Today, more than a century later, the city of Kingston (a smaller area than the town) contains only some 25,000 inhabitants, with perhaps 30,000 residing within the bounds of the antebellum township.

2. Rondout *Courier*, March 7, 1851.

3. Marius Schoonmaker, manuscript fragment intended for second volume of his history of Kingston, Senate House Museum, Kingston. Cited hereafter as Schoonmaker MS.

4. J. Disturnell, *A Gazetteer of the State of New York* ... (Albany, N.Y., 1842), pp. 347–48.

5. Rondout *Courier*, April 12, 1850.

6. Ibid., March 6, 1857.

7. Louis Wirth, "Urbanism as a Way of Life," *American Journal of Sociology* 44 (1938): 1–24. See chapter 1, above.

8. Much of the following analysis is based on complete enumeration of the state census of 1855 and the federal census of 1860 for the town of Kingston. These two sources vary slightly but significantly; for example, the state census lists the county of birth (for New York State natives) and the number of years each enumerated individual had lived in Kingston in 1855; and the federal census gives the value of real and personal property reported by each head of household. In most other respects the two censuses are alike. They have been collected in their entirety to provide sufficient numbers of cases for detailed analysis and to permit occasional cross-file linkages (see chapter 9 in particular). The 1850 census has not been collected, as it would have added no information not already included in the other two or significantly extended the period for which such information is available.

9. *Ulster Republican*, July 3, 1833, March 23, 1836.

10. Ibid., February 10, 1836.

11. Information is missing about 157 cases (3.6%). These are excluded from table 3. The numbers of cases in the tables that follow will generally vary by small amounts for this reason.

12. Oscar Handlin, *Boston's Immigrants: A Study in Acculturation*, rev. ed. (New York, 1968), p. 244; Peter R. Knights, *The Plain People of Boston, 1830–1860: A Study in City Growth* (New York, 1971), pp. 34–35.

13. Sam Bass Warner, Jr., *The Private City: Philadelphia in Three Periods of Its Growth* (Philadelphia, 1968), pp. 55, 139.

14. Theodore Hershberg, Michael Katz, Stuart Blumin, Laurence Glasco, and Clyde Griffen, "Occupation and Ethnicity in Five Nineteenth-Century Cities: A Collaborative Inquiry," *Historical Methods Newsletter* 7 (1974): 195.

15. Ibid.

16. Based on a 10% sample of the manuscript schedules of the United States census of 1860.

17. Marcus Lee Hansen, *The Atlantic Migration: 1607–1860* (Cambridge, Mass., 1940), p. 301.

18. Nathaniel Bartlett Sylvester, *History of Ulster County, New York* . . . , 2 vols. (Philadelphia, 1880) 1:233; *Ulster Republican*, June 18, 1845; *Kingston and Rondout Directory* . . . (New York, 1858), p. 134; *St. John's Parish Centennial* (Kingston, N.Y., 1932), p. 3.

19. Sylvester, *History of Ulster County*, 1:233–39; *Kingston and Rondout Directory*, p. 134.

20. Sylvester, *History of Ulster County*, 1:239; *Kingston and Rondout Directory*, p. 135.

21. Sylvester, *History of Ulster County*, 1:241; Works Progress Administration, Historical Records Survey, *Inventory of the Church Archives of New York State* . . . (Albany, 1939), p. 299.

22. Sylvester, *History of Ulster County*, 1:250, 251, 254.

23. Ibid., pp. 233–54; Works Progress Administration, *Inventory of the Church Archives*, pp. 294–99.

24. Manuscript schedules of the United States census of 1860.

25. Stuart Blumin, "Mobility and Change in Ante-Bellum Philadelphia," in Stephan Thernstrom and Richard Sennett, eds., *Nineteenth-Century Cities: Essays in the New Urban History* (New Haven and London, 1969), p. 204.

26. See James A. Henretta, "Economic Development and Social Structure in Colonial Boston," *William and Mary Quarterly* 22 (1965): 75–92; James T. Lemon, "Urbanization and the Development of Eighteenth-Century Southeastern Pennsylvania and Delaware," *William and Mary Quarterly* 24 (1967): 501–42.

27. During these years the proportion of improved land in Marlborough increased from 60% to more than 80% of the town's total area, and local agriculture began to shift toward the intensive cultivation of fruits and berries for nearby urban markets and resorts.

28. Rondout *Courier*, March 3, 1848.

29. Ibid., July 28, 1848.

30. An examination of the 1,500 households headed by Irish and Germans in 1860 yielded only 99 American-born sons or male relatives over the age of fifteen. There must have been others, of course, but the total could not have been more than 5% of the male work force. Of the 99 located, 82 were listed as members of the work force, and it is interesting that as a group they lay in between the old-stock natives and the foreign-born (e.g., 57.4% were unskilled workers, but fully 7.3% were clerical workers). This does not mean, of course, that the children of more recent immigrants would have had similar opportunities, but it does imply that the second generation were less "ethnic" than their immigrant parents. If their numbers were larger, they would best be handled here by being set up as a separate category.

31. In each of the following tables, the decision about which census file to use was made partly on the basis of the information required and partly on the basis of comparability to other tables. The two censuses are quite consistent with each other, so the choice in each instance may be regarded as a matter of convenience.

32. Two of these wealthy household heads were women. The accuracy of the property entries is a matter of some importance, and I have tried to test them whenever possible. Besides occasional references to the wealth of specific men in newspapers and the Booth diary, there are surviving credit reports of the Mercantile Agency, predecessor to Dun & Bradstreet. These have been compared to the property entries of the census. In almost every instance, the census entries conform closely to these other sources.

33. Occupational groups must be used here because the 1855 census does not provide property data, while the 1860 census does not record length of residence. Linked pairs would, in this instance, produce biased results. The substitution of occupations for property at this end of the scale is acceptable, however, as unskilled and semiskilled workers were the most homogeneous occupational groups in property ownership. 82.4% of the former and 76.0% of the latter reported $0–$500 in property in 1860, and these were all heads of household. If property entries existed for boarders and other nonhouseholders, these percentages would be still higher.

34. Two excellent analyses of the phenomenon of "repeated migration" are Peter A. Morrison, "Duration of Residence and Prospective Migration: The Evaluation of a Stochastic Model," *Demography* 4 (1967): 553–61; and Kenneth C. Land, "Duration of Residence and Prospective Migration: Further Evidence," *Demography* 6 (1969): 133–40.

35. Manuscript diary of Nathaniel Booth, Senate House Museum, Kingston, May 21, 1850. Hereafter cited as Booth diary.

36. Ibid., March 17, 1850.

37. *Ulster Republican*, May 17, May 24, 1854; Booth diary, January 19, October 2, 1849.

38. Examples of the first are *Ulster Republican*, November 25, 1857, and Rondout *Courier*, November 27, 1857; of the second, Booth diary, January 19, October 2, 1849, May 21, October 13, 1850.

39. Rondout *Courier*, August 4, 1854.

40. Ibid., April 6, 1849.

41. Ibid., December 20, 1850, January 3, 1851; *Ulster Republican*, December 25, 1850.

42. *Ulster Republican*, July 9, 1851.

43. Ibid.

44. Booth diary, July 4, 1851.

45. Rondout *Courier*, March 4, 1853.

46. *Ulster Republican*, March 9, 1853.

47. Booth diary, October 13, 1850.

48. Ibid., July 3, 1848.

49. Rondout *Courier*, November 7, 1851.

50. See, for example, ibid., March 2, 1849. William E. Rowley has argued that the existence of an Irish "aristocracy" in Albany in 1830 facilitated the peaceful infusion of more than 20,000 Irish into that city between 1830 and 1855. See Rowley, "The Irish Aristocracy of Albany, 1798–1878," *New York History* 52 (1971): 275–304. No such "aristocracy" existed in Kingston, however.

Chapter 6

1. See *Kingston and Rondout Directory* . . . (New York, 1858).

2. David Ward, *Cities and Immigrants: A Geography of Change in*

Nineteenth-Century America (New York, 1971), pp. 85–103.

3. Rondout *Courier,* August 6, 1852, March 18, 1853.

4. Ibid., May 7, 1852.

5. Manuscript diary of Nathaniel Booth, Senate House Museum, Kingston, May 1, 1849. Hereafter cited as Booth diary. The question of the extent of this institution is an interesting one. Howard Chudacoff writes of moving day in Omaha, Nebraska, and Richard C. Wade, in his Foreword to Chudacoff's book, implies that it was a general American institution. See Howard P. Chudacoff, *Mobile Americans: Residential and Social Mobility in Omaha* (New York, 1972), pp. v, 111.

6. See Chudacoff, *Mobile Americans;* Stephan Thernstrom and Peter R. Knights, "Men in Motion: Some Data and Speculations about Urban Population Mobility in Nineteenth-Century America," in Tamara K. Hareven, ed., *Anonymous Americans: Explorations in Nineteenth-Century Social History* (Englewood Cliffs, N.J., 1971), pp. 17–47; Stuart Blumin, "Residential Mobility within the Nineteenth-Century City," in Allen F. Davis and Mark H. Haller, eds., *The Peoples of Philadelphia* (Philadelphia, 1973), pp. 37–51.

7. See Gideon Sjoberg, *The Preindustrial City: Past and Present* (New York, 1960), pp. 80–107.

8. For a vivid description of the increasing congestion of nineteenth-century Manhattan, see Seymour J. Mandelbaum, *Boss Tweed's New York* (New York, 1965), pp. 12–17.

9. George Rogers Taylor, "The Beginnings of Mass Transportation in Urban America," pts. 1 and 2, *Smithsonian Journal of History* 1, no. 2 (1966): 35–50, 1, no. 3 (1966): 31–54; Sam Bass Warner, Jr., *Streetcar Suburbs: The Process of Growth in Boston, 1870–1900* (Cambridge, Mass., 1962).

10. See Ward, *Cities and Immigrants,* pp. 105–21.

11. Marius Schoonmaker, *The History of Kingston, New York* ... (New York, 1888), pp. 435–71.

12. See Conrad M. Arensberg, "American Communities," in Arensberg and Solon T. Kimball, *Culture and Community* (New York, 1965), pp. 112–13.

13. See Allan R. Pred, *The Spatial Dynamics of U.S. Urban-Industrial Growth, 1800–1914: Interpretive and Theoretical Essays*

(Cambridge, Mass., 1966), pp. 196–213.

14. Rondout *Courier*, January 12, 1849.

15. Ibid., May 21, 1852.

16. Ibid., May 27, 1859.

17. Ibid., April 2, 1850.

18. Booth diary, June 2, 1850.

19. Ibid., August 3, 1850.

20. Rondout *Courier*, February 28, 1851.

21. *Kingston and Rondout Directory* ... (New York, 1858) lists numerical addresses for North Front, Wall, and Crown streets in Kingston village, and Lackawanna, Ferry, Canal, Garden, and Division streets in Rondout.

22. Booth diary, July 11, 1849. See also *People's Press*, May 8, 1857.

23. Andrew S. Hickey, *The Story of Kingston* (New York, 1952), claims that Wall Street had no sidewalks (p. 68), but makes no mention of other streets.

24. *Ulster Republican*, January 22, 1851.

25. Rondout *Courier*, August 13, 1852.

26. Minutes of the Board of Directors of the Village of Kingston, City Hall, Kingston, 1854–63. Hereafter cited as Kingston Village Minutes.

27. Rondout *Courier*, April 27, 1860.

28. *Ulster Republican*, May 17, 1854; Rondout *Courier*, April 28, May 12, 1854.

29. Rondout *Courier*, June 13, 1851.

30. *Ulster Republican*, May 5, 1852.

31. Ibid., April 26, 1854.

32. Ibid., September 2, 1857.

33. *Kingston and Rondout Directory*, p. 130.

34. Booth diary, July 30, 1851.

35. Ibid.

36. Rondout *Courier*, March 2, 1849.

37. Ibid., November 17, 1854.

38. Ibid., August 8, 1858.

39. Ibid., October 5, 1849.

40. *Ulster Republican,* July 16, 1851.

41. Booth diary, August 20, 1849.

42. Rondout *Courier,* March 7, 1851.

43. *Ulster Republican,* January 15, 1851.

44. For example, Rondout *Courier,* May 5, 1847, April 12, 1850, March 6, March 20, 1857.

45. *Ulster Republican,* May 16, 1860.

46. Rondout *Courier,* November 30, 1849.

47. Ibid., March 13, 1857.

48. For a good summary, see ibid., March 27, 1857.

49. *Ulster Republican,* June 20–September 5, 1849, July 26–August 16, 1854.

50. Rondout *Courier,* March 13, November 27, 1857, March 25, 1859, January 15, 1858.

51. *Ulster Republican,* February 9, 1848.

Chapter 7

1. Minutes of the Board of Directors of the Village of Kingston, City Hall, Kingston, 1829–30. Hereafter cited as Kingston Village Minutes.

2. *Ulster Palladium,* September 9, 1830.

3. *Ulster Republican,* June 13, 1838.

4. Ibid., February 24, 1837. The 1821–22 report is in the *Craftsman,* April 10, 1822, and the 1829–30 figures were reconstructed from the village minutes.

5. *Ulster Republican,* April 10, 1839.

6. Ibid., March 24, 1841.

7. Ibid., April 20, April 27, May 11, May 18, 1842.

8. Ibid., May 11, 1842.

9. Ibid.

10. Kingston Village Minutes, 1854–63.

11. *Ulster Republican,* December 21, 1853.

12. Kingston Village Minutes, June 20, 1854.

13. Ibid., August 14, 1854.

14. Ibid., March 5, 1855.

15. *Ulster Republican,* July 4, 1855.

16. Ibid.

17. Ibid., May 27, 1857.

18. Kingston Village Minutes, 1860-61.

19. *Ulster Republican,* May 16, 1860.

20. Kingston Village Minutes, June 25, 1860.

21. Ibid., July 30, 1860.

22. Ibid., October 22, 1860.

23. Ibid., April 1, 1861.

24. Ibid., July 2, 1860. There does not appear to have been a charter amendment permitting this step, and it was probably illegal for the directors to transform the road tax in this manner.

25. Ibid., April 25, 1860.

26. *Ulster Republican,* March 5, March 12, 1834.

27. Ibid., August 6, 1845.

28. Ibid., June 16, 1847.

29. Ibid., August 4, October 6, 1847, October 16, 1850, January 15, January 22, 1851, February 4, March 31, May 5, October 20, December 15, 1852.

30. Ibid., April 18, 1860 is the first date.

31. *Ulster Palladium,* April 11, 1832.

32. *Ulster Republican,* April 2, 1834.

33. For example, ibid., April 6, 1836.

34. Ibid., April 3, 1839.

35. Ibid., April 1, 1840.

36. For an excellent discussion of antiparty attitudes as a general phenomenon in this period, see Ronald P. Formisano, *The Birth of Mass Political Parties: Michigan, 1827-1861* (Princeton, N.J., 1971), pp. 56-80.

37. *Ulster Republican,* March 31, 1841. Fall election returns for 1841 are in ibid., November 10, 1841.

38. Ibid., March 30, 1842.

39. Ibid., March 29, 1843, March 29, 1848, June 13, 1855. See also ibid., March 27, 1844, March 31, 1847, March 28, 1849, March 26, 1851, April 6, 1853, April 12, June 14, 1854, June 11, 1856, April 6, 1859, April 11, 1860.

40. Ibid., April 1, 1846.

41. Ibid., April 14, 1858.

42. Rondout *Courier*, January 4, 1844, February 4, February 25, 1848, January 19, January 26, March 30, April 20, April 27, May 4, 1849.

43. Ibid., July 6, August 17, 1849, July 5, July 19, December 13, 1850, March 7, 1851, August 13, August 20, 1852, April 28, 1854.

44. Before incorporation, a single fire engine was maintained by private efforts. But it was poorly maintained, at best, and did not always make it to local fires. The *Courier* based its appeal for incorporation largely on this issue. See ibid., January 26, 1849.

45. Ibid., January 4, 1844.

46. Ibid., February 4, 1848.

47. Ibid., April 27, May 4, 1849.

48. Minutes of the Trustees of the Village of Rondout, City Hall, Kingston, May 4–June 6, 1849. Hereafter cited as Rondout Village Minutes. Trustees in Rondout were equivalent to directors in Kingston.

49. Ibid., July 28, 1852; Rondout *Courier*, August 20, 1852.

50. Rondout Village Minutes, November 22, 1853, January 24, March 1, 1854; Rondout *Courier*, February 3, March 3, 1854. Popular support for the hospital was never achieved, and even the *Courier* approved when the trustees sold the property in 1858. See Rondout *Courier*, April 11, 1858.

51. *Ulster Republican*, June 6, 1849; Rondout Village Minutes, June 7, June 8, September 7, 1849.

52. Rondout Village Minutes, 1850–51.

53. Ibid., January 16, 1851, January 30, 1857; Rondout *Courier*, April 18, 1851, May 22, 1857.

54. Rondout Village Minutes, 1860–61.

55. Rondout *Courier*, April 9, 1858.

56. Ibid., April 4, 1856, April 9, 1858, April 6, 1860.

57. Ibid., April 6, 1860.

58. John Tappen, *The County and Town Officer* . . . (Kingston, 1816), preface, n.p.

59. *Ulster Sentinel*, April 11, March 21, 1827.

60. Ibid., March 19, 1828.

61. Ibid., April 9, 1828.

62. *Ulster Palladium*, March 23, 1831.

63. *Ulster Republican*, April 2, 1834.

64. Ibid., April 10, 1835.

65. The final issues of the *Palladium* advertise and recommend the New York *Whig*, support the Bank of the United States, and oppose Van Buren. The *Palladium* disappeared after November 27, 1833.

66. *Ulster Republican*, March 30, 1836. Italics added.

67. See ibid., March 23–April 6, 1838.

68. Ibid., April 3, 1839.

69. Ibid., March 14, 1860.

70. On the subject of continued Clintonian-Bucktail (Regency) rivalry, see Lee Benson, *The Concept of Jacksonian Democracy: New York as a Test Case* (Princeton, N.J., 1961), pp. 21–63; Richard P. McCormick, *The Second American Party System: Party Formation in the Jacksonian Era* (Chapel Hill, N.C., 1966), pp. 119–21.

71. *Ulster Palladium*, March 6, April 10, 1833.

72. *Ulster Republican*, July 31, 1833.

73. Ibid., August 14, 1833.

74. *Ulster Palladium*, August 14, 1833.

75. Ibid., September 11, 1833.

76. In the 1833 fall election, the Anti-Junto ticket carried Saugerties by approximately 420 to 30, while the Junto carried Kingston by approximately 435 to 250. *Ulster Republican*, November 30, 1833.

77. Ibid., November 19, 1834, January 21, February 7, April 10, April 13, 1835. A Junto leader's recollection of the entire affair appears in ibid., September 1, 1837.

78. Ibid., September 16, 1835.

79. Ibid., September 30, October 7, October 28, November 5, November 18, 1835.

80. Ibid., January 27, 1836.

81. Ibid., February 24, 1836.

82. Ibid., April 6, May 11, May 18, 1836.

83. Ibid., June 29, 1836.

84. Ibid., August 5, 1836.

85. Ibid., July 15, July 22, 1836.

86. Ibid., May 19, 1837.

87. Ibid., April 7, October 27, November 9, 1837, April 6, August 29, 1838.

88. Ibid., November 14, 1838.

89. Ibid., July 8, 1840.

90. *Ulster Palladium*, February 23, March 16, October 19, 1831.

91. *Ulster Republican*, May 11, 1842.

92. Ibid., July 18, 1849.

93. Ibid., May 20, May 27, July 15, August 26, September 2, 1846, April 28, May 5, 1847.

94. Ibid., September 26, 1855.

95. Ibid., April 3, 1844.

96. Ibid., January 29, February 13, 1845.

97. Ibid., March 26, 1845.

98. Ibid., April 5, 1854.

99. Ibid., March 7, March 14, May 23, June 13, 1855.

100. Ibid., March 12, April 9, June 11, 1856; Rondout *Courier* February 29, 1856, April 9, 1858.

101. *Ulster Republican*, March 11, June 10, 1857, March 3, March 10, April 14, 1858, March 9, 1859, March 14, 1860.

102. Ibid., January 29, 1845.

Chapter 8

1. *Ulster Palladium*, March 16, March 23, April 6, 1831, August 28, 1833; *Ulster Republican*, September 11, 1833.

2. *Ulster Palladium*, May 8, 1833; *Ulster Republican*, October 23, 1839. Kingston's lyceum was one of several founded in New York around this time. Most, including nearly all the successes, were in larger cities and towns. For an excellent discussion of the lyceum movement in America, see Carl Bode, *The American Lyceum: Town Meeting of the Mind* (New York, 1956).

3. Nathaniel Bartlett Sylvester, *History of Ulster County, New York* ... (Philadelphia, 1880), 1:266.

4. *Ulster Republican*, June 5, 1833, August 27, 1834, August 5, 1835.

5. Ibid., April 22, 1840, May 4, June 8, 1842.

6. Ibid., June 14, 1843.

7. Ibid., December 25, 1844, January 29, 1845.

8. Ibid., November 29, December 6, 1843, January 3, 1844.

9. Sylvester, *History of Ulster County*, 1:271.

10. *Ulster Republican*, January 8, 1840.

11. Ibid., December 29, 1841.

12. Ibid., November 7, 1850.

13. Ibid., October 17, 1860.

14. Ibid., January 14, 1852.

15. Manuscript diary of Nathaniel Booth, Senate House Museum, Kingston, December 19, 1851. Hereafter cited as Booth diary.

16. Ibid., January 8, 1849.

17. *Ulster Republican*, November 26, 1856.

18. Ibid., January 7, 1847.

19. Ibid., March 12, 1851, March 17, 1852, January 4, 1860; Rondout *Courier*, November 29, 1850; Booth diary, January 27, 1851.

20. *Ulster Republican*, January 24, 1855; Rondout *Courier*, February 1, 1856.

21. *Ulster Republican*, February 28, 1855, March 2, 1859.

22. Ibid., November 19, 1851. See Bode, *The American Lyceum*, pp. 145–46, on the expansion of the lyceum movement in the growing towns and cities of New York.

23. Rondout *Courier*, November 21, 1851.

24. Ibid., November 21, December 5, 1851.

25. Ibid., January 30, 1852.

26. *Ulster Republican*, January 21, 1852, December 7, 1853.

27. Ibid., February 8, July 19, September 6, 1854, October 17, 1855, January 25, 1860.

28. Ibid., September 9, 1846.

29. Ibid., August 2, 1848.

30. Ibid., September 7, 1853.

31. Ibid., August 17, 1859.

32. Ibid., August 24, September 7, September 14, 1859.

33. Rondout *Courier*, March 19, April 2, April 9, 1858.

34. Ibid., April 16, 1858.

35. Ibid., April 23, 1858.

36. Ibid., June 15, 1860.

37. *Ulster Republican,* August 6, 1851.

38. Booth diary, June 18, 1850.

39. *Ulster Republican,* July 10, 1833, June 18, 1834.

40. Ibid., June 18, 1834, July 6, 1842, July 9, 1845, July 8, 1846, July 7, 1847, July 5, 1848, June 26, 1850.

41. Ibid., July 5, 1843.

42. Ibid., July 7, 1852.

43. Ibid., July 8, 1857.

44. Ibid., July 6, 1859.

45. Ibid., June 27, 1860.

46. Ibid., June 3, 1846.

47. Ibid., December 6, 1854.

48. Ibid., May 31, 1854.

49. Ibid., March 20, 1855.

50. Ibid., March 19, April 9, 1856; Rondout *Courier,* March 21, 1856.

51. Sylvester, *History of Ulster County,* 1:267–71.

52. Rondout *Courier,* August 18, 1848.

53. See Manuscript Minutes, Washington Engine Company No. 3, 1857–76, in Office of the Clerk of Ulster County, Kingston, N.Y.

54. *Ulster Republican,* December 12, 1849; Rondout *Courier,* January 10, 1851.

55. Booth diary, November 17, 1854.

56. Minutes of the Board of Directors of the Village of Kingston, City Hall, Kingston, November 28, 1860.

57. Rondout *Courier,* December 10, 1858.

Chapter 9

1. Robert K. Merton, *Social Theory and Social Structure* (Glencoe, Ill., 1957), p. 122.

2. Organized community participation in Kingston was almost en-

tirely a male prerogative. The participation of women was restricted to a few types of organizations, mainly church auxiliaries and temperance societies, and these have left no records. The activities of women, moreover, received practically no attention in the local press. The study of this mid-nineteenth-century community's social participation, therefore, is necessarily the study of its men.

3. It should be noted that the scoring of participants was not accomplished by counting up incidents of participation, or by assigning specific weights to specific incidents, or by any other precise, mathematical means. Several methods of this sort were attempted, but each seemed to multiply rather than reduce the number of subjective decisions involved, and each new refinement seemed to produce less realistic results. Ultimately, I decided to evaluate, as a panel of one, the *total* participation of each individual and to assign him one score or another according to criteria described in the text. At a number of points I reviewed the results of my scoring to insure that my criteria had not changed as I went along, and at the end I reviewed all the categories to insure that they were both distinct and internally homogeneous. This method is, I believe, superior to one that either ignores the differences between different types of participation or presumes to know *precisely* what those differences are.

4. A more complete discussion of the methods on which this chapter is based is contained in appendix B.

5. Statistical procedures for analyzing the strength of association among the variables of complex contingency tables (where *all* the variables may be nominal or ordinal scale) are sadly lacking. One new procedure, called "log-linear modeling," is designed to evaluate any statement, or model, descriptive of the interactions within a complex table, principally by comparing it with other statements and with a hypothetical (but analytically useless) statement descriptive of all possible interactions. The purpose, according to Paul Holland, one of the developers of log-linear modeling, is to provide the researcher with a "better pair of eyes" for reading tables that can, in fact, become quite confusing. My interpretation of the following tables has been guided by this method, and I, and my two bleary human eyes, wish to thank Mr. Holland for his indispensable and cheerful assistance. Log-

linear modeling is described in Yvonne M. M. Bishop, Stephen E. Fienberg, and Paul W. Holland, *Discrete Multivariate Analysis: Theory and Practice* (Cambridge, Mass., 1975).

6. Property, as we have observed before, is not recorded on the 1855 census.

7. Separate analysis of the relationship between place of birth and participation indicates that English and Scottish immigrants participated at about the same levels as in-migrants from other counties and states of the United States. For this reason, the few Englishmen and Scotsmen recorded on the census are combined here with native-born in-migrants rather than with Irish, German, and other immigrants. Their category as a whole will be referred to as "other natives," or "native in-migrants," as a matter of convenience.

8. At least two of these three "workers," moreover, should be upgraded in status. One, Andrew Bostwick, listed his occupation as "teamster" but was really a fairly prosperous farmer and the street commissioner of Kingston village. Another, a "boatman" named Charles Brodhead, was almost certainly a boat captain, for he reported fully $20,500 in real and personal property on the federal census five years later. (The third worker was a young quarryman with the prestigious surname of Van Keuren. He does not appear in any other records.) But what these examples really illustrate is that our occupational data are rather crude, and that our simple categories estimate only roughly the distribution of wealth and prestige in the community.

9. English- and Scottish-born immigrants account for only two of the thirty "native" leaders.

10. This point could probably be made with more force if occupational data distinguished between master and journeyman craftsmen. Many of the members of the middle occupational category were independent businessmen, and it is quite possible that these were the more active members of this category.

11. These proportions are based on a sample of 244 workers traced to the 1860 census. They are subject to the numerous pitfalls inherent in the study of mobility and should be regarded as approximate. The period 1855–60 is a short one, and it did include a rather severe, brief depression. More on this in the following chapter.

12. These proportions are based on a sample of 68 workers traced to the 1860 census.

13. *Ulster Republican*, August 26, 1857.

14. Ibid., September 9, 1857.

15. Ibid., August 31, 1859.

Chapter 10

1. Rondout *Courier*, April 11, 1856.

2. *Ulster Palladium*, August 14, 1833.

3. Marius Schoonmaker, *The History of Kingston, New York* . . . (New York, 1888), p. 1.

4. Manuscript diary of Nathaniel Booth, Senate House Museum, Kingston, June 1, 1848. Hereafter cited as Booth diary.

5. Ibid., December 15, 1851; see also Rondout *Courier*, April 9, 1852.

6. Booth diary, May 31, 1851.

7. Rondout *Courier*, September 30, 1853; see also *Ulster Republican*, September 21, 1853.

8. See Rondout *Courier*, March 10, 1854.

9. Ibid., May 9, 1856.

10. Ibid., July 9, 1852.

11. Ibid., September 21, 1849.

12. Ibid., March 4, 1853.

13. But see Leonard L. Richards, *"Gentlemen of Property and Standing": Anti-Abolition Mobs in Jacksonian America* (New York, 1969).

14. See Joseph R. Gusfield, *Symbolic Crusade: Status Politics and the American Temperance Movement* (Urbana, Ill., 1963).

15. Rondout *Courier*, September 30, 1853; *Ulster Republican*, September 21, 1853.

16. Rondout *Courier*, October 14, December 16, 1853.

17. *Ulster Republican*, August 26, 1846.

18. The term is Richard Hofstadter's, by way of Algie M. Simons. See Hofstadter, *The American Political Tradition, and the Men Who Made It* (New York, 1948), p. 57. See also Lee Benson's discussion of the stimulating effects of the Erie Canal on enter-

prise in *The Concept of Jacksonian Democracy: New York as a Test Case* (Princeton, N.J., 1961), pp. 12–14.

19. For example, Robert A. Dahl, *Who Governs?: Democracy and Power in an American City* (New Haven, Conn., 1961), pp. 11–31; Stephan Thernstrom, *Poverty and Progress: Social Mobility in a Nineteenth-Century City* (Cambridge, Mass., 1964); E. Digby Baltzell, *Philadelphia Gentlemen: The Making of a National Upper Class* (Glencoe, Ill., 1958).

20. Rondout *Courier*, September 3, 1858.

21. Ibid., March 15, 1850.

22. The best discussion of rural tenancy in New York and of the struggle it produced is David M. Ellis, *Landlords and Farmers in the Hudson-Mohawk Region: 1790–1850* (Ithaca, N.Y., 1946).

23. See Rondout *Courier*, February 25, 1848.

24. *Ulster Republican*, March 12, March 19, 1845. See also Marius Schoonmaker, manuscript fragment intended for second volume of his history of Kingston, Senate House Museum, Kingston. Hereafter cited as Schoonmaker MS.

25. *Ulster Republican*, August 20, 1845.

26. Rondout *Courier*, January 7, 1853, November 19, 1852, March 31, 1854. See also Paul Goodman, "Ethics and Enterprise: The Values of the Boston Elite, 1800–1860," *American Quarterly* 18 (1966): 437–51.

27. Schoonmaker's history is laced with nostalgia, but it was written by a man in his seventies two decades after the close of the period examined here.

28. Rondout *Courier*, October 5, 1849.

29. *Ulster Republican*, July 25, 1838, May 1, May 15, June 5, July 31, August 7, September 4, September 25, 1839; *Political Reformer*, August 7, 1839.

30. *Ulster Republican*, June 27, 1855.

31. Ibid.

32. Rondout *Courier*, April 9, 1852.

33. Booth diary, April 28, 1851.

34. Ibid.

35. For example, see ibid., April 28, 1848.

36. See Stephan Thernstrom, "Urbanization, Migration, and Social

Mobility in Late Nineteenth-Century America," in Barton J. Bernstein, ed., *Towards a New Past: Dissenting Essays in American History* (New York, 1968), pp. 158–75.

37. Leon Sciaky, "The Rondout and Its Canal," *New York History* 22 (1941): 283. The original, published in a more discreet era, contains only underscored blanks after the word "You" in the final line. I can only presume that the reader agrees with my own interpretation of the missing words.

38. See Stuart Blumin, "The Historical Study of Vertical Mobility," *Historical Methods Newsletter* 1 (1968): 1–13; Clyde Griffen, "The Study of Occupational Mobility in Nineteenth–Century America: Problems and Possibilities," *Journal of Social History* 5 (1972): 310–30; Michael B. Katz, "Occupational Classification in History," *Journal of Interdisciplinary History* 3 (1972): 63–88.

39. Early Handwritten Credit Reporting Ledgers of The Mercantile Agency: New York, Ulster County, vol. 2–1, pp. 98–106. Hereafter cited as Mercantile Agency Ledgers.

40. Booth diary, March 9, 1852.

41. Ibid., January 1, 1853.

42. Mercantile Agency Ledgers, vol. 2–1, p. 110.

43. Ibid., p. 49.

Chapter 11

1. Letter by the Reverend Laurentius Van Gaasbeck, printed in *Ulster Republican*, August 30, 1843. See chapter 2.

2. See Stephan Thernstrom, *Poverty and Progress: Social Mobility in a Nineteenth-Century City* (Cambridge, Mass., 1964), pp. 33–56.

3. Winter passage was now possible by way of the Hudson River (or East Shore) Railroad, in conjunction with a ferry or sleigh ride across the Hudson.

4. The canal declined steadily in traffic after 1872, the year the city of Kingston was incorporated. In 1898 it was sold and thereafter carried only a few boats, the last in 1901. See Dorothy Hurlbut Sanderson, *The Delaware & Hudson Canalway: Carrying Coals to Rondout* (Ellenville, N.Y., 1965), pp. 27–29.

5. Patricia U. Bonomi argues that local government in eighteenth-

century Kingston was active and significant. This does not necessarily contradict my judgment about Kingston's governments at earlier and later dates. During the eighteenth century, Kingston enjoyed a significance in the region that it had not obtained by 1700 and that it had lost by 1800. It is only a variation on a major theme of this book to observe the correspondence between the significance of Kingston to the region and the significance of its purely local government to the Kingstonians themselves. See Bonomi, "Local Government in Colonial New York: A Base for Republicanism," in Jacob Judd and Irwin H. Polishook, *Aspects of Early New York Society and Politics* (Tarrytown, N.Y., 1974), pp. 29–50.

6. Based on a sample of 93 households drawn from the manuscript schedules of the United States census of 1800.

7. *Return of the Whole Number of Persons Within the Several Districts of the United States* . . . (Washington, D.C., 1802), p. 47.

8. See Stuart M. Blumin, "Rip Van Winkle's Grandchildren: Family and Household in the Hudson Valley, 1800–1860," *Journal of Urban History* 1 (1975): 293–315.

9. F. A. DeZeng to Robert R. Livingston, November 30, 1802: Robert R. Livingston Collection, New-York Historical Society.

10. See James T. Lemon, *The Best Poor Man's Country: A Geographical Study of Early Southeastern Pennsylvania* (Baltimore, 1972).

11. In his recent study of nineteenth-century Springfield, Massachusetts, Frisch describes an alteration in the "meaning of community" in which "the local orientation could [and did] remain hugely significant, and central to the processes of change." Specifically, Frisch finds that "community" in Springfield "was changing from an informal, direct sensation to a formal, perceived abstraction. As such, the emerging idea of community had considerable power and inspirational reach." Frisch goes on to suggest that this process was ultimately corrosive of community, but it is clear that this corrosion was not far advanced in 1880, the final year of his study. That is, "community" was altered, but not destroyed, in this growing Yankee town. See Michael H. Frisch, *Town into City: Springfield, Massachusetts, and the Meaning of Community, 1840–1880* (Cambridge, Mass., 1972), p. 247.

Bibliography

I. Primary Sources

A. Manuscripts and newspapers

Many types of documents were consulted in this study, and the following is a description of those manuscripts and newspapers that contributed in some significant way to the preceding pages. Understandably, much of the archival research was conducted in Kingston, New York. At the Kingston Area Library I utilized nearly all of the newspapers published in Kingston during the period covered by this study. These include: the *Craftsman*, 1820–22; Kingston *Democratic Journal*, 1840–60; *People's Press*, 1857; *Political Reformer*, 1839–40; Rondout *Courier*, 1848–54, 1856–60; *Ulster Palladium*, 1830–33; *Ulster Republican*, 1833–60; and the *Ulster Sentinel*, 1826–28. At the Office of the Clerk of Ulster County I made use of the manuscript population, agricultural, and industrial schedules of the New York State census of 1855, the Ulster County Mortgage Register, and the minutes of several local organizations, including the Washington Engine Company No. 3, 1857–76, the Ulster County Medical Society, 1806–83, and the Ulster County Agricultural Society, 1859–83. Kingston City Hall contains the Minutes of the Board of Directors of the Village of Kingston, vol. 1, 1805–30, vol. 3, 1854–63 (vol. 2, 1830–53, is missing), and the Minutes of the Trustees of the Village of Rondout, vol. 1, 1849–60. Among the many manuscripts available at the Senate House Museum, the most useful by far proved to be the diary of Nathaniel Booth. Also useful were the diary of Jonathan D. Ostrander, and a manuscript of the opening chapter of a second volume to Marius Schoonmaker's *History of Kingston*. In addition to these public archives I visited each of Kingston's pre–Civil War churches, and searched for the records of several churches that are now defunct. Useful manuscripts located by this search include: Record of the Proceedings of the Eldership and Consistory of the Reformed

Dutch Church of Kingston, 1841–78; Membership Record, 1855–
68, Clinton Avenue Methodist Church; General Record, Trinity
Methodist Church; Minutes of Session, Rondout Presbyterian
Church; and Consistorial Records and Elders' Book, Fair Street
Reformed Church. Other local documents, including the records of
several additional churches, are listed below in the printed sources
section.

A number of manuscripts I utilized were located in archives
outside of Kingston. The New-York Historical Society in New York
City contains the diary of Henry Vanderlyn, the Robert R.
Livingston Collection, and a small variety of other documents
relating to Kingston. At the New York State Library in Albany are
the Abstract of Civil Appointments, 1823–54, and Civil Officers
Elected by the People, 1828–53. The New York State National
Guard at Albany holds the Organization Rosters of Military
Officers, vol. 5, 1847–56, and vol. 6, 1857. At the Baker Library of
Harvard University are the Early Handwritten Credit Reporting
Ledgers of the Mercantile Agency: New York, Ulster County,
vol. 2-1, while the National Archives and Record Service, Wash-
ington, D.C., supplied microfilms of the manuscript population
schedules of the United States census of 1860.

B. Printed Sources

The Acts and Proceedings of the General Synod of the Reformed
    Dutch Church, in North America, at Kingston, October, 1817.
    Albany, N.Y., 1817.
Annual Report of the Board of Managers of the Delaware and
    Hudson Canal Co. to the Stockholders.... New York, 1832–61.
Barber, John W. Historical Collections of the State of New
    York, ... with Geographical Descriptions of the Counties, Cit-
    ies and Principal Villages.... New York, 1851.
Catalogue of the Trustees, Officers, and Teachers of Kingston
    Academy.... New York, 1848.
Census of the State of New York for 1855.... Albany, N.Y., 1857.
Connelly, Arthur C. St. James Methodist Church of Kingston, New
    York, Historical Account. N.p., n.d.
Darby, William. A Tour From the City of New York to De-
    troit.... 1819. Chicago, 1962.
Disturnell, J. A Gazetteer of the State of New York.... Albany,
    N.Y., 1842.

Documents Relative to the Manufactures in the United States. . . .
2 vols. Washington, D.C., 1833.

French, J. H. *Gazetteer of the State of New York*. Syracuse, N.Y.,
1860.

Gordon, Thomas F. *Gazetteer of the State of New York*. Philadelphia, 1836.

Kingston and Rondout Directory. . . . New York, 1858.

Manual of the Wurts Street Baptist Church of Rondout. Kingston,
N.Y., 1908.

Morse, Jedidiah. *American Universal Geography*. Vol. 1, 5th ed.
Boston, 1805.

[New York State] Division of Archives and History. *Historical
Account and Inventory of Records of the City of Kingston*.
Albany, N.Y., 1918.

*One Hundredth Anniversary of the First Baptist Church, 1831–
1931*. Kingston, N.Y., 1931.

Proceedings of the Ulster County Temperance Society. . . . Albany, N.Y., 1848.

St. John's Parish Centennial. Kingston, N.Y., 1932.

Spafford, Horatio G. *A Gazetteer of the State of New York*.
Albany, N.Y., 1824.

*The Statistical History of the United States from the Colonial
Times to the Present*. Stamford, Conn., 1965.

Tappen, John. *The County and Town Officer*. . . . Kingston, N.Y.,
1816.

Trollope, Frances. *Domestic Manners of the Americans*. 1832.
Reprint. New York, 1949.

United States Bureau of the Census. *Aggregate Amount of Each
Description of Persons within the United States of America*. . . .
Washington, D.C., 1811.

———. *Aggregate Value and Produce, and Number of Persons
Employed in Mines, Agriculture, Commerce, Manufactures,
Etc*. . . . Washington, D.C., 1841.

———. *Census for 1820*. . . . Washington, D.C., 1821.

———. *Fifth Census*. . . . Washington, D.C., 1832.

———. *Heads of Families at the First Census . . . 1790: New York*.
Washington, D.C., 1908.

———. *Population of the United States in 1860*. . . . Washington,
D.C., 1864.

———. *Return of the Whole Number of Persons within the Several*

Districts of the United States.... Philadelphia, 1791.

————. *Return of the Whole Number of Persons within the Several Districts of the United States....* Washington, D.C., 1802.

————. *Seventh Census of the United States.* Washington, D.C., 1853.

————. *Sixth Census....* Washington, D.C., 1841.

Werner, Edgar A. *Civil List and Constitutional History of the Colony and State of New York.* Albany, N.Y., 1888.

Works Progress Administration, Historical Records Survey. *Inventory of the Church Archives of New York State....* Albany, N.Y., 1939.

II. Secondary Sources

A. *The Study of Community: Theory and Practice*

Arensberg, Conrad M. "American Communities." In Conrad Arensberg and Solon T. Kimball, *Culture and Community*, pp. 97–116. New York, 1965.

————. "The Community as Object and as Sample." In Conrad Arensberg and Solon T. Kimball, *Culture and Community*, pp. 7–27. New York, 1965.

————. *The Irish Countryman.* New York, 1937.

Arensberg, Conrad M., and Kimball, Solon T. *Culture and Community.* New York, 1965.

————. *Family and Community in Ireland.* Cambridge, Mass., 1940.

Atherton, Lewis. *Main Street on the Middle Border.* Bloomington, Ind., 1954.

Baltzell, E. Digby. *Philadelphia Gentlemen: The Making of a National Upper Class.* Glencoe, Ill., 1958.

Blackwell, Gordon W. "A Theoretical Framework for Sociological Research in Community Organization." *Social Forces* 33 (1954): 57–64.

Boyer, Paul, and Nissenbaum, Stephen. *Salem Possessed: The Social Origins of Witchcraft.* Cambridge, Mass., 1974.

Bridenbaugh, Carl. *Cities in the Wilderness: Urban Life in America, 1625–1742.* New York, 1938.

————. *Cities in Revolt: Urban Life in America, 1743–1776.* New York, 1955.

Brown, A. Theodore. *Frontier Community: A History of Kansas City to 1870.* Columbia, Mo., 1964.

Bushman, Richard L. *From Puritan to Yankee: Character and the Social Order in Connecticut, 1690–1765*. Cambridge, Mass., 1967.

Curti, Merle. *The Making of an American Community: A Case Study of Democracy in a Frontier County*. Stanford, 1959.

Dahl, Robert A. *Who Governs? Democracy and Power in an American City*. New Haven, 1961.

Demos, John. *A Little Commonwealth: Family Life in Plymouth Colony*. New York, 1970.

Dollard, John. *Caste and Class in a Southern Town*. New Haven, 1937.

Duncan, Otis Dudley. "Community Size and the Rural-Urban Continuum." In Paul K. Hatt and Albert J. Reiss, eds., *Cities and Society*, pp. 35–45. Glencoe, Ill., 1954.

Dyos, H. J., ed. *The Study of Urban History*. New York, 1968.

Frankenberg, Ronald. *Communities in Britain: Social Life in Town and Country*. Baltimore, 1966.

French, Robert Mills, ed. *The Community: A Comparative Perspective*. Itasca, Ill., 1969.

Frisch, Michael H. *Town into City: Springfield, Massachusetts, and the Meaning of Community, 1840–1880*. Cambridge, Mass., 1972.

Gans, Herbert J. *The Urban Villagers: Group and Class in the Life of Italian-Americans*. Glencoe, Ill., 1962.

———. "Urbanism and Suburbanism as Ways of Life: A Reevaluation of Definitions." In Arnold Rose, ed., *Human Behavior and Social Processes*, pp. 625–48. Boston, 1962.

Grant, Charles A. *Democracy in the Connecticut Frontier Town of Kent*. New York, 1961.

Greven, Philip. *Four Generations: Population, Land and Family in Colonial Andover, Massachusetts*. Ithaca, 1970.

Hauser, Philip M., and Schnore, Leo F., eds. *The Study of Urbanization*. New York, 1965.

Hawley, Amos H. *Human Ecology: A Theory of Community Structure*. New York, 1950.

———. *Urban Society: An Ecological Approach*. New York, 1971.

Hiller, E. T. "The Community as a Social Group." *American Sociological Review* 6 (1941): 189–202.

Hillery, George A., Jr. *Communal Organizations: A Study of Local Societies*. Chicago, 1968.

———. "Definitions of Community: Areas of Agreement," *Rural*

Sociology 20 (1955): 111–23.

Hunter, Floyd. *Community Power Structure: A Study of Decision Makers.* Chapel Hill, 1953.

Jones, Emrys. *Towns and Cities.* New York, London, and Toronto, 1966.

Kaufman, Harold F. "Toward an Interactional Conception of Community." *Social Forces* 38 (1959): 8–17.

Knights, Peter R. *The Plain People of Boston, 1830–1860: A Study in City Growth.* New York, 1971.

König, Rene. *The Community.* Translated by Edward Fitzgerald. New York, 1968.

Land, Kenneth C. "Duration of Residence and Prospective Migration: Further Evidence." *Demography* 6 (1969): 133–40.

Laslett, Peter. *The World We Have Lost.* London, 1965.

Lemon, James T. *The Best Poor Man's Country: A Geographical Study of Early Southeastern Pennsylvania.* Baltimore, 1972.

————. "Urbanization and the Development of Eighteenth-Century Southeastern Pennsylvania and Delaware." *William and Mary Quarterly* 24 (1967): 501–42.

Lewis, Oscar. "Peasant Culture in India and Mexico: A Comparative Analysis." In McKim Marriott, ed., *Village India: Studies in the Little Community,* pp. 145–70. Chicago and London, 1955.

————. "Tepoztlán Restudied: A Critique of the Folk-Urban Conceptualization of Social Change." *Rural Sociology* 18 (1953): 121–34.

Lockridge, Kenneth A. *A New England Town: The First Hundred Years.* New York, 1970.

Lynd, Robert S. and Merrell, Helen. *Middletown: A Study in Modern American Culture.* New York, 1929.

MacIver, Robert M. *Community: A Sociological Study.* London, 1917.

Mandelbaum, Seymour J. *Boss Tweed's New York.* New York, 1965.

Marriott, McKim. "Little Communities in an Indigenous Civilization." In McKim Marriott, ed., *Village India: Studies in the Little Community,* pp. 171–222. Chicago and London, 1955.

————, ed. *Village India: Studies in the Little Community.* Chicago and London, 1955.

McKinney, John C. and Loomis, Charles P. "The Typological Tradition." In Joseph S. Roucek, *Contemporary Sociology,* pp. 557–82. New York, 1958.

Merton, Robert K. *Social Theory and Social Structure*. Glencoe, Ill., 1957.

Miner, Horace. "The Folk-Urban Continuum." *American Sociological Review* 17 (1952): 529–37.

———. *St. Denis: A French-Canadian Parish*. Chicago and London, 1939.

Morrison, Peter A. "Duration of Residence and Prospective Migration: The Evaluation of a Stochastic Model." *Demography* 4 (1967): 553–61.

Park, Robert E.; Burgess, Ernest W.; and McKenzie, Roderick D. *The City*. Chicago, 1925.

Powell, Sumner Chilton. *Puritan Village: The Formation of a New England Town*. Middletown, Conn., 1963.

Redfield, Robert. *The Little Community*. Chicago and London, 1955.

Redfield, Robert and Rojas, Alfonso Villa. *Chan Kom: A Maya Village*. 1934; Chicago and London, 1962.

Reiss, Albert J., Jr. "The Sociological Study of Communities." *Rural Sociology* 24 (1959): 118–30.

Rutman, Darrett B. *Winthrop's Boston: A Portrait of a Puritan Town, 1630–1649*. Chapel Hill, 1965.

Sanders, Irwin T. *The Community: An Introduction to a Social System*. New York, 1958.

Schnore, Leo F., ed. *The New Urban History: Quantitative Explorations by American Historians*. Princeton, 1975.

Simpson, Richard L. "Sociology of the Community: Current Status and Prospects." *Rural Sociology* 30 (1965): 127–49.

Sjoberg, Gideon. *The Preindustrial City: Past and Present*. New York, 1960.

Smailes, Arthur E. *The Geography of Towns*. Chicago, 1968.

Smith, Page. *As a City upon a Hill: The Town in American History*. New York, 1966.

Stirling, Paul. *Turkish Village*. New York, 1966.

Sutter, Ruth E. *The Next Place You Come To: A Historical Introduction to Communities in North America*. Englewood Cliffs, N.J., 1973.

Sutton, Willis A., Jr., and Kolaja, Jiri. "The Concept of Community." *Rural Sociology* 25 (1960): 197–203.

Thernstrom, Stephan. *Poverty and Progress: Social Mobility in a Nineteenth-Century City*. Cambridge, Mass., 1964.

Thernstrom, Stephan and Sennett, Richard, eds. *Nineteenth-Cen-*

tury Cities: Essays in the New Urban History. New Haven and London, 1969.

Thomlinson, Ralph. *Urban Structure: The Social and Spatial Character of Cities.* New York, 1969.

Tolles, Frederick B. *Meeting House and Counting House: The Quaker Merchants of Colonial Philadelphia, 1682–1763.* Chapel Hill, 1948.

Vidich, Arthur J. and Bensman, Joseph. *Small Town in Mass Society: Class, Power and Religion in a Rural Community.* Princeton, 1958.

Wade, Richard C. *The Urban Frontier: The Rise of Western Cities, 1790–1830.* Cambridge, Mass., 1959.

Walker, Mack. *German Home Towns: Community, State, and General Estate, 1648–1871.* Ithaca, 1971.

Warner, Sam Bass, Jr. "If All the World Were Philadelphia: A Scaffolding for Urban History, 1774–1930." *American Historical Review* 74 (1968): 26–43.

———. *The Private City: Philadelphia in Three Periods of Its Growth.* Philadelphia, 1968.

———. *Streetcar Suburbs: The Process of Growth in Boston, 1870–1900.* Cambridge, Mass., 1962.

Warner, W. Lloyd and Lunt, Paul A. *The Social Life of a Modern Community.* New Haven, 1941.

Warren, Roland L. *The Community in America.* Chicago, 1963.

———, ed. *Perspectives on the American Community: A Book of Readings.* Chicago, 1966.

West, James. *Plainville, U.S.A.* New York, 1945.

Wirth, Louis. "Urbanism as a Way of Life." *American Journal of Sociology* 44 (1938): 1–24.

Wylie, Lawrence, ed. *Chanzeau: A Village in Anjou.* Cambridge, Mass., 1966.

Wylie, Lawrence. *Village in the Vaucluse: An Account of Life in a French Village.* Cambridge, Mass., 1957.

Yang, Martin C. *A Chinese Village: Taitou, Shantung Province.* New York, 1945.

Zimmer, Basil G. "Participation of Migrants in Urban Structures." *American Sociological Review* 20 (1955): 218–24.

Zuckerman, Michael. *Peaceable Kingdoms: New England Towns in the Eighteenth Century.* New York, 1970.

B. Kingston and New York State

Albion, Robert Greenhalgh. *The Rise of New York Port: 1815–1860.* New York, 1939.

Alexander, De Alva S. *Political History of the State of New York, 1774–1882.* 3 vols. New York, 1906–9.

Benson, Lee. *The Concept of Jacksonian Democracy: New York as a Test Case.* Princeton, 1961.

Blumin, Stuart M. "Rip Van Winkle's Grandchildren: Family and Household in the Hudson Valley, 1800–1860." *Journal of Urban History* 1 (1975): 293–315.

Bonomi, Patricia U. "Local Government in Colonial New York: A Base for Republicanism." In Jacob Judd and Irwin H. Polishook, *Aspects of Early New York Society and Politics,* pp. 29–50. Tarrytown, N.Y., 1974.

A Century of Progress: History of the Delaware and Hudson Company, 1823–1923. Albany, N.Y., 1925.

Clark, Colonel Emmons. *History of the Seventh Regiment of New York, 1806–1889.* 2 vols. New York, 1890.

Clearwater, Alphonso T. *The History of Ulster County, New York.* Kingston, N.Y., 1907.

Cross, Whitney R. *The Burned-over District: The Social and Intellectual History of Enthusiastic Religion in Western New York, 1800–1850.* Ithaca, 1950.

DeWitt, William C. *People's History of Kingston, Rondout and Vicinity.* New Haven, 1943.

Ellis, David M. *Landlords and Farmers in the Hudson-Mohawk Region: 1790–1850.* Ithaca, 1946.

Ellis, David M.; Frost, James A.; Syrett, Harold C.; and Carman, Harry J. *A History of New York State.* Ithaca, 1967.

Elting, Irving. "Dutch Village Communities on the Hudson River." In *Municipal Government and Land Tenure.* Johns Hopkins University Studies in Historical and Political Science, 4: no. 1, 5–68. Baltimore, 1886.

Ernst, Robert. *Immigrant Life in New York City: 1825–1863.* Port Washington, N.Y., 1949.

Flick, Alexander C., ed. *History of the State of New York.* 10 vols. New York, 1933–37.

Fox, Dixon Ryan. *The Decline of Aristocracy in the Politics of New York.* New York, 1919.

————. *Yankees and Yorkers.* New York, 1940.

Ginsberg, Stephen F. "Above the Law: Volunteer Firemen in New York City, 1836–1837." *New York History* 50 (1969): 165–86.

————. "The Police and Fire Protection in New York City, 1800–1850." *New York History* 52 (1971): 132–50.

Griffen, Clyde. "Making It in America: Social Mobility in Mid-Nineteenth Century Poughkeepsie." *New York History* 51 (1970): 479–99.

Hammond, Jabez D. *History of Political Parties in the State of New York.* 2 vols. Cooperstown, N.Y., 1846.

Hedrick, Ulysses Prentiss. *A History of Agriculture in the State of New York.* New York, 1966.

Hickey, Andrew S. *The Story of Kingston.* New York, 1952.

Ironside, Charles Edward. *The Family in Colonial New York: A Sociological Study.* New York, 1942.

Kass, Alvin. *Politics in New York State, 1800–1830.* Syracuse, N.Y., 1965.

Litt, Robert Stephen. "Urbanization and Social Control: An Analysis of Kingston, New York, 1820–1872." Unpublished Senior Honors Thesis, Harvard University, 1971.

McKinley, Albert E. "The English and Dutch Towns of New Netherland." *American Historical Review* 6 (1900): 5.

Merritt, Edward L. "Kingston Academy," *Proceedings of the Ulster County Historical Society* (1937–38) pp. 22–53.

Miller, Douglas T. "Immigration and Social Stratification in Pre-Civil War New York." *New York History* 49 (1968): 157–88.

————. *Jacksonian Aristocracy: Class and Democracy in New York, 1830–1860.* New York, 1967.

Miller, Nathan. *The Enterprise of a Free People: Aspects of Economic Development in New York State during the Canal Period, 1792–1838.* Ithaca, 1962.

Nordstrom, Carl. *Frontier Elements in a Hudson River Village.* Port Washington, N.Y., 1973.

Rosenberg, Charles E. *The Cholera Years: The United States in 1832, 1849 and 1866.* Chicago and London, 1962.

Rowley, William E. "The Irish Aristocracy of Albany, 1798–1878." *New York History* 52 (1971): 275–304.

Sanderson, Dorothy Hurlbut. *The Delaware and Hudson Canalway: Carrying Coals to Rondout.* Ellenville, N.Y., 1965.

Schoonmaker, Marius. *The History of Kingston, New York.* New York, 1888.

Sciaky, Leon. "The Rondout and Its Canal." *New York History* 22 (1941): 272–89.

Scisco, Louis D. *Political Nativism in New York State.* Columbia University Studies in History, Economics and Public Law, vol. 13. New York, 1901.

Sylvester, Nathaniel Bartlett. *History of Ulster County, New York....* 2 vols. Philadelphia, 1880.

Van Wagenen, Jared, Jr. *The Golden Age of Homespun.* New York, 1963.

Whitford, Noble E. *History of the Canal System of the State of New York....* Albany, N.Y., 1906.

C. General

Bender, Thomas. *Toward an Urban Vision: Ideas and Institutions in Nineteenth-Century America.* Lexington, Ky., 1975.

Bidwell, Percy W. "The Agricultural Revolution in New England." *American Historical Review* 26 (1921): 683–702.

Billington, Ray Allen. *The Protestant Crusade, 1800–1860: A Study of the Origins of American Nativism.* New York, 1938.

Bishop, M. M. Yvonne; Fienberg, Stephen E.; and Holland, Paul W. *Discrete Multivariate Analysis: Theory and Practice.* Cambridge, Mass., 1975.

Blumin, Stuart. "The Historical Study of Vertical Mobility." *Historical Methods Newsletter* 1 (1968): 1–13.

———. "Mobility and Change in Ante-Bellum Philadelphia." In Stephan Thernstrom and Richard Sennett, eds., *Nineteenth-Century Cities: Essays in the New Urban History,* pp. 165–208. New Haven and London, 1969.

———. "Residential Mobility within the Nineteenth-Century City." In Allen F. Davis and Mark H. Haller, eds., *The Peoples of Philadelphia,* pp. 37–51. Philadelphia, 1973.

Bode, Carl. *The American Lyceum: Town Meeting of the Mind.* New York, 1956.

———. *Ante Bellum Culture.* Carbondale, Ill., 1970.

Boorstin, Daniel J. *The Americans: The National Experience.* New York and Toronto, 1965.

Brown, Richard D. "The Emergence of Urban Society in Rural Massachusetts, 1760–1820." *Journal of American History* 61 (1974): 29–51.

Bruchey, Stuart. *The Roots of American Economic Growth, 1607–1861: An Essay in Social Causation.* New York, 1965.

Cochran, Thomas C., and Miller, William. *The Age of Enterprise: A Social History of Industrial America.* New York, 1958.

Commons, John R. "American Shoemakers, 1648–1895." *Quarterly Journal of Economics* 24 (1909): 39–84.

———, et al. *History of Labour in the United States,* vol. 1. New York, 1921.

Chudacoff, Howard P. *Mobile Americans: Residential and Social Mobility in Omaha, 1880–1920.* New York, 1972.

Fish, Carl Russell. *The Rise of the Common Man.* New York, 1927.

Formisano, Ronald P. *The Birth of Mass Political Parties: Michigan, 1827–1861.* Princeton, 1971.

Goodman, Paul. "Ethics and Enterprise: The Values of the Boston Elite, 1800–1860." *American Quarterly* 18 (1966): 437–57.

Griffen, Clyde. "The Study of Occupational Mobility in Nineteenth-Century America: Problems and Possibilities." *Journal of Social History* 5 (1972): 310–30.

Gusfield, Joseph R. *Symbolic Crusade: Status Politics and the American Temperance Movement.* Urbana, Ill., 1963.

Handlin, Oscar. *Boston's Immigrants: A Study in Acculturation.* Cambridge, Mass., 1941; rev. ed. New York, 1968.

Hansen, Marcus Lee. *The Atlantic Migration: 1607–1860.* Cambridge, Mass., 1940.

Harlow, Alvin. *Old Towpaths: The Story of the American Canal Era.* New York and London, 1926.

Henretta, James A. "Economic Development and Social Structure in Colonial Boston." *William and Mary Quarterly* 22 (1965): 75–92.

Hershberg, Theodore; Katz, Michael; Blumin, Stuart; Glasco, Laurence; and Griffen, Clyde. "Occupation and Ethnicity in Five Nineteenth-Century Cities: A Collaborative Inquiry." *Historical Methods Newsletter* 7 (1974): 174–216.

Jensen, Merrill, ed. *Regionalism in America.* Madison and Milwaukee, 1951.

Katz, Michael B. "Occupational Classification in History." *Journal of Interdisciplinary History* 3 (1972): 63–88.

Krout, John Allen, and Fox, Dixon Ryan. *The Completion of Independence, 1790–1830.* New York, 1944.

Martin, Edgar W. *The Standard of Living in 1860: American Consumption Levels on the Eve of the Civil War.* Chicago, 1942.

McCormick, Richard P. *The Second American Party System: Party Formation in the Jacksonian Era.* Chapel Hill, 1966.

McKelvey, Blake. *American Urbanization: A Comparative History.* Glenview, Ill. and Brighton, England, 1973.

Meyers, Marvin. *The Jacksonian Persuasion: Politics and Belief.* Stanford, 1957.

Miller, Douglas T., ed. *The Nature of Jacksonian America.* New York, 1972.

Mood, Fulmer. "The Origin, Evolution, and Application of the Sectional Concept, 1750–1900." In Merrill Jensen, ed., *Regionalism in America,* pp. 5–98. Madison and Milwaukee, 1951.

Mott, Frank Luther. *American Journalism: A History of Newspapers in the United States through 250 Years, 1690–1940.* New York, 1941.

———. *A History of American Magazines.* 2 vols. [1741–1850] [1850–1865]. New York and London, 1930; Cambridge, Mass., 1938.

North, Douglas C. *The Economic Growth of the United States: 1790–1860.* Englewood Cliffs, N.J., 1961.

Nye, Russel Blaine. *The Cultural Life of the New Nation: 1776–1830.* New York, 1830.

Odum, Howard W., and Moore, Harry E. *American Regionalism: A Cultural-Historical Approach to National Integration.* New York, 1938.

Ostrogorski, M. *Democracy and the Party System in the United States: A Study in Extra-Constitutional Government.* New York, 1910.

Pessen, Edward. "The Egalitarian Myth and the American Social Reality: Wealth, Mobility, and Equality in the 'Era of the Common Man.'" *American Historical Review* 76 (1971): 989–1,034.

———. *Jacksonian America: Society, Personality, and Politics.* Homewood, Ill., 1969.

———. *Riches, Class, and Power Before the Civil War.* Lexington, Mass., 1973.

Pred, Allan R. *The Spatial Dynamics of U.S. Urban-Industrial Growth, 1800–1914: Interpretive and Theoretical Essays.* Cambridge, Mass., 1966.

———. *Urban Growth and the Circulation of Information: The United States System of Cities, 1790–1840.* Cambridge, Mass., 1973.

Reps, John W. *Town Planning in Frontier America.* Princeton, 1969.

Richards, Leonard L. *"Gentlemen of Property and Standing":* *Anti-Abolition Mobs in Jacksonian America.* New York, 1969.

Riegel, Robert E. *Young America: 1830–1840.* Norman, Okla., 1949.

Rostow, W. W. *The Stages of Economic Growth: A Non-Communist Manifesto.* Cambridge, Mass., 1960.

Rothman, David J. *The Discovery of the Asylum: Social Order and Disorder in the New Republic.* Boston and Toronto, 1971.

Schlesinger, Arthur M., Jr. *The Age of Jackson.* Boston, 1945.

Segal, Harvey H. "Canals and Economic Development." In Carter Goodrich, ed., *Canals and American Economic Development,* pp. 216–48. Port Washington, N.Y., and London, 1972.

Taylor, George Rogers. "American Urban Growth Preceding the Railway Age." *Journal of Economic History* 27 (1967): 309–39.

―――. "The Beginnings of Mass Transportation in Urban America," parts 1 and 2. *Smithsonian Journal of History* 1, no. 2 (1966): 35–50; 1, no. 3 (1966): 31–54.

―――. *The Transportation Revolution: 1815–1860.* New York, 1951.

Thernstrom, Stephan. "Urbanization, Migration, and Social Mobility in Late Nineteenth-Century America." In Barton J. Bernstein, ed., *Towards a New Past: Dissenting Essays in American History,* pp. 158–75. New York, 1968.

Thernstrom, Stephan and Knights, Peter R. "Men in Motion: Some Data and Speculations about Urban Population Mobility in Nineteenth-Century America." In Tamara K. Hareven, ed., *Anonymous Americans: Explorations in Nineteenth-Century Social History,* pp. 17–47. Englewood Cliffs, N.J., 1971.

Tryon, Rolla Milton. *Household Manufactures in the United States, 1640–1860.* Chicago, 1917.

Turner, Frederick Jackson. *The United States, 1830–1850.* New York, 1935.

Tyler, Alice Felt. *Freedom's Ferment: Phases of American Social History from the Colonial Period to the Outbreak of the Civil War.* Minneapolis, 1944.

Ward, David. *Cities and Immigrants: A Geography of Change in Nineteenth-Century America.* New York, 1971.

Weber, Adna Ferrin. *The Growth of Cities in the Nineteenth Century: A Study in Statistics.* Columbia University Studies in History, Economics and Public Law, vol. 11. New York, 1899.

Williamson, Jeffrey G. "Antebellum Urbanization in the American
    Northeast." *Journal of Economic History* 25 (1965): 592–608.
Wish, Harvey. *Society and Thought in Early America: A Social
    and Intellectual History of the American People through 1865.*
    New York, 1950.
Wright, Carroll D. *The History and Growth of the United States
    Census. . . .* Washington, 1900.

Index

Academy. *See* Kingston Academy
Acquaintance, extent of, 43–44, 49
Addresses, 118
Advertisements, newspaper, 18, 59, 60, 61–62, 116, 253 n. 36
Age: and poverty, 92, 94; and social participation, 231, 234
Agriculture, 14–15, 73–74, 75, 200–201, 218, 257 n. 27
Albany Regency (Bucktail) party, 18, 25–26
Albion, Robert G., 16–18
Alcohol. *See* Drunkenness; Temperance movement
Anti-Junto, 142, 143, 156
Anti-Masons, 138, 139
Anti-Regency party, 141–42
Anti-rent war, 200–201
Arensberg, Conrad, 8
Autonomy: of community, 16, 216–18; of households, 47, 222 (*see also* Manufacturing, home)

Baggs, Bob, 98–100, 178, 209
Balls, 152–53, 154, 158
Banks, 57, 58; bank war, 142–44, 202; political importance of, 141–42
Barter system, 15, 59–60, 61
Benson, Lee, 48
Bible societies, 4, 28, 31, 150, 164
Birthplace: and length of residence, 95; and social participation, 173, 178–89, 231–32, 237, 270 n. 7; and wealth, 91–92. *See also* Ethnic group; Immigrants; In-migrants; Native Americans

Bishop, Yvonne M. M., et al., 235
Blacks, 14–15, 35–36, 39, 219
Board of directors: meetings of, 22–23, 127, 128, 129, 136, 214; membership of, 129, 187–88; powers of, 22–23, 127–30; for Rondout, 136. *See also* Government, village
Bonomi, Patricia, 40, 42
Booth, Nathaniel: business affairs, 210–11; on commerce, 68, 71–72, 117, 123, 204–5, 219; on moving day, 109; on social life, 153, 156, 161–62, 166; on social structure, 118, 193; value system, 190; on violence, 96–97, 98, 101
Boston, trade with, 16–18
Breweries, 65
Bruyn, Johannes, 170
Bucktail party, 18, 25–26
Buildings: character of, 119–20; number of, 120–21. *See also* Kingston, physical structure of
"Bumble Bee Boys," 98–99, 178, 197–98, 209
Business. *See* Businessmen; Commerce; Economy; Industry; Manufacturing; Stores; Trade
Businessmen: characteristics of, 102, 194–95, 207, 209–11; failure of, 207–11. *See also* Commerce; Craftsmen

Campaigning, political, 139–40, 145, 214–15
Canal: cultural impact of, 52; effect on economy, 2–3, 51, 56–57, 216;